The Many Faces of Sacha Baron Cohen

The Many Faces of
Sacha Baron Cohen

Politics, Parody, and the Battle over Borat

ROBERT A. SAUNDERS

LEXINGTON BOOKS

A division of
ROWMAN & LITTLEFIELD PUBLISHERS, INC.
Lanham • Boulder • New York • Toronto • Plymouth, UK

LEXINGTON BOOKS

A division of Rowman & Littlefield Publishers, Inc.
A wholly owned subsidiary of The Rowman & Littlefield Publishing Group, Inc.
4501 Forbes Boulevard, Suite 200
Lanham, MD 20706

Estover Road
Plymouth PL6 7PY
United Kingdom

British Library Cataloguing in Publication Information Available

Library of Congress Cataloging-in-Publication Data

Saunders, Robert A., 1973–
  The many faces of Sacha Baron Cohen : politics, parody, and the battle over Borat /
Robert A. Saunders.
    p. cm.
  Includes bibliographical references and index.
  ISBN-13: 978-0-7391-2336-2 (cloth : alk. paper)
  ISBN-10: 0-7391-2336-X (cloth : alk. paper)
  ISBN-13: 978-0-7391-3120-6 (electronic)
  ISBN-10: 0-7391-3120-6 (electronic)
  1. Baron Cohen, Sacha, 1971– 2. Comedians—Great Britain—Biography. I. Title.
  PN2598.B426S38 2008
  792.702'8092—dc22
  [B]   2008025706

Printed in the United States of America

∞™ The paper used in this publication meets the minimum requirements of American
National Standard for Information Sciences—Permanence of Paper for Printed Library
Materials, ANSI/NISO Z39.48–1992.

For Kairat

Contents

Figures

Acknowledgments

The first time I saw Borat was shortly after returning from Kazakhstan in 2002. I was there conducting dissertation research on the country's fast-evolving national identity. A friend, who vaguely remembered something about Kazakhstan being mentioned, recommended that I watch *Da Ali G Show* on HBO. After viewing a few minutes of Sacha Baron Cohen parading in front of spectators at a minor league baseball game in the Deep South, I was perplexed. I asked myself, Why Kazakhstan? No good answers came to mind. Certainly, a host of other countries would have made better covers for this shtick.

Over the next couple of years, I watched the waning of Ali G and the waxing of Borat as I completed my dissertation. A few months after I defended my thesis, Borat hosted the MTV Europe Music Awards and sparked the fury of Kazakhstan. As a scholar of national identity, an expert on Kazakhstan, and a fan of British humor, this proved to be an unavoidable academic temptation. While I should have persevered with my efforts to turn my dissertation into a publishable manuscript, I ultimately tabled that endeavor in favor of researching an English mountebank and his battle with one of the world's largest and newest countries.

More than once, I tried to talk myself out of writing this book. Since you are reading this, it is obvious that I failed. For that spectacular failure, I would first and foremost like to thank Alexander J. Motyl, whose encouragement provided the fuel for this undertaking. Had he shown even the slightest apprehension at my "Borat book," it is likely that I would have abandoned the project forthwith.

From the very start, this project has been a collective effort. However, one person's efforts overshadow those of all others: Vlad Strukov. Throughout this adventure, Vlad has served as my friend, critic, sounding board, and sage. I would also like to take this opportunity to give formal thanks to others who contributed to this book in both large and small ways: Joel Vessels, for asking the tough questions and allowing me to pilfer from his intellectual wellspring; Eliot Borenstein for his thorough and thoughtful review of the text; the ever sanguine Pablo Castillo-Diaz for his unflagging enthusiasm and constant feedback; Kevin Dooley for reading and commenting on drafts of key chapters; George Kassimeris for encouraging me to write a prospectus for the book; Ky Krauthamer and Ken Silverstein for their patience and patronage; Joseph Parry, Mark Steinberg, and Thomas Wilson for believing that writing about Borat was not as silly as it sounded; Irina Del Genio, Yana Dimitrovich, and Dennis Babkov for their help on Kazakhstan; and the seminal figures of Richard Langhorne, Yale Ferguson,

Valters Ščerbinskis, Oded Eran, Alexander Golovko, and Maria Todorova for their dutiful guidance and for sparking my interest in the various themes of this text.

I would like to thank Matthew Johnson of the law firm Ziffren, Brittenham, Branca, Fischer, Gilbert-Lurie, Stiffelman, Cook, Johnson, Lande & Wolf LLP for his kind support in granting permission to use images of Sacha Baron Cohen that appeared on HBO. Justin Ide of the Harvard News Office also deserves my thanks for allowing me to use an image from Ali G's Class Day speech in 2004. I apologize to the reader for not including any images from the film *Borat: Cultural Learnings of America for Make Benefit Glorious Nation of Kazakhstan*. My request to use stills from the movie was denied by Twentieth Century Fox without explanation.

While researching this book, I had the great fortune to meet many people whose lives have been impacted by the grand trickster Sacha Baron Cohen. Their help has been invaluable. Particularly, I would like to offer my gratitude to Roman Vassilenko, who graciously provided his time and support for this project. Others who gave of themselves include Tony Badger, Niall Ferguson, and Roger Lancaster, among others who must go unnamed. I thank the dozens of proud parents of Kazakhstani children who shared their thoughts on Borat and Sacha Baron Cohen. I would also like to thank those Kazakhstanis who spoke with me about their lives, their loves, their hopes, and their fears. May all their dreams come true.

I would also like to extend my thanks to Richard Vogel, Jeff Gaab, and other members of the Department of History, Economics and Politics at Farmingdale State College for their encouragement. I am also indebted to Ligia Rodriguez and Eugenio Villareal for their support. A special thanks is due to Frank Pellegrini for his help in securing a course reduction to allow me to put the finishing touches on the manuscript. I would also like to thank my students at Farmingdale, Rutgers University, and elsewhere for their queries and comments about Borat, each one of which pushed me to work harder and smarter. This undertaking was possible only though access to the vast array of electronic and print materials of the library of Rutgers, The State University of New Jersey.

I thank my parents, Robert Franklin Saunders and Suzanne Hamby, and my grandparents—Carter, George, Louise, and Irene—for igniting my life-long interest in identity (political, ethnic, religious, and otherwise). I also wish to express my appreciation to my in-laws, Ray and Sandra, for everything they have done for me. My sincerest thanks, however, go to my wife, Michelle E. Fino. Throughout this project, she has been my inspiration, intellectual partner, and long-suffering copy-editor.

Several segments of Chapter 4 previously appeared in "In Defence of *Kazakshilik*: Kazakhstan's War on Sacha Baron Cohen," *Identities: Global Studies in Culture and Power* (May 2007). Chapter 5 is adapted from my spring 2008 article "Buying into Brand Borat: Kazakhstan's Cautious Embrace of Its Unwanted 'Son,'" which appeared in the American Association for the Advancement of Slavic Studies' journal *Slavic Review*, and is reprinted with the permission of the publisher. Certain passages in both these chapters also appeared in my brief article "Cultural Learnings: Welcome to Boratistan" published by *Transitions Online* (November 2006), and in Ken Silverstein's piece, "A Recap from the World's Leading Boratologist," which appeared on *Harper's* web site in October 2006.

Introduction
Who Is Sacha Baron Cohen and What
Does He Want?

Few comedians can boast a resume as impressive as that of Sacha Baron Cohen. By his mid-thirties, the Cambridge-educated Londoner had broken box office records with his motion picture *Borat: Cultural Learnings of America for Make Benefit Glorious Nation of Kazakhstan*, won a Golden Globe and dozens of other film and television awards, been named one of *Time*'s 100 most important people, and begun a promising career as a Hollywood leading man. Along the way, he had also been threatened by the government of the world's ninth largest country, been condemned by the Anti-Defamation League, triggered multiple investigations of obscenity and impropriety by media regulators, and provoked dozens of lawsuits.

Baron Cohen's humor is built on the use of exaggerated ethnic personae. In the 1990s, he developed three characters: Ali G, a wannabe gangster from the middleclass London suburb of Staines; Bruno, a gay Austrian fashionista with a Nazi fetish; and Borat, an anti-Semitic, Gypsy-baiting journalist from Kazakhstan. Over the years, he has added details to these creations, but their substance has changed little since their original inception. Baron Cohen's ability to remain loyal to these avatars is even more impressive given that the comedian is loath to appear in public, at least out of character. Each of his alter egos poses as a journalist for some fictitious news organization. This cover provides Baron Cohen with the ability to mine humor from a number of sources, including embarrassing politicians, provoking laughably bad behavior among the hoi polloi, and exposing the ignorance of both.

Ali, Bruno, and Borat have all become insoluble facets of global popular culture. The argot, phonation, and malapropisms of these characters can be heard in schoolyards and college dorms across the Western world, while products emblazoned with their images can be bought in shops from California to Krakow. Ali G has become an international symbol for a "lost generation" of young Britons seduced by conspicuous consumption and suburban mimicry of the ghetto-fabulous "thug life." Bruno has re-opened the wounds of Austria's Nazi past, while concurrently inflicting new ones surrounding the nation's contemporary Eurotrash culture. Baron Cohen's most famous creation, Borat, has gone even further. The bumbling faux reporter from Kazakhstan has emerged as a powerful and timely trope of foreignness, misogyny, and anti-Semitism. He single-handedly wrenched the Republic of Kazakhstan from post-Soviet obscurity, placing it squarely in the international spotlight. Simultaneously, Borat has become a cultural lodestone for American politics during a time of intense societal divisiveness. All this while obsessing over his bowel movements, the sexual conquest of *Baywatch* star Pamela Anderson, and the malevolent threat of Gypsy magic.

For many, Sacha Baron Cohen represents a bright future for comedy—a reinvigoration of Britain's contribution to world humor reminiscent of Oscar Wilde, Benny Hill, and Monty Python. Some have even gone so far as to label him a latter-day Jonathan Swift for his biting satire and keen insight into contemporary social issues. Others are not so kind. More than once, Baron Cohen has been condemned as a modern-day Al Jolson, profiting from grotesque stereotypes of minorities that border on unreconstructed minstrelsy. His parody of anti-Semitism has been especially inflammatory, particularly given Baron Cohen's own Orthodox Jewish origins. His critics are confined neither to his homeland of Great Britain, nor his adopted country of the United States. The government of Kazakhstan carried on a six-year campaign against his depiction of the Central Asian republic as a medieval backwater. At one point, Kazakhstan even publicly threatened him with legal action, intimating he was a foreign agent. Baron Cohen has also been condemned in Germany, Russia, and the Arab world.

Baron Cohen's humor has been politicized at every turn. Given his background, this is likely his intention. Baron Cohen was already politically conscious in his early teens, participating in anti-fascism demonstrations and marching against apartheid. He opted for a year-long sojourn on an Israeli kibbutz before returning to England to study history at Christ's College in Cambridge. After conducting field research in the US, he wrote his senior thesis on the complicated relationship between blacks and Jews during the American Civil Rights Movement (1955-1968). His revisionist interpretation of black-Jewish cooperation won him accolades from his peers and professors alike. While he certainly could have continued in academia, he opted for a decidedly different path. Having developed a flare for filmmaking in Israel and finding success on the stage while at Cambridge, he decided to make a career for himself as an entertainer. After five trying years in cable television obscurity, he joined the cast of a ribald fake news program on Britain's Channel 4. *The 11 O'Clock Show* gave Baron Cohen the freedom to develop his comedic personae and probe political sore spots in British society.

The sociologist Peter L. Berger once wrote, "Benevolent satire is an oxymoron."[1] Baron Cohen seems to have taken this notion to heart. Early in his career, he proved that he had no respect for sacred cows, political, religious, social, or otherwise. His militant humor targeted the Left and the Right, Jews, Christians, and Muslims, patricians and plebs, men and women, and gays and straights with equal fervor. Yet his true talent proved to be his ability to expose the stultifying ignorance of the political elite vis-à-vis the masses they purportedly served. His poseur gangster character Ali G ultimately served this undertaking most effectively. Ali flourished in the late 1990s, a time when British youth had all but abandoned politics. His affected urban style and recondite language functioned as the perfect façade for Baron Cohen's satire. The victims of his barbs—British MPs, US presidential candidates, and even a former UN Secretary-General—suffered his idiocy at the price of their reputations. Ali G soon became politically important in his own right. Initially, various ethnic groups (Greeks, Sikhs, etc.) competed to claim him as their own when it was unclear who was behind the ethnic tranvestism of the character. Once Baron Cohen was unveiled as an affluent and well-educated British Jew, cultural commentators tied themselves up in knots over his role in multicultural "Cool Britannia," while identity police within the black community condemned his "wigger" presentation as retrograde and racist. Baron Cohen did more than take the criticism in stride; he further provoked it by refusing to break from character.

Sacha Baron Cohen's personal revulsion at appearing out of character contrasted sharply with the comedian's unflagging promotion of his various personae. He rarely passed up an opportunity to generate controversy or parade publicly as Ali, Bruno, or Borat. His tireless self-marketing as Borat bordered on the absurd; he appeared on dozens of talk and news shows in character, even calling a press conference in front of Kazakhstan's embassy to the United States before trying to gain entry to the White House. However, Baron Cohen's abiding commitment to stay in character did not prevent details about his personal life from coming to light. Once his religious, class, and academic backgrounds were made public, the media refashioned its approach to commenting on his humor. His lampooning of the rougher edges of black culture as Ali G became more tolerable because of his intellectual investigation of the history of the Civil Rights Movement. His Cambridge education ultimately became a permanent part of his biography for any and all journalists writing on his humor. Likewise, his Jewishness was now accentuated in accounts of his humor. This effectively attenuated previously-held concerns about his (i.e., Borat's) purported anti-Semitism. In other words, if you are smart, it's satire, if you're not, it's just plain racist.

This was especially true when he was denounced by the Anti-Defamation League for his now infamous "Throw the Jew Down the Well" skit in 2004. In the aftermath of the controversy, Baron Cohen made a rare break from character to address the issue directly stating, "Part of the idea of Borat is to get people to feel relaxed enough that they fully open up. And they say things that they never would on normal TV. So if they are anti-Semitic . . . they'll say it."[2] In the face of an investigation by Britain's broadcast television regulator, Baron Cohen enjoyed the media's support for his unorthodox approach to the issue of religious bigotry. Reporters regularly equated Baron Cohen with the left-leaning star of *All in the Family* Carroll O'Connor, who aped racial prejudice in 1970s America in an effort to dispel it. Baron Cohen readily embraced the mantle of a satirical campaigner against anti-Semitism. In 2006, he famously quoted Ian Kershaw, the esteemed historian of the Third Reich, who wrote, "The path to Auschwitz was paved with indifference."[3] According to Baron Cohen, fear of such apathy is a driving force behind his own humor; however, a critical reading of Baron Cohen's career suggests this explanation is both mawkishly self-serving and overly simplistic.

Over time, the press has increasingly ascribed political meaning to Borat's untoward buffoonery, Bruno's fascist ramblings, and Ali's abject ignorance. As Baron Cohen turned his bit player success on *The 11 O'Clock Show* into nation-wide fame on *Da Ali G Show*, this tendency to politicize his work only intensified. As a fixture in British (and later American) popular culture, this trend should be neither underestimated nor taken lightly. Acclaimed French sociologist Pierre Bourdieu once noted, "When one speaks of 'popular culture,' one is speaking about politics."[4] This maxim is frighteningly realized through Sacha Baron Cohen's normative satire, global minstrelsy, and ambush journalism. In 2002, *Ali G Indahouse* became the most successful British film of the year, forever banishing Ali's anonymity. Once Ali G had become as recognizable an icon of the country as the Queen Mother, Baron Cohen found it increasingly difficult to continue his burlesque in England. This happy inconvenience forced him across the pond, where he began targeting Americans with his Swiftian wit. There he netted Newt Gingrich, James Baker, and Pat Buchanan among other luminaries and politicos. In the American heartland, he found homicidal homophobic football fans, anti-Semitic big game hunters, and a Southern gentry pining for the return of the "peculiar institution," i.e., slavery.

In America, his humor proved to be an acquired taste. While Baron Cohen was unable to replicate the level of fame he enjoyed in Britain, he did gain entry into the inner sanctum of Hollywood elite. After *Da Ali G Show* was cancelled, he landed a memorable cameo in the animated film *Madagascar* before scoring a key supporting role in the summer 2006 blockbuster *Talladega Nights: The Ballad of Ricky Bobby*. However, his success in the US was just beginning. That autumn, *Borat* became the surprise hit of the season. Surprisingly, the film also ended his long-running feud with the Kazakhstani government, which decided, after painful consideration, to embrace the curious fame Baron Cohen's pantomime had generated. Financial success, however, proved to be a magnet for legal troubles. Romanian Gypsies, etiquette coaches, frat boys, and almost everyone else associated with the film sued (or threatened to sue) Baron Cohen, hoping to either quash *Borat* or profit from it. Not surprisingly, Baron Cohen's star rose with every new controversy. In the immediate aftermath of the film's success, he signed a $40 million deal to develop a motion picture featuring his third alter ego, Bruno.

The purpose of this book is two-fold. My primary aim is to provide a political analysis of Sacha Baron Cohen and his various avatars. I explore the political, social, religious, and personal sources of Baron Cohen's humor and ethnic pantomime. While this book is not a biography, I have attempted to produce an exhaustive account of how Sacha Baron Cohen has been consumed in popular culture, as an actor, a comedian, and an activist. Importantly, I am more interested in how Baron Cohen is perceived than who he actually is. I similarly endeavor to understand and deconstruct the multivariate interpretations of Ali G, Bruno, and Borat by academics, the media, everyday viewers, politicians, and cultural critics. In doing so, my aim is to take the temperature of the Anglophone world at a critical stage in its cultural evolution. I hope to provide the reader with a greater understanding of the postmodern metamorphosis currently underway in satirical ethnic comedy, and how globalization and multiculturalism influence this shift. As a political scientist, my analysis consistently returns to the political ramifications of such subtle changes in the various power structures of America, Britain, and the larger international system.

Secondarily, I hope to elucidate the curious state of affairs that have allowed a mass-mediated persona (Borat) to do battle with a sovereign state (the Republic of Kazakhstan). Back in 2000 when Borat first claimed to represent Kazakhstan, the country's politicians could ill-afford Baron Cohen's interference in their brand management of the country's national image. Still suffering from the deleterious effects of a post-Soviet hangover, they demanded he be banned. However, the country's diplomats quickly decided that they had to take matters into their own hands rather than relying on London or Washington to "do something" about Borat. In the second half of this book, I explore how and why Kazakhstan decided to go to war with Baron Cohen over the right to determine its national image, and what this tells us about diplomacy in the era of globalization.

For whom is this text intended? The obvious answer is anyone interested in the back-story of Sacha Baron Cohen's precipitous rise from local cable TV hoaxster to a globally-recognized anti-hero. This book looks at Baron Cohen through the lens of politics—specifically identity politics, thus making it of particular interest to those in the fields of cultural and media studies, political communication, and sociology. With its focus on Kazakhstan's mobilization against Sacha Baron Cohen, this text is also a study in postmodern statecraft, and an interrogation of national identity in the 21st century. As such, it provides value to students of diplomacy, nationalism studies, and international public policy. I have endeavored, however, to write an accessible and even humorous account of Baron Cohen, his characters, and their misadventures. Therefore, it may also be intriguing to those with an interest in contemporary popular culture and ethnic humor.

A few words about the structure of the text are now in order. This book is divided into two parts: Part I: Being Baron Cohen and Part II: The Battle over Borat. The first is dedicated to Baron Cohen's rise to global fame, and includes a political analysis of his comedy. In Chapter 1, "From Hertfordshire to Kibbutz to Cambridge: The Making of a Social Critic," I detail Baron Cohen's early life, education, religious upbringing, and comedic influences. The second chapter, "*Da Ali G Show*: Building a Brand as Bamboozler Extraordinaire," explores the comedian's successes with his character Ali G on *The 11 O'Clock Show* and his eponymously-named program. Chapter 3, "*Personae Comicae*: The Postmodern Politics behind Ali G, Borat, and Bruno," attempts to provide a theoretical analysis of how Baron Cohen's various alter egos were interpreted in Britain and, to a lesser extent, in the United States.

In Part II, I address the international ramifications of what I call the Boratistan pantomime, i.e., Baron Cohen's construction of fictional and grotesque Kazakhstan which bears no resemblance to the actual country. Chapter 4, "Defending and Defining Kazakhstan: The Battle over Borat Begins," provides the reader with an introduction to the history, culture, and politics of the Central Asian republic with an eye towards explaining the political establishment's vociferous, often hysterical, denunciations of Borat. As the title suggests, Chapter 5: "Learning to Love Boratistan: Kazakhstan Buys into Brand Borat" delineates Kazakhstan's about-face on Baron Cohen's international charade. I go into some detail about how the country's diplomatic corps used the postmodern practices of state branding to tame their out-of-control country image in the wake of the premiere of *Borat*. In Chapter 6: "Under Fire and Loving It: The Cultural Impact, Criticisms, and Controversies of *Borat*," I provide a critical analysis of Baron Cohen's 2006 motion picture, and investigate the wildly politicized reception it triggered from some unexpected sources. I conclude the chapter with a discussion of the various individuals who sued him or threatened legal action because of the film. In the conclusion, "The Global Minstrel Show," I attempt to place Baron Cohen within a larger setting, one shaped by deterritorialized, denationalized, decentralized media products. I also offer some thoughts on the future of identity in a mass-mediated world of iPods, YouTube, pirated DVDs, and satellite television.

Let the reader beware: this is not a paean to Baron Cohen. I do not shy away from criticizing his actions where appropriate. Furthermore, I have been careful not to overstate his importance. While Sacha may be the subject of college courses, political protests, presidential summits, and partisan hackery, he remains a funnyman, a jester, a comic. Regardless, his humor has acutely resonated in his home country and abroad, and like many wits who preceded him, he has come to represent a political force in his own right. As such, this study is, at its core, an attempt to buttress Bourdieu's previously-mentioned truism that popular culture is politics. I will leave it to the reader to judge if this text lives up to that goal.

Notes

1. Peter L. Berger, *Redeeming Laughter: The Comic Dimension of Human Experience* (New York and Berlin: Walther De Gruyter, 1997), 157.

2. Virginia Heffernan, "The Cheerful Confessions of Ali G, Borat and Bruno," *New York Times*, 15 July 2004.

3. See Neil Strauss, "The Man behind the Moustache," *Rolling Stone* 1014 (11 November 2006): 58-70.

4. Pierre Bourdieu, "La sociologie de la culture populaire," in *Le Handicap socioculturel en question* (Paris: ESF, 1978), 118.

Part I
Being Baron Cohen

Chapter 1
From Hertfordshire to Kibbutz to Cambridge: The Making of a Minstrel

While Borat, Bruno, and Ali G are known for their propensity for sharing inappropriate personal details about themselves, Sacha Baron Cohen is ironically tight-lipped about his own background. Despite his worldwide fame, he is visibly annoyed when photographed out of costume. The actor gives few interviews out of character, and has refused to do any interviews in the United Kingdom since 2000. Baron Cohen has, however, granted a handful of interviews to select American media, initially to promote the second season of *Da Ali G Show* on HBO (2004) and, more recently, the release of *Borat: Cultural Learnings of America for Make Benefit Glorious Nation of Kazakhstan* in the winter of 2006-2007.[1] Despite the guarded nature of the comedian, much of his life has now become public record.

"Da Voice of Youf": The Early Years

Sacha Noam Baron Cohen was born on 13 October 1971 in Hammersmith, London, England to an Orthodox Jewish family. He is the youngest of three sons of parents Gerald Baron Cohen and Daniella Weiser. Baron Cohen's youth was spent in the comfortable, almost exclusively middle-class Hampstead Garden Suburb of north London. His father, Gerald, owned a menswear shop named the House of Baron in Piccadilly Circus—the commercial hub of London's kinetic West End. Sacha's paternal line hails from picturesque Pontypridd in south Wales. In fact, the family still maintains garment shops in Cardiff. In what may be seen as a nod to his Welsh heritage, Baron Cohen's character Ali G offered this now famous critique of Cymru as part of his manifesto for a re-branded, "well wicked" Britain: "The first thing I would do is get rid of Wales . . . I would swap it for Jamaica."[2] *The Western Mail*, the self-described "national newspaper of Wales," subsequently pondered: "Ali neglects to mention whether his proposed swap with Jamaica would involve a straight transplantation of populations between the two countries, which might well be welcomed more by the Welsh than the Jamaicans, given the relative weather conditions."[3]

Sacha's mother, who is of German- and Persian-Jewish origin, was born in Israel. She is reportedly very close to her son. *The Observer* has described Daniella as "forceful Jewish mother," who would "regularly encourage her talented boys to give musical recitals to guests after Friday night Shabbat meals."[4] She is a teacher at a dance school, continuing a family tradition. Her mother, who lives in Haifa, Israel, was an acclaimed ballet dancer in Germany before fleeing the country during the Third Reich.[5] Sacha once recounted in an interview that "She was the last Jewish girl to be taught ballet in Germany."[6] At 91, she was not yet too frail to brave a midnight showing of *Borat* in Haifa. After watching the risqué film, she called Sacha to "compliment him and dissect the scenes in detail."[7]

Sacha's brother Erran Baron Cohen is a composer and trumpet player; he is also a founding member of the British electronica world-music group *ZOHAR*.[8] His band has played some of London's tonier clubs including Chinawhite, Momo and Bagley's, as well as the Glastonbury and Womad music festivals. Erran produced the music for *Da Ali G Show* and, more recently, lent his talents to the *Borat* film, including composing the fictitious anthem, "O, Kazakhstan."[9] Sacha's other brother, Amnon Baron Cohen, is a computer chip designer.

"Heducation": Only the Best for the Baron Cohen Boys

The brothers Baron Cohen all attended Haberdashers' Aske's Boys' School, an independent day school in Elstree, Hertfordshire. At school, they were regarded as "clever but eccentric."[10] Sacha Baron Cohen's friend and future collaborator, Dan Mazer, attended the school as well, thus beginning a long and fruitful relationship. Other pupils included future comedy writers William Sutcliffe and Matt Lucas who ultimately came to join the *Ali G* writing team.[11] Aske's is nominally Church of England in its orientation; however, today its students come from a variety of ethnic and religious backgrounds. The school is well known across Britain and is "much in demand" among London's Jewish community due to its prestige and high academic standards.[12] Speaking of their shared alma mater, co-creator and producer of *Da Ali G Show* Dan Mazer waxed nostalgic. "It's basically a factory of comedy. . . . It's just cocky young Jews. And because we are too weak to fight each other, we compensated with verbal jousts."[13]

Unlike his alter ego Ali G, Sacha Baron Cohen was an excellent student. While at Haberdashers' Aske's, he contributed an essay to the *Times Literary Supplement* at the tender age of eight (one out of only 11 published). The future Ali G extolled the virtues of studying English, history, and most interestingly "maffs:"

> All sorts of things may have happened over the weekend. Russia may have invaded Afghanistan, England may have lost against the West Indies at cricket, and the price of Smarties has jumped 5p. But in our maths lesson nothing has changed. One plus one still equals two. After Monday morning's maths lesson, the world does seem a bit more reliable and less insane than it did on Sunday night.[14]

In a 2002 documentary on his early life, one of his history teachers at Aske's, David Cooper, described him as "ambitious, articulate, and hard working."[15] "Habs"—as the school is colloquially known—was one of the

most important influences on Sacha's life. In her 2002 profile of Baron Cohen for *The Daily Mail,* Glenda Cooper stated, "It was where he made
friends with a brilliant clique to which he has stayed close ever since. . . .
Increasingly, his privacy is his main concern and he surrounds himself with
his family and friends from Habs whom he can trust not to go to the press.
'Non-Habs' people have been gradually squeezed out of his life."[16]

From Habs, he went on to Christ's College at the University of Cambridge where he studied history under such prominent historians as Niall
Ferguson and Anthony Badger. At Cambridge, Baron Cohen impressed
peers, professors, and administrators alike; the former head of Christ's College, Sir Hans Kornberg, remembers Baron Cohen as a likeable and "social"
college student.[17] In "Borat's Guide to Britain," one of Borat's first televised
appearances, the Kazakhstani journalist visited the hallowed halls of Britain's top university. He described Baron Cohen's alma mater as the "greatest university in world—Cambridge, where most famous men in world
study: Isaac Newton, William Shakespeare, [footballer] Kenny Dalglish,
[and 1980s synth-pop band] Thompson Twins." Noticeably, the bumbling
Borat did not include his own alter ego in the auspicious (and not so auspicious) list of celebrities.

In his final year at Christ's College, Sacha Baron Cohen wrote his thesis, "The Black-Jewish Alliance—A Case of Mistaking Identities" (1993).
The work investigated Jewish involvement in the American Civil Rights
movement. His emphasis was on the 1964 murders of James Chaney, Andrew Goodman, and Michael Schwerner in Mississippi. The 1964 slayings
of Chaney, a young black man from Mississippi, Goodman, a 20-year-old
Jewish anthropology student from New York, and Schwerner, a 24-year-old
Jewish social worker also from New York, galvanized the US federal government against institutionalized racism and the culture of violence it perpetuated in the Deep South. In death, the three emerged as posthumous symbols of what came to be known as the "Freedom Summer"—a grassroots
campaign to register disenfranchised southern blacks to vote.

Baron Cohen's principal findings were that while "official" Jewish organizations supported the Civil Rights movement, they provided little in the
way of substantive support. Instead it was student-activists that made a difference, and in doing so, used the struggle as a tool for managing their own
identity issues.[18] Speaking of his thesis, Baron Cohen states:

> I was writing this at the time of the Crown Heights riots when the Jewish
> community was obsessed with black anti-Semitism and I argued that this
> obsession came out of Jews feeling betrayed by their old blood brothers
> from the civil-rights movement. But while it was perceived in the Jewish
> community that Jews were disproportionately involved in civil rights, my
> conclusion was that black Americans didn't see Jews as being more in-
> volved than any [other] white Americans.[19]

In the conclusion of his thesis, Baron Cohen states, "The 'Black-Jewish alliance' is a misnomer. An alliance implies a reciprocal relationship, acknowledged and supported from both sides. This was not the case. . . . Ever since
the meeting of the Jews and Blacks in urban America, there have been tensions between them" (1993: 41). In conducting his thesis research, Baron
Cohen scored a research coup by securing an interview with Robert Parris
Moses, the Harvard-educated activist and Co-Director of the Council of

Federated Organizations (COFO), an umbrella organization which united the various groups associated with the Freedom Summer movement.

Bob Moses' reputation as a recluse did not deter Baron Cohen. His history tutor, Professor Anthony Badger, who is now the master of Cambridge's Clare College, stated, "I know from my colleagues who are civil rights historians that Bob Moses is notoriously reluctant to be interviewed and very difficult to pin down. You really needed to work at it to get to him. That is what impressed me about Sacha being able to get an interview with Moses."[20] His ability to secure the Bob Moses interview impressed both his colleagues and professors. One of his friends from those days told me, "He just had that kind of chutzpah and the ability to ingratiate himself with somebody. He gave clear indications that he did possess a high level of inner strength and sense of self." This key interview was a harbinger of things to come for Baron Cohen, who went on to interrogate the likes of a former United Nations Secretary-General, various advisors to US presidents, and internationally-recognized experts and academics .

In 1992, Sacha's research brought him to the ghettoes of Atlanta, Georgia where he saw American racism—white on black, black on white, and black on black—up close and personal. Undoubtedly, these experiences were formative ones for the young Baron Cohen. As Rich Cohen recently pointed out in his 2006 *Vanity Fair* interview of the comedian, "Much is made of this [thesis]—the implication being . . . that Borat's travels in the [American] south are a continuation of Baron Cohen's earlier studies. In fact, every article about the comedian mentions Cambridge [because] it makes the disturbing parts of his act less unacceptable. Because it's coming from a smart man, an educated man."[21] In other words, if he was under-educated he would just be a racist, but his Oxbridge degree affords him a greater level of tolerance among the culture police.

At one time, Sacha's parents—especially his mother—had even envisioned a career in academia for their youngest son; however, this was not to be.[22] He soon began to dedicate much of his time to acting and comedy, though frequently infusing his performances with political and cultural references gleaned from his investigations of class and race. Niall Ferguson, who describes Baron Cohen as "highly intelligent" and someone who had "obvious academic potential," repines the fact that Baron Cohen chose a career in entertainment over that of an academic. In response to my question "Is there anything that you remember about Sacha that made you think he was destined for greatness?," he retorted imperiously, "That you call greatness? If only he had followed my advice, he could have been a serious historian."[23]

Heedless of such urgings, he focused his attention on the stage. At the Cambridge University Amateur Dramatic Club, Baron Cohen acted in plays such as *My Fair Lady, Biloxi Blues, Cyrano de Bergerac,* and *Fiddler on the Roof,* in which he played Tevye. He also took on the role of Tamburlaine the Great, the 13th century Turkic conqueror of Central Asia, a curious happenstance given how much his future fame would depend on the region. Baron Cohen's long-time collaborator, Dan Mazer, also attended the University of Cambridge. It was Mazer who introduced him to the Cambridge University Footlights Dramatic Club (Mazer would later go on to be the group's president). The Cambridge Footlights troupe has produced such comic geniuses as *Monty Python Flying Circus*' Eric Idle, Graham Chapman, and John

Cleese, as well as Hugh Laurie, star of Britain's dark comedy *Black Adder* and, more recently, the FOX medical drama *House, M.D.*[24] Although Baron Cohen himself was not a member of Footlights, he performed in a number of the group's productions. In an interview with *National Public Radio* in 2004, he fondly recounted his time at university, stating "very little work gets done there [at Cambridge]," but that "it's a great place to learn acting and comedy."[25] He would return to Cambridge again, but in the guise of Borat irreverently sending up effete professors and cocksure students alike.

"Relijon": The Impact of the Jewish Faith

Despite the fact that *CNN*'s movie reviewer Tom Charity described the *Borat* film as "the most anti-Semitic American movie ever made," Sacha Baron Cohen's Jewish credentials are solid. [26] In high school, he belonged to the international Socialist-Zionist youth movement *Habonim Dror* ('Builders of Freedom')—an organization dedicated to peace with Israel's neighbors and the Palestinian people, strengthening Jewish culture among the diaspora, and the promotion of a new social order based on egalitarianism, individual liberty, and social justice. He relished his time as a *madrich* (youth leader) within the organization. According to one of his charges, "I think all of us 10-year-olds hero-worshipped him. He had this ability to capture a roomful of people with his wit and charm and just make us all laugh."[27]

Upon graduation, he spent his "gap year" working and studying on a kibbutz in the north of Israel, in what has become a common practice among many Orthodox Jews in the diaspora. At 18, the experience reportedly helped Baron Cohen overcome any lingering shyness, especially amongst the opposite sex.[28] Describing the budding actor in his third year at Cambridge, a former colleague told me, "He had such a large personality—extremely extroverted. He didn't convey any sense of being a wallflower. He flirted with everyone from the women working in the cafeteria all the way up. He conveyed an overwhelming sense of confidence and had that ability to light up the room." This is a far cry from the teen-aged Baron Cohen who left the security and reliability of Habs for Israel. Travel photographer Joel Brandon-Bravo recently recounted his time at the Rosh Hanikra kibbutz with Baron Cohen, "He was likeable and friendly, if a little geeky, and seemed to find it easier to overcome social barriers by fooling around and cracking jokes."[29] Israel became a turning point for the young jokester, as he began making short films and soon gained a reputation as the funniest man in the kibbutz.[30]

Baron Cohen still remains close to the land of his mother's birth. He made headlines there in 2002 when he survived a stray bullet that struck his hotel mirror in Tel Aviv's David Intercontinental Hotel after two guests in an adjoining room killed themselves. At first blush, the local police assumed someone was trying to assassinate the man known as Ali G. However, the shootings were entirely coincidental. According to the Israeli daily newspaper *Haaretz*, "Baron Cohen has since returned for several visits, his Hebrew is excellent and he has a good understanding of Israeli culture."[31] A friend from his Cambridge days told me that Baron Cohen's long-term aspiration while he was in college was to resettle in Israel; he simply considered that to be the natural trajectory of his life. Interestingly, Baron Cohen's creation Borat regularly employs Hebrew in his otherwise incomprehensible faux Kazakh mutterings. A writer for the *Jerusalem Post* commented that "just about every 'Kazakh' sentence Borat Sagdiyev utters in the entire movie [*Borat*] is Hebrew—near-accentless flawless slang-filled modern Hebrew. My fellow Jerusalem audience members loved every word of it heaving hysterically at each idiomatic pearl."[32]

Religion has always been a part of Baron Cohen's comedic repertoire. The comedian keeps kosher, considers himself to be "almost a teetotaler," and is observant, including keeping the Sabbath when possible.[33] In accordance with Jewish tradition, he regularly spent his Friday nights with his immediate family until moving to Los Angeles to pursue a career in Hollywood.[34] Reportedly, he does not work from sundown on Friday to sundown on Saturday, including even refusing to answer the telephone. Baron Cohen's decision to appear on the 28 October 2006 episode of *Saturday Night Live* was made only after a good deal of soul-searching.[35] Former classmates have described him as "quite religious" as a young man.[36]

While the press has made much of his religiosity, he does not claim to be especially devout. In a 2007 *NPR* interview he paradoxically stated, "I wouldn't say I am a religious Jew . . . I am proud of my Jewish identity and there are certain things I do and customs I keep."[37] Despite such protestations, he did accept the rather prestigious task of reciting the Yom Kippur "priestly blessing" at a New York synagogue in 2005.[38] This is curious given that Britain's *Sunday Times* referred to Baron Cohen's practice of his religion as "Church of England Jewish," suggesting that he attends synagogue only twice per year.[39] Regardless, his fiancée and the mother of his child, Isla Fisher, converted to Judaism in advance of the couple's pending nuptials.[40]

Is Sacha Baron Cohen a "Jewish Comedian"?

If you have to ask, the answer is probably "yes." Sacha Baron Cohen's "Jewishness" is always simmering beneath the surface of his comedy. Just as his Cambridge education is mentioned in every profile, so is his Jewish heritage—again as a way to "explain" his comedy (and frequently to blunt his critics' invective).[41] Take for instance the first line in a 2006 *Houston Chronicle* cover story on Borat which read: "It's a good thing Sacha Baron Cohen is Jewish or he probably would have more than angry Kazakhstanis after his bare tuchis."[42] Speaking more generally of Jewish comedians, the late A. Roy Eckardt, an expert on Jewish-Christian relations, stated, "the clown, provided he is significantly amusing, is forgiven everything, even, where necessary, his Jewishness."[43] In the case of Baron Cohen, it seems he is forgiven *only* because he is Jewish, whether it is his anti-Semitism, homophobia, misogyny, Gypsy-baiting, racism, or run-of-the-mill bad taste. In her review of *Borat*, the *New York Times* film critic Manohla Dargis remarked, "Commentators often imply that Borat wouldn't be funny if Mr. Baron Cohen were not Jewish, which is kind of like saying that Dave Chappelle wouldn't be funny if he were not black."[44]

Such a comparison is worth exploring. Dave Chappelle is the creator and star of *Chappelle's Show*, which ran for three successful seasons on the

Comedy Central cable television network before Chappelle walked away from the show due to stress, creative disputes with network executives, and a desire to "check his intentions."[45] *Chappelle's Show*'s biting satire and parody included short films of "racial daring" on topics such as the civil rights movement, slavery, and "questionable behavior" within contemporary black culture.[46] One of Chappelle's most touted sketches was about a blind white supremacist who does not realize he is actually a black man. The skit was filmed in a mock documentary style reminiscent of PBS's *Frontline* news program. In other sketches, Chappelle imagines how America would be altered if the government agreed to pay reparations to the descendents of slaves and how the war in Iraq would have been prosecuted if President George W. Bush and his cabinet were all black. Both Baron Cohen and Chappelle tap into racism as a way to expose it. According to Dargis, "For these performers, the existential and material givens of growing up as a Jew in Britain or as a black man in America provide not only an apparently limitless source of comic material, but they are also inseparable from their humor."[47] While Dave Chappelle derailed his own career, in part, as a response to his growing angst that his audience was "laughing at the wrong jokes for the wrong reasons at the wrong times," Baron Cohen seems to have paid little attention to why they are laughing—as long as they continue laughing.[48]

Just as Chappelle is not simply a "black" comedian, Baron Cohen is more than "just" a Jewish comic. He is a trailblazer of 21st century ethnic humor. Ethnic humor can be defined as "humor directed at racial and nationality groups, denigrating alleged attributes of those groups."[49] Since time immemorial, aspirant and venerable comedians alike have plumbed their societies' collective insecurities about the "other" for laughs. Jokes about Poles, blacks, and Italians are so prevalent in American culture that they each warrant separate sections in collections such as the *Truly Tasteless Jokes* series. With the advent of political correctness some two decades ago, ethnic humor, as well as jokes about gays, women, the handicapped, and other minorities, became almost taboo. However, today's ethnic humor is generally freed from both the cultural policing of the 1980s and early 1990s and the hateful and derogatory caricaturing of earlier eras. The dual shift likely is a by-product of workaday globalization and the maturation of identity politics (see Chapter 3). Today, such humor is typically (though not exclusively) "insider" joking made by members of various groups who use it as a "means to develop and reflect group pride."[50] Baron Cohen's central role in contemporary Jewish humor was underscored by a 2005 graduate course in English which was offered at the University of Wisconsin-Madison entitled "Performing Jewishness: William Shakespeare to Ali G."[51] In addition to lending his character's name to college courses, he is regularly invoked in academic discussions of Jewishness in contemporary British and American society.[52]

Few would dispute the notion that Jewishness and humor have become inextricably linked since the late 19th century, especially in the German- and English-speaking worlds.[53] Social marginalization has influenced multiple generations of Jewry, causing them to view the world from a slightly different perspective than their gentile counterparts. As outsiders looking in, many gravitated to careers which were also on the fringes of society, e.g., theater, popular music, vaudeville, etc.[54] According to historian Stephen J. Whitfield:

> Humor has become one of the enduring features of communal life, an adhesive that has exhibited about as much staying power as religious belief and that has helped to bind Jews to one another. Humor has served as an index of both memory and identity. . . . Jewish wit is . . . a consequence of the ambiguities of emancipation, and was sparked by the friction of encounters with the incongruities of civil society.[55]

According to a friend of Baron Cohen's, "Growing up Jewish in a Britain that is still profoundly suspicious of outsiders and institutionally racist, identity is always in 'question.' Baron Cohen had to think about his identity as a Jew."[56] While Baron Cohen's style has been trumpeted as a new form of comedy that uses ethnic stereotyping and often overtly racist pantomime to expose societal prejudice, it in fact is simply a modern manifestation of an established tradition of ethnic humor as performed by the minority in question.

Sacha Baron Cohen fits within a paradigm based on the exaggeration of stereotypes as a trigger for laughter. Being on the receiving end of such stereotyping provides minority comedians with a wealth of ideas for their own humor. These ideas need not be solely confined to their own ethnic or religious group. According to sociologist and theology professor Peter L. Berger:

> The margins of society have been the Jewish habitat for many centuries. From a marginal position one sees things more clearly and therefore more comically! It may be that the same social forces which have produced such a great number of Jewish analysts and interpreters of society also underlie the phenomenon of Jewish humor. The humorous capacity to put oneself in the other's position, to look at oneself doubtfully and self-critically, to take all serious matters with a grain of salt—these classically Jewish characteristics may all be seen as the fruits of marginality.[57]

Echoing Berger, Eckardt argues that Jewish humor is founded upon marginality and shares certain traits with the comedy of blacks, Hispanics, and other marginalized peoples.[58] What makes Sacha Baron Cohen so interesting is that he both manipulates the internal boundaries of marginality and uses marginality itself as a weapon. In traditional ethnic humor, the use of self-deprecating jokes is directed inward as an "adaptive move to avoid ultimate victimization."[59] In the case of Jews, humor often includes an additional component: it becomes an element of identity-building for those who have left the ghetto or the *shtetl* but not yet assimilated into the majority society. These partially assimilated Jews are able to laugh at "traditional" Jews because of the latter's perceived backwardness, and thus the "transitional Jew" is able to "cement his or her association with the larger host culture."[60] This is a peculiarly Jewish form of humor which is not fully replicated among other immigrant groups, though shades of such mirth can be found among certain indigenous minorities.

Such forms of humor *cum* critique are central to Jewish humor according to Eckardt:

Jewish humor is usually substantive; it is about something. It is fascinated by the intricacies of the mind and logic. As a form of social or religious commentary, it may be sarcastic, complaining, resigned, or descriptive. It tends to be anti-authoritarian, ridicules grandiosity and self-indulgence, exposes hypocrisy, kicks pomposity in the pants, and is workably democratic. It frequently has a critical edge that tends to create discomfort. Lastly it mocks everyone—including God and religion, while nevertheless seeking a new understanding of the difference between the holy and the mundane.[61]

There are shades of the American Jewish comedian Woody Allen's humor in the works of Baron Cohen. Ali G excels at what Eckardt refers to as the *"comedy of deflation—whose* basic trope is a sudden thrusting downward from the exalted to the workaday."[62] But unlike Woody Allen whose observations on life sublimely mix transcendental rumination with the banalities of everyday life (e.g., the scene from *Hannah and Her Sisters* in which Allen's character's father declares "How the hell do I know why there were Nazis? I don't know how a can opener works!"), Baron Cohen's humor expands well beyond the narrow confines of Manhattanite mores into a world of thug rap (Ali G), Hitlerian fashion (Bruno), and post-Soviet faux pas (Borat).[63]

Rock critic Jody Rosen explicitly links Baron Cohen to a long-established tradition of Jewish anti-Semitism as spectacle: vaudeville.[64] Rosen, an expert on Jewish minstrelsy, argues: "Sacha Baron Cohen in 'Borat' is portraying a kind of . . . newly arrived, greenhorned immigrant, who's mangling the English language and kind of bumbling around the country, misapprehending the customs and getting himself into all kinds of trouble in the process."[65] This character evokes the vaudevillian panorama of inebriated Irish, opium-eating Chinese, violently mercurial Italians, and unctuous Jews of *fin-de-siècle* America.[66] However, Baron Cohen's brand of Jewish humor turns this relationship on its head. As a perfectly well-established London Jew with excellent schooling and even better connections, he need not distance himself from his Jewishness. Instead, he has broadened his comic focus by taking aim at those well-heeled whites (including other Jews) who want to affect "blackness" through appearing violent, uneducated, and marginal. In doing so, he has become a sort of postmodern vaudevillian.

Psychologists Samuel Juni and Bernard Katz liken the Jewish comedic tradition to an updated form of that of the medieval court jester, i.e., "a hapless individual [who] is often both the perpetrator and the subject (butt) of his own humor." Baron Cohen adds a twist.[67] Not only does he accomplish the time-honored duty of the court jester to make society laugh at itself by parodying its malevolence, he also provides a multilayered social critique of the purported subject of parody (wannabe-blacks, clueless foreigners, and campy gays). Regardless, the effect on the audience is the same as it has always been when confronted with "aggressive" ethnic humor, i.e., "an unsettling feeling of suffering and triumph."[68]

If the Jews' sensibility rarely exults in the catharsis of physical violence or of sadism, their jokes often exhibit plenty of psychological competitiveness and verbal aggressiveness. Because anger could not often be turned outward against the dominant majority, because the expression of such hostility to the powerful might be risky, animus had to be channeled against one's self, or perhaps against other Jews: relatives, rabbis, cantors, the rich.[69]

Baron Cohen's assumption of the identity of other marginalized groups is telling. As journalist Richard Brookhiser contends, "Jewish comics are being sabotaged by their own tribe; the success of the ethnicity has made the persona of the underdog hard to pull off."[70]

Baron Cohen may be just the first in a slew of Jewish comedians to hunt for humor in the once protected preserves of other minorities' ethnic stereotypes. In fact, he is frequently compared to the Jewish-American comedian Sarah Silverman who employs unapologetic and unrefined racist joking in her film *Sarah Silverman: Jesus is Magic* (2005). While Silverman's defenders claim that she, like Baron Cohen, attempts to undermine racist stereotypes by embracing them, this is debatable. Michael Musto of the *Village Voice* opined that "she's the upscale cousin of Sacha Baron Cohen's Borat, draping herself in insensitivity in order to use it as a mirror and reflect everyone else's."[71] However, his claim that "Silverman probably is politically correct" fails to pass the red-face test when viewing her comedy, which includes one-liners like "The best time to have a baby is when you're a black teenager" and song lyrics such as "I love you more than Asians are good at math. . . . I love you more than black people don't tip. . . . I love you more than Puerto Ricans need baths."[72]

Unlike Sarah Silverman, who proudly basks in her Jewishness, e.g., declaring herself "one of the chosen people" and lampooning her boyfriend's Catholicism as believing "Jesus is magic," Baron Cohen is disinclined to do likewise. Reportedly, he has been dissuaded from defaming Jews and Judaism by his more religious friends "who fear that it might be offensive to the Jewish community."[73] Today, Baron Cohen is frequently accused of anti-Semitism (as will be explored later); however, his act is based on assuming gentile personae who engage in "every possible anti-Semitic canard," rather than parodying Jewishness as an "insider," a comedic mainstay of an earlier generation of Jewish comedians that included Jackie Mason, Alan King, and Woody Allen.[74]

Despite his apparent decision to swear off parodying Jewishness, Sacha Baron Cohen's early comedic performances were closely linked to his Jewish faith. According to the *Sunday Times,* "It was thanks to the Jewish tradition that he got his first taste of showbiz: his breakdancing group provided the entertainment at his bar mitzvah."[75] Once deciding to make the leap to comedy upon graduation from Cambridge, he ran a comedy club in West Hampstead with his brother Erran. Here the Baron Cohen boys made a name for themselves doing send-ups of their own community. At the club, their keystone act was a ditty called "Shvitzing" (Yiddish for 'sweating'), lampooning two Hassidic Jews who strip to their Speedos because their black garb is too stifling. Sacha submitted a video of the skit to BBC's *Comedy Nation*; it was initially rejected on the grounds it was too offensive, but later aired. In the video, Erran jams on a portable synthesizer as Sacha raps in an affected Yiddish accent. The skit ends with Sacha dancing around impersonating a chicken before ultimately deciding to shave his beard, arms, and back to cool off. In a similar (though even less humorous) vein, one of his earliest short films, "The Golders Green Formation Leaning Team," parodies Orthodox Jews in prayer.[76] However, as Baron Cohen started to break into mainstream television with his appearances on Britain's *The 11 O'Clock Show,* he traded mockery of Jews for a multi-layered political pantomime employing misogyny, anti-Semitism, and homophobia among other tools of the ethnic comedy trade.

An "Undertow of Rage"? Deconstructing Baron Cohen

In its late 2006 cover story on *Borat,* the Film Society of Lincoln Center's journal *Film Comment* opined, "What gives this postmodern performance piece its edge, why it's a cultural phenomenon for reasons beyond funny haha, is the undertow of rage. It's funny because it's true, and the truth is there are a lot of assholes out there."[77] While there is undoubtedly a wellspring of politics seething beneath Baron Cohen's comedy, open aggression is never apparent. Instead, the comedian is a contemporary scion of a long line of social critics who have chosen to manifest their voice through parody, pantomime, and the occasional fart joke.

Molding a Satirist: Sacha's Political Foundations

Since his debut on British television, there has been an almost endless stream of palaver dedicated to Sacha Baron Cohen's politics. Every major media outlet from *The Sun* to the *Wall Street Journal* has speculated on the political orientations of the actor behind the ethnically-ambiguous gangsta-wannabe Ali G, the hyper-amphierotic fashionista Bruno, and the Gypsy-baiting Semitophobe Borat. However, as Simon Weaver, editor of the academic journal *Ethnicities,* points out,

> [T]he media have been unable to confirm Baron Cohen's "true" motivations, influences or intentions. The effect of this general lack of interaction with the media [as himself] and specific silence concerning the meaning of the character is the construction within the media of Baron Cohen as a personality that exhibits a semantic void. Because of this semantic void, Baron Cohen is specifically not constructed as a celebrity and Ali G is reified or becomes the celebrity that Baron Cohen could have been.[78]

When interviewed out-of-character, Baron Cohen deliberately oversimplifies his comedy and his characters in "a further attempt to subvert or confuse" his viewers, the press, and the political establishment.[79]

Understanding Baron Cohen's political background is no trivial matter considering the fact that in March 2007, *GQ* ranked him as the nineteenth most powerful man in Britain. This put the comedian one place behind Prince William and only two spots behind the country's Conservative Party leader, David Cameron.[80] In the words of *GQ* editor Darius Sanai, "Not since John Lennon has an English entertainer had such an effect on the world . . . [US President] George Bush was briefed on him, the Kazakh government briefed against him and the film *Borat* . . . hit the No. 1 spot in America last autumn."[81]

In today's interconnected world of creolized global culture, one might argue that his import outstrips that of the Beatles simply because barriers to access are only a shadow of what they were during the Cold War. The commodification and trasnationalization of media has given any cultural product a resonance which is a hundred times stronger than would have been possible only a few decades ago. Sacha Baron Cohen's internationally-recognized influence would come as no surprise to his late mentor and producer of *The 11 O'Clock Show*, Harry Thompson, who commented in 2002, "He has got the power to make people want him and reveal their true nature."[82] After being hoaxed by Ali G, Labour MP Tony Benn, who is perhaps Britain's most prominent leftwing politician, paid the comedian a great compliment stating that his act is a "very important piece of political education."[83]

It is clear that Baron Cohen is politically astute, if for no other reason than his fondness for political sore spots, his selection of interviewees, and the questions he poses to them (each one containing a seductive kernel of genuine perspicacity surrounded by a nearly impenetrable coating of buffoonery and vulgarity). Despite the seemingly obvious political content of his humor, those who know him tend to discount the importance of politics in his life. According to his thesis director Tony Badger, "I would not say that Sacha Baron Cohen was exceptionally political. He was highly intelligent and therefore inevitably interested in contemporary issues. His political orientation was relatively standard for the time."[84] Concerning Baron Cohen's 1993 undergraduate thesis "The Black-Jewish Alliance," his advisor states: "The dissertation was challenging a comfortable Jewish orthodoxy concerning African American-Jewish cooperation—one which is prevalent in the British Jewish press." Namely, that Jewish participation was an integral part of the struggle. Badger elaborated, "He was criticizing the celebratory Jewish convention [about the American Civil Rights movement] which will inevitably make people feel uncomfortable." Writing in the *Observer*, Oliver Marre opined, "The existence of this thesis suggests that Baron Cohen has more than a passing interest both in Borat's specific American targets and in the wider challenges of social integration and bigotry with which his comedy deals."[85] However, deeper inspection suggests that Baron Cohen's thesis sought not only to expose the bigotry of the American South, but also to challenge the self-congratulatory positions of established elites and their pervasive, often fallacious assumptions about the society which supports them. Despite having traded in his academic robes for comedic drag, he continues to pursue both missions today.

While Sacha Baron Cohen was not overtly political by the definition of the times, he did establish his political bona fides early in life. While still in secondary school, he was photographed at an anti-fascist rally with MP Ken Livingstone, who went on to become the mayor of London.[86] He marched against fascists and racists in London, and demonstrated against South African apartheid in the 1980s.[87] Baron Cohen was also involved in Britain's Anti-Racist Alliance (ARA) for many years—a black-led coalition which also includes many Jewish groups. Ironically, the ARA would later condemn Baron Cohen for his comedic portrayals of blacks.[88] In response to a question about the criticisms of Baron Cohen's humor as racist and anti-Semitic, Tony Badger told me:

How you interpret that form of satire is very much a matter of personal taste or definition of humor. Particular audiences respond in different ways. I never detected a semblance of racism in him. Actually, this is not strong enough. There is no evidence of Sacha Baron Cohen being racist. No one can see a racist intent in the humor. Everything about him was consistent with an anti-racist orientation. The $64,000 question here is about the danger of parody when one takes a ludicrous or extremist view or approach. This has been a problem for humorists forever. He faces it now. That sort of humor lends itself to criticism and contestation.

A friend from Baron Cohen's college days echoes the sentiment: "I don't see how he can be anti-Semitic. He's passionately Jewish—ethnically and religiously. Instead, he seems to be constantly exposing anti-Semitism. . . . His work is not racist." Returning to Baron Cohen's Jewishness, his sustained interest in political subjects can, according to Whitfield, be partially connected to his Jewish upbringing: "A value system from which [Jewish] comedy has sprung also includes political passions more intense than how their fellow citizens have generally felt."[89] Comedy has long been employed as a complement to political action among Jewish immigrants to the United States and other countries. Baron Cohen embodies this tradition in myriad ways.

By lampooning politicians, he may also be criticizing society at large for its abandonment of politics. In the words of one Ali G's victims, MP Tony Benn, "There has been a notable de-politicization of young people, many of whom tend to think of the prime minister as if he were the well-liked manager of a successful United Kingdom football team, whom they admire as spectators without much sense of personal involvement . . . [Ali G's skits are] genuinely educational in that anyone watching them would be bound to question their own prejudices and think about the real issues raised."[90] It would be absurd for Ali G to break from character and urge British (or American) youth to "get out there and vote," yet his approach to humor certainly leaves the watcher feeling a bit uneasy about the current raft of politicians.

While Baron Cohen's humor lacks the overt political content of comedians like Bill Maher and Dennis Miller in the US and Rory Bremner and Mark Thomas in the UK, he does fit into a new category of politically-oriented satirists which includes Dave Chappelle, Stephen Colbert of *The Colbert Report*, and others. However, according to Jaime J. Wienman, "The difference between Cohen and some of these other comics is that he doesn't try to reassure the audience."[91] For instance, Chappelle is openly critical of segments of his audience that do not grasp his satire, while Colbert's *modus operandi* employs regular cues that evoke the comedian's left-of-center agenda despite his miming of far right demagoguery.

Having developed his humor outside the mainstream, Baron Cohen is perhaps more willing to push the envelope than his peers. The noted historian of ethnic humor, Christie Davies, notes, "It is possible that Jewish humor has become bolder, and the playing with aggression rougher, in countries like contemporary Britain and America where the non-Jewish population is far less hostile and oppressive than was the case in Central and Eastern Europe."[92] According to Eckardt:

There is also a decisive sense in which Jewish humor is anything but humorous. It is sometimes said that Jewish humor is humor of aggression against others, but even against Jews. It is not easy to disassociate this charge of antisemitism but it is sometimes seen as reflecting Jewish self-hated or least self-mockery. . . . Jewish humor is in truth a form of counteraggression—the historically enduring act of fighting off enemies of Jews. Counteraggression is a moral response to the aggression of others. The laughter involved is in essence sardonic, a mark of triumph over persecution.[93]

By constantly blending political satire, ribald humor, and pointed social commentary in a media environment that rewards the outrageous, Sacha Baron Cohen has earned the mantle of comedic trailblazer.

Forming a Funnyman: Baron Cohen's Comedic Influences

While religion and politics seem to have deeply shaped Baron Cohen's unique brand of comedy, there have been other important influences as well. He frequently cites the actor Peter Sellers as the most seminal force in shaping his early ideas on comedy. He was even rumored at one point to be under consideration for the role of his idol in the biopic *The Life and Death of Peter Sellers* (the role ultimately went to Australian actor Geoffrey Rush).[94] In fact, he is often compared to Sellers. In the words of actor Paul Rudd, "He's got more guts and is more inventive than anyone except Peter Sellers. I actually, as a diehard Peter Sellers fan, think he might actually be better, because he's a very nice guy, too." In his 2004 *Vanity Fair* interview with Sacha Baron Cohen, Jim Windolf echoed the sentiment:

Baron Cohen, in his combination of dramatic skills and devotion to comedy, has a lot in common with Sellers—a gift for playing foreigners for laughs being the most obvious thing. Also, they're both British Jews who bury themselves in character, for whatever that's worth. But there's one major difference: Sellers was good in front of the camera and, famously, a shit when he was away from it. Baron Cohen is the converse: a shit in front of the camera and, by all accounts, a decent person in real life.

In addition to the *Pink Panther* star, Sacha Baron Cohen includes an illicit viewing of Monty Python's *Life of Brian* (1979) among his most formative experiences in early life.[95] The film recounts the misadventures of Brian Cohen who is born in Judea at the same time as Jesus of Nazareth (just a few doors down). After joining an anti-Roman revolutionary organization in his early life, he is proclaimed a prophet but tries to convince his followers that they should think for themselves (they slavishly parrot his advice back to him). He meets his end—like Jesus—on the cross, but is reminded to "Always Look on the Bright Side of Life." Upon its release, the film was picketed, banned, and lambasted as blasphemous for its ridicule of organized religion. Such humor seems to be a natural byproduct of elite British education. According to his former history professor Niall Ferguson:

Clearly there's a tradition of Oxbridge humor that goes back through *Not the Nine O'Clock News* and *Monty Python* to *Beyond the Fringe*. [Sacha] wanted to be a part of that, I think, hence the early involvement in the

Footlights. At root, this kind of humor consists of making fun of stupidity. What Sacha and John Cleese have in common is that they do not suffer fools gladly. However, the grotesque characters they play are so funny that mass audiences can laugh at them. It is in fact the masses that the comics are laughing at. The success of the movie *Borat* illustrates this perfectly. Quite probably the most cruelly anti-American film ever made was hugely popular in America.[96]

Like his Monty Python idols, Sacha Baron Cohen reveled in tipping sacred cows. While on the kibbutz, he made a short film where he pretended to be the Messiah ascending to heaven.[97] Such irreverent humor was later to become a mainstay of Baron Cohen's own style from his "Shvitzing" of the late 1990s to his infamous reporting on Kazakhstan's (fictitious) "Running of the Jews" in *Borat*.

Sacha Baron Cohen was also a great fan of Derek and Clive, the controversial characters created by the comedic team of Dudley Moore and Peter Cook. The duo produced a series of comedy albums and the feature film *Derek and Clive Get the Horn* (1979); the recordings—sometimes little more than drunken tirades ad-libbed by Moore and Cook—represented the pinnacle of anti-establishment humor in the late 1970s. The album sleeve of *Derek and Clive Live* (1976) lauded the comedy team's talents as such: "At a time when British influence is declining throughout the world, Derek and Clive represent welcome evidence of what this great country could be. They are a ray of hope on a darkening horizon. Their philosophy is both an inspiration to youth and hope for the senile." Upon playing the record, one encounters a stream of foul—even taboo—language: bodily function blather, discussion of Winston Churchill's bogeys, and an exchange about mutual masturbation.

Such low brow, satyric comedy infects nearly every aspect of Baron Cohen's pantomime. Taking their name from the mythical companions of Pan and Dionysius, 5th century Athenian satyric dramas burlesqued the serious events of the mythic past through lewd pantomime and subversive mockery. In his review of *Borat*, Richard Alleva states:

> Like the short satyr plays that followed Greek tragedies, this film both mocks and revels in the absurdities of the human body, its sexual and excretory functions, and how those functions embarrass and disgust us, yet amuse us precisely because they embarrass and disgust us. This is the hilarity of shock, not the hilarity of moral criticism that satirists such as Aristophanes and Swift employ.[98]

Despite Alleva's attempt to disabuse his readers of Baron Cohen's ability to produce effective satire, more than a few film critics and cultural commentators have likened him to Jonathan Swift, the Dublin-born writer who suggested the Irish save themselves from famine by eating their own children in his infamous *A Modest Proposal* (1729).[99] Perhaps the most auspicious of these critics was ambassadorial assistant and press secretary for Kazakhstan's U.S. embassy Roman Vassilenko (who is discussed in detail later) who stated, "Like Jonathan Swift wrote 'Gulliver's Travels' and invented a country, Lilliput, to make a satire of England, this is the same thing. He invents a Kazakhstan in order to make a satire of a very different country."[100] Peter L. Berger defines satire as "the deliberate use of the comic for purposes of attack."[101] As a satirist, Baron Cohen has an agenda; his humor is meant as an attack on political and religious institutions, as well as the bourgeoisie, the ruling classes, and other social groups. It is also educational in that it is meant to teach the audience something about the undesirability of that which is being attacked.[102]

In addition to standard satire, Baron Cohen's humor is also characterized by its obsession with the body and its functions. Writing on Ali G's impact on British culture, London School of Economics professor Paul Gilroy commented that Sacha Baron Cohen possesses a "carnivalesque contempt for the pompous and powerful people he is still able to ambush, manipulate and even humiliate."[103] The term 'carnivalesque' was used by the Russian literary critic Mikhail Bakhtin to describe the "temporary liberation from the prevailing truth and from the established order [and] the suspension of all hierarchical rank, privileges, norms, and prohibitions."[104] Drawing on Renaissance fêtes, Bakhtin discussed how the peasantry used ribald celebration as a tool of liberation, escaping the constrictive and often soul-crushing hierarchies of church and state.[105] Carnivalesque humor relies on the "'merry' weapons of excess" employing "turnabout," i.e., "a continual shifting from top to bottom, from front to rear, of numerous parodies and travesties, humiliations, profanations, comic crownings and uncrownings."[106]

Central to the carnival atmosphere was grotesque realism: a form of below-the-belt humor which valued the nether regions of the body over their loftier counterparts. In the words of sociologist Sean Brayton, "rationality and mental resolve are replaced with bodily fluids and defecation."[107] Bakhtin reminds us, "Not only parody in its narrow sense but all other forms of grotesque realism degrade, bring down to earth, turn their subject into flesh."[108] Baron Cohen's humor revels in such methodologies of mirth. Paradoxically, his obsession with feces, genitalia, and sexual congress set him apart from the archetypal Jewish comic. According to Berger, "Jewish humor contains almost no scatology and remarkably little sexuality. . . . One can say that Jewish humor is at a great distance from the raucous carnival laughter that Mikhail Bakhtin goes on about."[109] While Ali G tends to be Baron Cohen's most effective carivalesque trope, his other personae also engage in the merry weapons of excess mentioned above and do not eschew the baser elements of human existence: bowel movements, excretion of bodily fluids, etc.

Despite his various disguises, he cannot hide his commitment to upsetting the accepted order of things. While it would be hyperbole to describe him as a revolutionary, at the very least, he is an effective and innovative social critic. As such, Baron Cohen is the modern epitome of *homo ludens* whose job it is to "loosen the rigors of a structured society and 'infuse' through the system at least temporarily the values of an egalitarian community."[110] The modern equivalent of such popular humor is undoubtedly burlesque—an entertainment form "that is grounded in the aesthetics of transgression, inversion, and the grotesque."[111] Unlike the (literally) stripped down "girlie shows" of the 1940s and 50s, late Victorian burlesque featured pointed social critique, particularly directed at the upper classes. According to historian Robert Clyde Allen:

> Burlesque is emblematic of the way that popular entertainment becomes an arena for 'acting out' cultural contradictions and even contestations and is exemplary of the complexities and ambiguities of that process. . . . [Burlesque was] disturbing—and threatening—because it presented a world without limits, a world turned upside down and inside out in which nothing was above being brought down to earth. In that world, things that should be kept separate were united in gross hybrids. Meanings refused to stay put. Anything might happen. And the burlesque performer . . . literally and figuratively embodied this world. [112]

Articulating a more parsimonious or more accurate description of Baron Cohen's humor would be difficult. Over a decade, Baron Cohen's transgressive style, obsession with nether regions of the human physique, and satirical barbs have blended together to produce a unique form of postmodern humor. However, there was a time when he was not so funny.

The Five-Year Plan: Sacha Before He Was "Massiv"

In 2002, Britain's Channel 5 spliced together a half-hour documentary on the works of Sacha Baron Cohen entitled "Ali G Before He Was Massiv." The aim of the special was to portray the creator of "Ali G" before his rise to fame on *The 11 O'Clock Show*. In the words of one reviewer of the piece, "It's fair to say that even dedicated comedy enthusiasts had barely heard of Baron Cohen before he made his first appearances as Ali G on Channel 4's *The 11 O'Clock Show*, and so the casual observer could be forgiven for thinking that there is hardly likely to be a treasure trove of undiscovered early performances gathering dust in the archives."[113] Despite this dismal review, the program does provide key insights into the early professional career of Sacha Baron Cohen. This was a critical time for the aspiring comedian when, according to the sneering voice-over: "He spent years wallowing in cable TV hell."[114]

Recounting the lean years after graduating Cambridge, the comedian told *Rolling Stone* in 2006, "I gave myself five years to start earning money from being an actor, a comedian. . . . If it didn't work out, I was going to move onto something else, become a barrister or something."[115] While he committed most of the next five years to acting, he briefly took a job with the financial services firm J.P. Morgan & Co. and flirted with modeling, appearing in an ill-advised fashion spread in the December 1994 issue of British "lad's" magazine, *Loaded*. He tried his lot at stand-up comedy, though his early onstage performances reportedly left much to be desired. Failing to take the comedy world by storm, he moved on to television, almost totally avoiding the "traditional" British route to comedic success which forces comics to plod a tortured path through the Edinburgh Comedy Festival and clubs like the Comedy Store in Soho.

By 1995, he landed his first television appearance on Channel 4's *Jack and Jeremy's Police 4*, a spoof of reality crime programs. The show's special constables prided themselves on the fact that they were "trained to hit people properly."[116] From there, he moved onto the short-lived local cable show *Pump TV* (broadcast from Slough—the dreary setting of the UK version of *The Office*) where he clumsily tried to affect cool with big lapels, chunky gold necklaces, and shades. For the next few years, he spent time in

Slough, Staines, and Ealing—England's suburban equivalent of Hollywood—working in front of and behind the camera.[117] Baron Cohen's occupational pursuits then led him to host a teen-oriented chat show entitled *F2F* on Granada Talk TV (the network itself lasted less than one year). While Baron Cohen once hyped *F2F* as the "most cultural ever youth show," another commentator described the program as such: "This was no intellectual student comedy: it was a terrifyingly chaotic, seat-of-the-pants broadcast, with a changing guest audience of surly teenagers from local comprehensives and D-list guests."[118] *F2F*, the self-billed "first program for the cyber generation," died in the crib.

According to a profile in *The Scotsman*, "Aspects of Cohen's comedy were evident in his TV persona, but there was no sign of the phenomenon which was to follow."[119] Upon viewing some of these early clips of Sacha Baron Cohen, there is little to suggest the indefatigable confidence he would later manifest with his Ali G, Bruno, and Borat personae. Instead, Baron Cohen seems uneasy in his own skin, making funny faces and jerky body movements whenever the camera points his way. Only when he is given the chance to introduce Richard Whiteley, the longtime host of Channel 4's daytime game show *Countdown*, does Baron Cohen shine. His litany of pre-interview kudos includes: "colossus of quiz shows, the master of mathematical equation, the archbishop of afternoon wordplay, the king of conundrums, the prince of puns, he's the one, he's the only, he's the legendary Richard Whiteley." His delivery is flawless and full of energy; it is clear that he is developing both style and confidence.[120]

It was only when Sacha found a spot on Granada's Talk TV show *London Weekend Television* that his career started to take shape. There he met Mike Toppin who would serve as his mentor and help him develop a prototype of "Ali G." Inspiration for this new character was found in Tim Westwood. In the 1990s, the BBC Radio One hip-hop DJ and son of a Church of England bishop became a sensation in Britain with his "wigger" style and outrageous personality.[121] Paradoxically, Westwood—sometimes known as the "Gangster of Rap"—had, by the end of the decade, become both "hugely influential" and "a laughable figure" in popular culture with his Jamaican-American accent and over-the-top clothing choices.[122] Taking a cue from Westwood, Baron Cohen developed a character named MC Jocelyn Cheadle-Hume (named after an area outside of Manchester in the north of England). Over time, Baron Cohen honed the shtick by introducing a more street-oriented style *à la* Westwood, as well as employing his own idiosyncratic argot such as "Boyakasha!"

By early 1998, Baron Cohen was appearing on the late night *Coming Soon*, which allowed him to expand into the raunchy netherworld of British comedy. By this point, he had developed incipient versions of his other comedic vehicles: Bruno and Borat. His first appearance as the Austrian fashionista Bruno was on the skit "Funk Off: Austria's Krrrazy Clothes Show Presents . . . *Unter dem Fleisch mit* . . . Bruno" for the Paramount Comedy Channel. In 1998, he also appeared on BBC's *Comedy Nation* as Kristo reporting for the fictional "Albanian Televiska" (the forerunner of Borat with a similar gray suit, thick accent, and thicker moustache). Despite his success in developing new characters, he had not yet been able to build a respectable career in entertainment. Sacha Baron Cohen was a hair's breadth from abandoning comedy altogether when Talkback Productions contacted him about doing a pilot for *The 11 O'Clock Show*. In 2006, he told *Rolling Stone*:

> I was sitting on a beach in Thailand. It was four years and ten months since I'd graduated, and I had just come back from my brother's wedding in Australia. . . . I was thinking about staying in Thailand, because I was having this very nice life on a pound-fifty a day. And that's when I got a call from my agent saying there's this audition for *The 11 O'Clock Show*, this satirical late-night show, and they were looking for a host. I remember telling her that I didn't know if I wanted to come back. I had been rejected so many times that I didn't know if it was worth it.[123]

However, Baron Cohen chose to pursue the opportunity—a decision that would forever change his life. He gave the producers a tape of his proto-Boratian "reportings" at a pro-fox hunting rally where he "elicited monstrously right-wing views from the foxhunting set simply by pretending to be a bewildered Albanian TV presenter."[124] He was quickly hired and the next stage of his career was about to begin.

Notes

1. Both *Vanity Fair* and *National Public Radio* (NPR) have published two out-of-character interviews with Sacha Baron Cohen. *The Los Angeles Times* (2007), *Rolling Stone* (2006), *The New York Times* (2004), *The Daily Show with Jon Stewart* (2004), *Late Night with David Letterman* (2004), and *The Howard Stern Show* (2004) have all interviewed the comedian (as himself) as well.

2. Ali G's "Well Wicked Britain" mocks New Labour's "Cool Britannia" late 1990s media campaign which marketed England (and to a lesser extent, the rest of the United Kingdom) as a hip, modern, and multicultural "destination country;" see, for instance, Bruce Wallace, "Cool Britannia," *Maclean's* 110, no. 17 (28 April 1997): 38-41 and John Lloyd, "Cool Britannia Warms Up," *New Statesman* 127, no. 4376 (12 March 1998): 10-11; "Valley G's Wicked Welsh Rootz," *BBC News*, 28 March 2002, http://news.bbc.co.uk/2/hi/uk_news/wales/1898402.stm (22 March 2007). In an interview with Welsh politician Ronald Davies he asked, "What is so good about Wales? Because with no disrespect, but me heard it's crap."

3. Richard Evans, "Is It 'Cos We is Welsh?" *Western Mail*, 22 March 2002, 11.

4. Jay Rayner, "The Observer Profile: Sacha Baron Cohen: Mutha of Invention," *The Observer*, 24 February 2002, 27; during his tenure on the teen-oriented *F2F* in the late 1990s, Baron Cohen once foppishly introduced the show playing the piano in a tuxedo replete with a maestro-style tailcoat.

5. Neil Strauss, "The Man behind the Moustache," *Rolling Stone* 1014 (11 November 2006): 58-70.

6. Roland White, "Borat's Easy . . . Being Me is Odd; Interview: Sacha Baron Cohen," *Sunday Times*, 21 January 2007.

7. Strauss, "The Man behind the Moustache," 61.

8. Zohar is considered to be the most important work in Kabbalah, or Jewish mysticism. It contains revelations about the nature of God, the origins and structure of the universe, the relationship between good and evil, and the purpose of man.

9. Interestingly, Erran Baron Cohen was invited to collaborate with the Turan Alem Kazakhstan Philharmonic Orchestra in 2007. His previous Borat accompaniments had no artistic connections to Kazakhstan, deriving instead from Romani music. Since the movie's premiere, he has begun to experiment with traditional Kazakh melodies; see "A Symphony for Kazakhstan," *Telegraph*, 30 April 2007.

10. Ruki Sayid, "It's Ali in De Mirror . . . Ali in De Mirror. Massive Scoop! Ali In," *Mirror*, 12 January 2000.

11. William Sutcliffe's first and best-known novel *New Boy* (1996) recounts certain incidents from his life at Haberdashers' Aske's. Besides bringing together a sizable chunk of the *Da Ali G Show* team, Aske's is also the alma mater of comedian David Baddiel, also of Welsh-Jewish origins.

12. Clifford, "The Great Pretender . . . Innit?" *Sunday Tribune*, 24 March 2002, 15. In March 2007, the school's Web site (http://www.habsboys.org.uk/) greeted visitors with scenes from the school's recent "Purim extravaganza," as well as photos of pupils of African, Asian, and European descent.

13. Strauss, "The Man behind the Moustache," 64.

14. Neil Tweedie and Thomas Harding, "The Polite Little Swot Who Grew into Ali G," *Telegraph*, 8 March 2002.

15. *Ali G Before He Was Massiv*. Produced by Tony Moss and directed by Viv Ellis. 25 min. Chrysalis Entertainment, 2003. Channel 5 (UK).

16. Glenda Cooper, "Secret World of Sacha B," *Daily Mail*, 19 March 2002.

17. Hans Kornberg. Email interview by author, 26 March 2007.

18. Brendan O'Neill, "Backstory: Borat Write Thesis," *Christian Science Monitor* 98, no. 250 (21 November 2006): 20.

19. Quoted in Patrick Goldstein, "Out of Character," *Los Angeles Times*, 9 January 2007.

20. Anthony Badger. Telephone interview by author, 18 April 2007.

21. Rich Cohen, "Hello! It's Sexy Time!" *Vanity Fair* 556 (December 2006): 262-270.

22. Had he chosen such a path, he would have been following in the footsteps of his cousin Professor Simon Baron-Cohen, a Fellow at Trinity College, Cambridge and world-renowned autism expert. I contacted Professor Baron-Cohen while conducting research for the manuscript. He politely—but firmly—declined to comment on any aspect of his relationship with the Baron Cohen family or the impact of Sacha Baron Cohen's success on his own career as an academic stating, "I get so many similar enquiries, and if [I] made an exception for you I'd not be able to stem the tide;" Simon Baron-Cohen, personal communication, 25 March 2007.

23. Niall Ferguson. Email interview by author, 30 June 2007.

24. Coincidentally, Hugh Laurie hosted *Saturday Night Live* the same night Sacha Baron Cohen appeared on the show in character as Borat to promote his 2006 film. On their way for drinks after the taping, Borat's pranks provoked an assault by a passer-by on a Manhattan street. Borat approached the man asking, "I like your clothings. Are nice! Please may I buying? I want have sex with it." The man responded by punching Baron Cohen repeatedly before being pushed away by Laurie as Baron Cohen struggled to his feet; see Emily Smith, "Borat Spanked by Angry Yank," *The Sun* web site, 13 November 2006, http://www.thesun.co.uk/article/0,,2-2006520669,00.html (22 March 2007). Curiously, Hugh Laurie later denied any heroics telling *E! Entertainment Television* at the 2007 Emmy Awards that "there's absolutely no truth to it whatsoever."

25. Robert Siegel, "Ali G: Fooling Serious Interviewees, All for a Laugh," All Things Considered, *NPR*, 23 July 2004.

26. Tom Charity, "Review: 'Borat' is Most Excellent Comedy," *CNN* web site, 6 November 2006, http://www.cnn.com/2006/SHOWBIZ/Movies/11/02/review.borat/index.html (22 March 2007).

27. Sayid, "It's Ali in De Mirror."

28. Peter Dyke, "Da Real Ali G's a Shy Geezer Innit," *Daily Star*, 20 March 2002, 19.

29. Joel Brandon-Bravo, "Israel, My Pride and My Shame," *Sunday Times*, 21 April 2002.

30. See Cooper, "Secret World of Sacha B."

31. "Sacha Baron Cohen Slips Out of Borat Role to Collect Golden Globe," *Haaretz* web site, 16 January 2007, http://www.haaretz.com/hasen/spages/814147.html (22 March 2007).

32. David Horovitz, "In My Country There Is Problem—With Borat," *The Jerusalem Post,* 1 December 2006, 24.

33. Virginia Heffernan, "The Cheerful Confessions of Ali G, Borat and Bruno," *New York Times,* Sec. E, Col. 1, The Arts/Cultural Desk, 15 July 2004, 1.

34. On one occasion, he brought home the pop star and Kabbalah enthusiast Madonna and her film director husband, Guy Ritchie, to meet his folks on the Sabbath; see Clifford, "The Great Pretender," 15.

35. Devin Gordon and Ginanne Brownell, "The Brain Behind Borat," *Newsweek* 148, no. 20 (13 November 2006): 69.

36. Cooper, "Secret World of Sacha B."

37. Terry Gross, "Meet the Real Sacha Baron Cohen," Fresh Air from WHYY on *NPR,* 4 January 2007.

38. Jaime J. Weinman, "Did Bunker Beget Borat?" *Maclean's* 119, no. 44 (6 November 2006): 62-64.

39. White, "Borat's Easy," 2007.

40. Fisher, who was born to Scottish Presbyterian parents in Muscat, Oman, also learned Hebrew and how to prepare kosher meals as part of her preparation for joining the Jewish faith.

41. According to film critic Peter Bradshaw, "only Jewish people are allowed to tell Jewish jokes;" see Peter Bradshaw, "Bear-Baiting in Bushville," *Guardian* (27 October 2006), 7.

42. Lana Berkowitz, "Cover Story: Borat," *Houston Chronicle,* 5 November 2006. Retrieved via *Factiva.*

43. A. Roy Eckardt, "The Heirs of Itzhak," *Society* 24, no. 4 (May/June 1992): 34-42.

44. Manohla Dargis, "Satire is Not Pretty," *New York Times,* 3 November 2006, WD1.

45. Christopher John Farley and Simon Robinson, "Dave Speaks," *Time* 165, no. 21 (23 May 2005): 68-73.

46. Farley and Robinson, "Dave Speaks," 68-70.

47. Dargis, "Satire is Not Pretty," 1.

48. Prior to unexpectedly leaving the US for South Africa in the middle of filming the third season of his show, Chappelle had begun to express reservations about the content of his own humor which—like that of Baron Cohen—could be interpreted on multiple levels, one of which was being racist and playing to grotesque stereotypes of blacks. Chappelle began to worry that he "had gone from sending up stereotypes to merely reinforcing them;" see Farley and Robinson, "Dave Speaks," 69.

49. Charles Schutz, "The Sociability of Ethnic Jokes," *Humor* 2, no. 2 (April 1989): 165–177.

50. Alleen Pace Nilsen and Don L. F. Nilsen, "Just How Ethnic is Ethnic Humor?" *Canadian Ethnic Studies* 38, no. 1 (2006): 131-139.

51. For the course listing and syllabus, see http://www.wisc.edu/english/walkowitz/519/.

52. See, for instance, Rachel Garfield, "Ali G: Just Who Does He Think He Is?" *Third Text* 54 (Spring 2001): 63-70; Dan Friedman, "Genuine Authentic Gangsta Flava," *Zeek: A Jewish Journal of Thought and Culture* (April 2003): 1-4, http://www.zeek.net/; and Richard Howells, "'Is It Because I Is Black?': Race, Humor and the Polysemiology of Ali G," *Historical Journal of Film, Radio and Television* 26, no. 2 (June 2006): 155-177.

53. According to Halkin, Jewish humor dates back to the baptized Jew Heinrich Heine (1797-1856) and attained full development with the Yiddish writer Sholom

Aleichem (1859-1916); see Hillel Halkin, "Why Jews Laugh at Themselves," *Commentary* 121, no. 4 (April 2006): 47-54. Jewishness also influenced an important subset of humor within the Soviet Union.

54. Nilsen and Nilsen, "Just How Ethnic is Ethnic Humor?," 131-32.

55. Stephen J. Whitfield, "Towards an Appreciation of American Jewish Humor," *Journal of Modern Jewish Studies* 4, no. 1 (March 2005): 33–48.

56. Friedman, "Genuine Authentic Gangsta Flava," 2.

57. Quoted in A. Roy Eckardt, "The Heirs of Itzhak," *Society* 24, no. 4 (May/June 1992): 34-42.

58. Eckardt, "The Heirs of Itzhak," 34.

59. Samuel Juni and Bernard Katz, "Self-Effacing Wit as a Response to Aggression: Dynamics in Ethnic Humor," *The Journal of General Psychology* 128, no. 2 (April 2001): 119-142.

60. Juni and Katz, "Self-Effacing Wit as a Response to Aggression," 122.

61. Eckardt, "The Heirs of Itzhak," 37.

62. Eckardt, "The Heirs of Itzhak," 38.

63. In another evocative scene from *Hannah and Her Sisters*, as Allen prepares for his conversion to Catholicism, he buys a spectral image hologram of Christ and a crucifix (symbolizing the transcendental elements of the religion) along with a jar of Hellman's mayonnaise and a loaf of Wonder Bread (the banal trappings of the gentiles).

64. Rosen recently produced an anthology of early 20th century Jewish vaudeville entitled *Jewface* (2006) which included such Jewish-crafted anti-Semitic tunes as "Cohen Owes Me 97 Dollars" and "I'm a Yiddish Cowboy."

65. Jody Rosen, "Borat Owes Me 97 Dollars," *Slate,* 3 November 2006, http://www.slate.com/.

66. Rosen, "Borat Owes Me 97 Dollars."

67. Juni and Katz, "Self-Effacing Wit as a Response to Aggression," 122-23

68. Juni and Katz, "Self-Effacing Wit as a Response to Aggression," 119-142.

69. Whitfield, "Towards an Appreciation of American Jewish Humor," 43.

70. Richard Brookhiser, "Jokers Wild and Mild," *National Review* 55, no. 2 (10 February 2003): 52.

71. Michael Musto, "Sarah Silverman Is My Kind of Cunt," *Village Voice*, 23 January 2007, http://www.villagevoice.com/nyclife/0704,musto,75611,15.html (14 August 2007).

72. Musto, "Sarah Silverman Is My Kind of Cunt."

73. Cooper, "Secret World of Sacha B."

74. Joshua Muravchik, "Borat!" *Commentary* 123, no. 1 (January 2007): 44-47.

75. White, "Borat's Easy," 2007.

76. Golders Green is a suburban commercial district in north London. It has a strong Jewish, especially Orthodox, presence which dates back to the early 1900s and numerous kosher food shops, yeshivas, and synagogues are to be found in the borough.

77. Nathan Lee, "Persona Non Grata," *Film Comment* 42, no. 6 (November/December 2006): 22-24.

78. Simon Weaver, "Comprehending Ambivalence: Ali G and Conceptualisations of the 'Other.'" Paper presented at The Connections Conference, University of Bristol, 2005, 5.

79. Weaver, "Comprehending Ambivalence," 3.

80. Interestingly, Prince William was filmed doing an impression of Ali G during his gap year in Chile; see Cooper, "Secret World of Sacha B."

81. David Byers, "Sacha Baron Cohen among 20 Most Powerful Men in UK," *European Jewish Press* Web site, 4 February 2007, http://ejpress.org/article/13693# (28 March 2007).

82. *Ali G Before He Was Massiv.*

31

83. *Ali G Before He Was Massiv.*

84. A contemporary at Cambridge agreed with this evaluation with one caveat: the Middle East. Sacha Baron Cohen was avidly pro-Israel during college, a position that would set him apart from many of his peers and professors alike.

85. Oliver Marre, "Sacha Baron Cohen: Our Man from Kazakhstan," *Observer,* 10 September 2006. A former confidant told me that Sacha Baron Cohen had a personal interest in the topic of Black-Jewish relations while at Cambridge, as his girlfriend at the time was black. According to the source, "He knew the relationship would not last because he would have to marry a Jewish woman."

86. David Winner, "Minimum Respect," *The Jerusalem Report* 11, no. 8 (14 August 2000): 42. Interestingly, Livingstone has been dogged by accusations of anti-Semitism in recent years, particularly after an exchange with a Jewish reporter whom he likened to a Nazi concentration camp guard. The mayor has a particularly antagonistic position towards the policies of Israel which has further fueled this fire.

87. Twentieth Century Fox, "Sacha Baron Cohen Fact Sheet Awards," Academy of Motion Pictures Arts and Science Web site, 2006, http://www.oscars.org/press/presskit/nomannc/pdf/bios_notes/36_cohen_sacha_baron_borat.pdf (8 April 2007).

88. Tyler Hernandez, "It's Nice! Very Nice!" *Tulane Hullabaloo,* 10 November 2006, http://www.thehullabaloo.com/ (5 May 2007).

89. Whitfield, "Towards an Appreciation of American Jewish Humor," 38.

90. Tony Benn, "How I Tamed Ali G," *Guardian,* 30 March 2000, 17.

91. Jaime J. Weinman, "Did Bunker Beget Borat?"*Maclean's* 119, no. 44 (6 November 2006): 62-64.

92. Christie Davies, *The Mirth of Nations* (New Brunswick, NJ: Transaction Publishers, 2002), 58.

93. Eckardt, "The Heirs of Itzhak," 41.

94. "Battle to be Best Sellers," *Daily Star,* 27 August 2001.

95. See Strauss, "The Man behind the Moustache," 64.

96. Ferguson, 2007.

97. See Cooper, "Secret World of Sacha B."

98. Richard Alleva, "British Invasion," *Commonweal* 133, no. 22 (15 December 2006): 15-16.

99. Though, for what are perhaps obvious reasons, Sacha Baron Cohen is less often compared to Aristophanes who commands the undeniably august title, "the father of comedy;" see, for instance, Peter Travers, "Comedy of the Year," *Rolling Stone* 1013 (16 November 2006): 134; Nigel Andrews, "Rude, Appalling, Irresistible," *Financial Times* (London), 2 November 2006, 13; Lou Lumenick, "Kazakh It To Me!" *New York Post,* 2 November 2006, 65; and Bill Maxwell, "Look at Borat, Then Look at Yourself," *St. Petersburg Times* (Florida), 26 November 2006, 3. Maxwell comments: "Borat, in my estimation, is a splendid mockumentary because it tolerates no sacred cows. Everything is up for ridicule, as it should be in unapologetic satire. And Borat is quintessential satire, on par with Swift's *Gulliver's Travels.* If you do not believe me, reacquaint yourself with Lemuel Gulliver's experiences with the petty Lilliputians, the foul Brobdingnagians and the brutish Yahoos and then watch Borat again."

100. Steven Rosen, "Will Offensive Volley Miss Its Mark?" *Denver Post,* 3 November 2006, F3.

101. Peter L. Berger, *Redeeming Laughter: The Comic Dimension of Human Experience* (New York and Berlin: Walther De Gruyter, 1997), 157.

102. Berger, *Redeeming Laughter,* 158.

103. Paul Gilroy, "Ali G and the Oscars," *Open Democracy* Web site, 4 April 2002, http://www.opendemocracy.net/arts-Film/article_459.jsp (9 April 2007).

104. Mikhail Bakhtin, *Rabelais and His World,* translated by Helene Iswolsky (Cambridge, MA: The MIT Press, 1968), 10.

105. David Gasperetti, "The Carnivalesque Spirit of the Eighteenth-Century Russian Novel," *Russian Review* 52, no. 2 (April 1993): 166-183.

106. See Gasperetti, "The Carnivalesque Spirit of the Eighteenth-Century Russian Novel," 167 and Bakhtin, *Rabelais and His World*, 11.

107. Sean Brayton, "MTV's *Jackass*: Transgression, Abjection and the Economy of White Masculinity," *Journal of Gender Studies* 16, no. 1 (March 2007): 57-72; Brayton's own work explores the Bakhtinesque qualities of *Jackass* creators' "series of self-deprecating stunts." The antics of Johnny Knoxville, Steve-O, *et al.* are regularly compared to those of Baron Cohen, though important stylistic differences exist; see, for instance, Lisa Kennedy, "Masochism's Light Side," *Denver Post*, 26 December 2006, F1.

108. Bakhtin, *Rabelais and His World*, 20.

109. Berger, *Redeeming Laughter*, 88.

110. See Johan Huizinga, *Homo Ludens: A Study of the Play-Element in Culture* (Boston: The Beacon Press, 1950) and Natalie Zemon Davis, *Society and Culture in Early Modern France* (Stanford: Stanford University Press, 1975), 103.

111. Robert Clyde Allen, *Horrible Prettiness: Burlesque and American Culture* (Chapel Hill: University of North Carolina Press, 1991), 26.

112. Allen, *Horrible Prettiness*, 27-29.

113. TJ Worthington, "Review: Ali G Before He Was Massiv," *Off The Telly*, 27 March 2002, http://www.offthetelly.co.uk/reviews/2002/aligmassiv.htm (1 April 2007).

114. *Ali G Before He Was Massiv.*

115. Strauss, "The Man behind the Moustache," 67.

116. "Jack and Jeremy's Police 4," *The bbc.co.uk Guide to Comedy*, 2007, http://www.bbc.co.uk/comedy/guide/articles/j/jackandjeremyspo_1299000866.shtml (1 April 2007).

117. For instance, he provided the English-language narration for the 1997 Hebrew documentary *Yatzati L'Hapes Ahavah: Techef Ashuv* (Out for Love . . . Be Back Shortly).

118. Vicky Allan, "Ali G Indahouse: Wigger Happy TV," *Scotland on Sunday*, 17 March 2002, 7.

119. "Saturday Profile: Sacha Baron Cohen Hiding behind the Magic of Ali G," *Scotsman*, 23 March 2002, 12

120. It is also possible that Baron Cohen was simply more comfortable with the attention focused on his guest rather than himself. Despite his worldwide fame, he still seems uncomfortable in front of the camera when not in costume.

121. "Wigger" or "wigga" is a portmanteau of 'white' and 'nigger.' It refers to a white who affects the caparison, rarefied speech, and anti-authoritarian behavioral patterns of black urban youths. For more, see Bakari Kitwana, *Why White Kids Love Hip-Hop: Wankstas, Wiggers, Wannabes, and the New Reality of Race in America* (New York: Basic Civitas Books, 2005).

122. Richard Cook, "The White DJ in Black Culture," *New Statesman* 128, no. 4447 (2 August 1999): 18-19.

123. Strauss, "The Man behind the Moustache," 68.

124. Harry Thompson, "G Force," *Guardian*, 27 April 1999, 19; one of the questions posed was whether prison overcrowding could be reduced by turning inmates loose to be chased by hounds. The response from many in the crowd: "Bloody good idea."

Chapter 2
Da Ali G Show: Building a Brand as Bamboozler Extraordinaire

After five years of cable TV obscurity, Sacha Baron Cohen began his rapid rise to stardom on Channel 4's *The 11 O'Clock Show*. The program melodramatically marketed itself with the tagline: "Live fast, die young, stay up late." Thanks to his expertise at the unscripted mock interview, the Cambridge graduate steadily developed a following of young Britons who laughed at the missteps and naïveté of the governing classes. However, Baron Cohen's growing fame made his style of "hoax journalism" ever more difficult to perpetrate as Ali G became nearly as ubiquitous a fixture in British popular culture as the Prime Minister. Consequently, Baron Cohen was forced to take his show on the road. In America, Baron Cohen plumbed new depths of humor, attracted controversy at every turn, and made himself into an international superstar.

Ali Unleashed

The 11 O'Clock Show was a half hour-long, thrice-weekly late-night satirical sketch show that was taped on the day of broadcast to ensure topicality. The program lasted for five series (seasons), ending in December 2000. In addition to Sacha Baron Cohen, the show also launched the careers of Ricky Gervais and Mackenzie Crook, both of whom went on to star in the highly successful British comedy *The Office*. When it premiered in 1998, *The 11 O'Clock Show* was integral to Channel 4's attempt to reverse its creeping abandonment of "British" programming. Until that point the network's evening lineup had been dominated by mainstream American fare, such as the situation comedies *Friends* and *Frasier*. Ironically, by jumpstarting the careers of Gervais and Baron Cohen, Channel 4 effectively reversed the flow of content across the Atlantic, prompting stentorian declarations of a new "British Invasion" of comedic talent.[1]

The 11 O'Clock Show was intended to ride the heels of Channel 4's *Brass Eye*, a series of satirical spoof documentaries which ridiculed British politicians and celebrities. Cultural critic Sally O'Reilly described *Brass*

Eye's "transgressive" model as such: "Its genre was fairly conventional, following the vein of grotesque satire from Jonathan Swift to Steve Bell, yet the butt of *Brass Eye*'s satire was not necessarily what is represented, but the way in which it is presented. . . . The more pointed and useful critique being proffered, though, was of the hyperbolic rhetoric of politicians and the media."[2] In one episode, a Conservative Member of Parliament was fooled into appearing in an elaborate video warning against the dangers of a fictional Eastern European drug called "cake." MP David Amess, while holding a massive yellow pill, declared, "This is a made-up drug." He went so far as to pose a question about it in the House of Commons, thus endowing Channel 4's jokesters a permanent place in the Parliamentary record.[3] *Brass Eye*'s humor was forged in the over-the-top and sometimes aggressive antics of Chris Morris, who undoubtedly paved the way for future spoof comedians like Sacha Baron Cohen.[4] Presaging the popularity of Ali G, Morris even developed his own gangsta rapper persona, Fur-Q. The insidiously-named character was created for a sketch satirizing hip hop's glamorization of guns and violence years before the debut of Staines' favorite son, Ali G.[5]

Baron Cohen's style was perfect for the budding genre of "hoax TV" which was gaining ground in the UK (though it would take a few more years to catch on in the US).[6] While it was his bumbling foreign reporter shtick that won him the job, Baron Cohen's hip-hop gangster persona actually launched his career. Ali G—once Baron Cohen's most famous creation—is the leader of the West Staines Massiv, as well as a part-time drug dealer, aspirant rapper, and stultifyingly ignorant buffoon.[7] In a 1999 interview, *The 11 O'Clock Show* producer Harry Thompson stated,

> I commissioned Sacha to come up with a new character. He created a youth presenter who would report from raves and festivals. I added only the name and the suggestion that if he were to interview Establishment figures instead, posing as a pig-ignorant Channel 4 "Voice of Youth," then his victims would immediately feel themselves superior. They would have to explain themselves—and therefore reveal themselves—more fulsomely than if confronted by a conventional-looking interviewer.[8]

Thompson, the man behind BBC2's long-running satirical quiz show *Have I Got News For You*, re-named the character (as mentioned earlier, Baron Cohen's rapper persona had previously gone by the ridiculous handle of MC Jocelyn Cheadle-Hume) hoping to create a safety net for his pranks. Thompson explained, "If he had a whiff of Islam about him, we thought people would be afraid to challenge him."[9] While 'Ali' implied Islam, the 'G' is a signified for 'gangsta' as in 'g-money.' Ironically, Ali G's real name is the Scottish-sounding and thoroughly unthreatening Alistair Leslie Graham.

The new and improved Ali was purportedly further influenced by a well-publicized appearance of BBC Radio One DJ Tim Westwood at the 1997 Notting Hill carnival, a venue where Westwood has been the headliner for some years.

> People were in a celebratory mood. Westwood, however, was not a happy disc jockey. He felt he wasn't getting to the people who really mattered. To sort out the problem he stopped the music, thought for a second or so and addressed the crowd: "Right, I want all the white people to move to

the back and let my big dick niggers come to the front." A roar of approval went up—whites cheering just as vociferously as blacks.[10]

According to *The Independent,* the outrageousness of a white son of a clergyman draping himself in black culture (and being celebrated for it) impacted Baron Cohen deeply. Both Westwood and Baron Cohen could ultimately attribute their careers to successfully "mimicking the manners of a culture that is increasingly reliant on stereotypes designed to increase visceral appeal . . . [specifically] hungry materialism: a ferocious hankering after jewelry, cars and girls (women are seldom more than objects here), along with a very big gun to ward off anyone else who wants to cut in."[11]

Yet, from their earliest successes, both were recognized by their fans as whites parading as black. Neither "blacked-up;" instead they affected the speech and dress of a particular black subculture. Both authenticity and marketability were realized through performance, not background. As such, they turned the expectations of the hip-hop world on their head. Hip-hop scholar Mickey Hess argues that success in the genre paradoxically demands that "artists work to produce marketable music for mainstream listeners yet at the same time to maintain a necessary level of authenticity to a place of cultural origin."[12] "Gagsta" rappers Westwood and Ali G are miles away from "genuine" gangster rappers like Ice Cube and Ice T. Instead, they resemble constructed or "masked" personae such as Marshall Bruce Mathers III's dual alter egos "Eminem"[13] and "Slim Shady," and Digital Underground's "Shock G" and "MC Humpty Hump" (both performed by Greg Jacobs). Such personae (Baron Cohen's "Ali G" and "Big Dawg" Westwood included) "specifically critique the existing ideologies of authenticity and marketability within hip-hop music of their specific eras."[14] Rachel Garfield echoes the sentiment:

> Sacha Baron-Cohen's choice of [the Ali G] character goes to the heart of Hip Hop's confusion of culture with consumerism . . . he was exposing the very manufactured essence of the fashion of Hip Hop with all of the reactionary politics of its performers and followers. It was crucial that Ali G be that very form of black cipher to critique that particular form of consumer 'identity,' the very consumer identity aspect that allows it to travel so easily into the white world.[15]

Newly-named, remade for primetime, and ready to probe the fringes of the British *zeitgeist,* "Ali G—Channel 4's Voice of Youth" was unleashed on the world in the autumn of 1998. However, producers Harry Thompson and Andrew Newman conducted Channel 4's launch of the *11 O'Clock Show* without fanfare to avoid the pre-premiere critical bloodbath that had afflicted many similar offerings like *TV Offal* (1997).

Stealth was integral to *The 11 O'Clock Show*'s success. Interviewees were generally in the dark about what they were getting themselves into. The show was pitched to its unwitting participants as a current affairs program. However, after an Independent Television Commission (ITC) ruling that shows must not deceive contributors about their purpose, the producers proceeded very carefully in their interactions with interviewees.[16] In fact, Ali G's first interview was with Dr. Madsen Pirie of the Adam Smith Institute, a free market think tank. The skit never aired due to a technicality regarding misrepresentation of a show's content (Dr. Pirie was asked to de-

scribe the British economy to the youth in terms of club culture). In retro-
spect, Channel 4 was playing with fire when it signed the unpredictable Baron Cohen. While Channel 4 is a commercial network and is supported by
paid advertising, at the time it was ultimately publicly owned and was therefore regulated by ITC.[17] Such regulation placed a heavy public service bur-
den on the network, including the requirement to "appeal to the tastes and
interests of a culturally diverse society." Ali G's antics were probably not
what Parliament had in mind when they penned that bit of legislation. Ali
did become a bit of an embarrassment for the network in 2002 when he appeared on a BBC Radio 1 breakfast program during a time when children
were off from school. He complained about his record being censored, asking "How comes people on this station is allowed to say the c-word and m-
o-t-h-e-r blank, blank, blank fucker but me can't say pooney. How is that
not racialist—answer me that." The incident provoked effusive apologies
from the BBC and was headline news around the country.

    While a part of *The 11 O'Clock Show*, Baron Cohen honed his inter-
view style, quickly adopting new techniques and adapting to new challenges. In his earliest skits, the joke was always on his various personae
(i.e., the nascent versions of Borat, Bruno, or Ali G). Later on, Baron Cohen
tilted his humor against those whom he was interviewing. According to series' producer Dominic English:

> The great strength of [Ali G] is that he's not setting out to trip people up or
> make fools of [politicians]. He's the fool in the equation and he shows up
> the weakness of their argument by asking the most banal and mundane
> questions. . . . The point of a satire is not necessarily to bring down the
> government, but to prick the pomposity bubbles by asking questions that
> people really should be able to answer."[18]

While these earlier interviews were rarely malicious, their tone grew increasingly provocative. With each question, the guests became more deeply
entangled in a web from which they could not gracefully extricate themselves—or to use Harry Thompson's phrase, "trapped in the mire like a
drowning mammoth." The Ali G character best embodied Baron Cohen's
change in tactics. As examples later in the chapter will demonstrate, his language grew coarser and his ignorance more preposterous—yet his targets of
ridicule continued to brook his nonsense in an attempt to salvage what they
could from the interview.

    It was during this time that Baron Cohen's reticence to do "out-of-
character" interviews began to genuinely add to the allure of his comedic
project. According to one profile, "[T]hroughout every furor, Baron Cohen
has kept his own counsel, leaving the media to tie itself in knots debating
the rights or wrongs of Borat and Ali G. . . . Like a great Hollywood star of
old, Baron Cohen never gives interviews. He's always available for comment as Ali G (or Borat or Bruno), but never as himself."[19] But many critics
have been less than forgiving of his press-shy ways, suggesting that Baron
Cohen is a coward who refuses to face his critics.

> Keeping himself and his creation separate makes an awful lot of sense
> for Baron Cohen. It means he never has to engage with the debate over
> his act. Is Ali G taking the piss out of the macho, misogynist excesses of
> black youth culture? Is he taking the piss out of Wiggers, white boys

who want to be black, or—with the name Ali—is it Asians he's after? There are many who say it doesn't matter; that the only thing which counts is that he's funny. As to Baron Cohen, he never apologizes, never explains.[20]

Recognizing the intrinsic value of distancing himself from Ali, Borat, and Bruno—both in terms of personal privacy and free professional exposure—Baron Cohen continued to build his brand as a new type of British comedian.

Baron Cohen's weekly appearances on *The 11 O'Clock Show* as Ali G included a trip to Northern Ireland to solve the problems between the "Catholics and the Muslims." Once there, he asked George Patton, Executive Officer of the Protestant Grand Orange Lodge of Ireland, if he would ever marry a Catholic girl. When his quarry demurred on account of his religious identity, Ali G continued to pester him on the issue, adding: "Even if she was really fit?" and then "What if she had her own car and sound system and wasn't gonna be stealing money off you all the time?" When Ali G interviewed royal watcher James Whittaker about Princess Diana, he asked: "Why was she nobbing that Pakistani?" (i.e., the Egyptian-born Dodi Al-Fayed) before getting the *Daily Mirror*'s royal correspondent to agree that Diana was "very tasty." Making such jokes a few short years after the Princess' tragic death proved that Ali was never going to shy away from Britain's sore spots; in fact, he would seek them out.

Playing on generational differences, he interrogated Sir Rhodes Boyson (Parliamentary Under-Secretary at the Department of Education and Science 1979-1983) as to whether he thought children should be "caned" in school.[21] Boyson then proceeded to doggedly extol the merits of caning while Ali G mimes the smoking of marijuana (getting "caned" means getting high to young Britons, though this nuance was lost on their elders). In a send up of class in Britain which included such questions as "What if someone was so rich dey had a swimming pool, would they be upper class?" and "What class is a Paki?" Ali tried to entice fellow Cambridge alumnus Jacob Rees-Mogg into "getting busy" with Ali's sister to produce offspring of a higher social class (the son of a former editor of *The Times*, Rees-Mogg's 1999 run for Parliament was purportedly tarnished by his "anachronistically posh accent").[22] In one of his more famous interviews, Ali attempted to persuade Euroskeptic Sir Teddy Taylor into a more pro-European stance with tantalizing promises of "Amsterdam quality" porn in the UK. He then condemned the fact that Jamaica is not part of the EU, intimating that such exclusion is a bit "racialist." Taylor subsequently penned a letter to the *Mail on Sunday* futilely attempting to lessen his shame: "As a longstanding Bob Marley fan—who often plays his songs on the road from the Commons to Southend—I felt quite at home with Ali's West Indian accent."[23] Taylor's invocation of the Rastafarian reggae master only made the joke funnier.

Ali G did not limit himself to media personalities and politicos. Early in his career, he interviewed fashion designer Tomasz Starzewski, asking if he welcomed Gianni Versace's murder since it reduced competition in his field. He also interviewed noted feminist activist and scholar Sue Lees for *The 11 O'Clock Show*, a curious honor which was noted in her 2003 obituary in the academic journal *Gender and Education*: "Perhaps she became best known because of her cameo appearance on the Channel 4 11 o'clock show with Ali G, immortalized on the Ali G video for her mocking defense of feminism as being more serious than an evening event."[24] The oblique reference stems from Ali G's conflation of feminism and lesbianism during Lees' appearance on *The 11 O'Clock Show*. He asked Dr. Lees if she thought that all girls should "try feminism when they is drunk at a party." She replied, "Feminism is not about sex. Having sexual relationships with other women." To which, Ali gleefully asserted, "Aiii, it ain't only about that." He also interviewed controversial Judge James Pickles, infamous for handing down a light sentence to a rapist because the victim had, in Pickle's words, "asked for it." Ali questioned Judge Pickles about pleading the (American) Fifth Amendment in Britain (it is not an option). Ali was also interested to learn that it is still illegal to murder someone even "when they call your mum a slag." He concluded the interview by suggesting that women should be banned from juries during menstruation.

In the third series of *The 11 O'Clock Show*, having made an inconvenient (though not necessarily unwanted) name for himself in the British Isles, Ali G took his show on the road. This change of venue naturally necessitated a reworking of Baron Cohen's humor to fit British stereotypes of Americans, as well as to maximize the comedic opportunities of filming overseas. Not surprisingly, he found a surfeit of new game in America. In the US, General Alexander Haig represented his biggest "get." Ali's opening question of "America. Well important, innit?" left Ronald Reagan's former Secretary of State scrambling to make sense of the interviewer. Ali then moved on to America's relations with Russia: "Do you think it's worth nukin' it now, while it's weak?" He concluded the session by probing into a possible sexual relationship between the co-authors of the 1980s Conservative Revolution: "Is it true, looking back now, that Reagan and Thatcher were actually, well, doing it?" By this point, Haig seems to have caught onto the gag and replies, "Doing it? I think that, at that point in Reagan's life, he couldn't have done it if he'd wanted to."

In his Tocquevillian travels, Ali G also enjoyed the opportunity to chat up the eminent economist John Kenneth Galbraith. He asked the best-selling author and advisor to four American presidents, "Could I be a millionaire with only £17,000?" Naturally, Galbraith responded in the negative. Ali G coolly retorted, "Ain't that racist?" He also inquired about the intricacies of microeconomics: "What is supply and demand? Is it like with me Julie? I supply it and she demand it." Ali then invited the grandee to join him in a preposterous venture selling slippers on the Internet. It was this moment that the man who had famously stated "Politics is not the art of the possible, it consists of choosing between the disastrous and the unpalatable" came face to face with the harsh reality of his own maxim. Like so many of Ali's unwitting victims, Galbraith had been forced to choose between condemning the extraordinarily daft urban baboon for his ignorance, a decision which might entail disastrous consequences, or pursue the unpalatable, but less risky approach of "keeping up appearances." Again and again, Baron Cohen demonstrated his cultural fluency in both American and British traits regarding such uncomfortable situations nearly always making the most out of such exchanges.

Baron Cohen also hornswoggled Admiral Stansfield Turner, former Director of the CIA. Ali G uses his opening question to get some basic information: "So, Mr. Stansfield, what does the CIA stand for?" The interview predictably went downhill from there. He interviewed Alan Dershowitz, Harvard law professor and famed defender of Claus von Bülow and O.J. Simpson, stupidly asking, "Can I sue you if you 'as murdered me?" On one of Ali's favorite topics, sex, the dialogue went as such:

> DERSHOWITZ: Every state has a different age of consent for having sex with somebody. Some states it's seventeen, some states it's fourteen, some states it's eighteen.
> ALI G: In which state is it fourteen?

In what seemed a rather inappropriate choice of subject matter, Ali G went to Los Angeles to discuss gang violence with the genuinely sincerely Alex A. Alonso, the creator of Streetgangs.com—a non-governmental organization dedicated to reducing street violence. The respected filmmaker and social geographer calmly attempted to stay on message as Ali G continued to trivialize gang violence. Alonso writes on his website: "I knew that this chap could not be taken seriously and I was not prepared for the questions he was about to ask. After the interview began, I was not sure how to behave, because he was asking some really silly questions, I wanted to laugh, but I just maintained a calm demeanor and continued to do the interview."[25] Ali pestered the seemingly imperturbable Alonso by questioning him about the problems a gang member would have if his "nan" (grandmother) knitted him a blue sweater but he lived in a 'hood where red was the color of the gang. The interview showed a callousness which would increasingly surface in Baron Cohen's subsequent projects.

Baron Cohen's humor—unlike that of stand-up comedy—relies on willing participants. From his earliest days on *The 11 O'Clock Show*, the comedian demonstrated a singular talent for securing unsuspecting victims and, more importantly, keeping them on the line once the interview had started. Much of Baron Cohen's success is due to a coterie of bright and responsive producers who are careful to project a veneer of professionalism that attenuates Ali's ridiculousness. One must also remember the power of a live camera. Once the red light is on, respondents are careful not to respond too aggressively or rashly. Baron Cohen knows this and turns such caution into a powerful tool of manipulation.

The Bruno and Borat interviews, which target the "man on the street" (with minor exceptions), are fairly easy to secure; however, Ali G's interviews with political, cultural, and media elites require a great deal more finesse. Baron Cohen and his production team are infamously guarded when it comes to the secrets of their success. However, a few of his high profile prey (Sam Donaldson, Tony Benn, et al.) have gone on record to discuss how they were duped. The process is initiated with an official-looking letter from a seemingly genuine production company. Over the years, a variety of front organizations have been employed, including Somerford Brooke Productions, Talkback Productions, United World Productions, One America Productions, etc. All claim to be developing a program for a major British television network. The nature of the program is often represented rather fuzzily, e.g., "late night factual-entertainment," "a series on American life," etc. Lavish praise is heaped upon the "mark" with references to previous media appearances. Modest remuneration, genuine phone numbers, and functional web sites provide an additional veneer of authenticity for those who are initially skeptical (many "victims" are not).

If the participant agrees to be interviewed, he or she is cautioned prior to meeting their host that he is somewhat unorthodox, but has a "great rapport with the young people." Enter Ali G. George Mason University anthropology professor Roger Lancaster recounted his own experiences with *Da Ali G Show*:

> I met Ali G a few minutes before taping, at an impromptu studio in DC. I knew something was fishy then—he was very much overdressed in hip hop regalia, and pretended to be unable to read my name (the producer helped him sound it out). Taping itself lasted about three hours. The first two-plus hours were pretty conventional fare, with the host basically asking serious questions. It was only during the last forty minutes or so that he started asking wonderfully daft questions, which confirmed my take that this was a set-up.[26]

While Lancaster suspected a ruse, other guests were surprised to learn they had been duped by a trickster. In an editorial in *The Guardian,* Tony Benn wrote, "At no stage during our talk did I suspect for a second that it was other than a genuine program, and when the interview was broadcast and someone rang to tell me about it, I was very angry."[27] According to *Slate,* every Ali G interview is the humor equivalent of navigating the straits between Scylla and Charybdis. "Ali G relies on his victims' reluctance to challenge his intellectual credentials or Brit-hop patois. The joke won't work when they know he's a fiction."[28] However, Baron Cohen does possess one advantage. According to Professor Lancaster, the fear of the editing process is a powerful motivator for those victims who end up on the couch with Ali. "There's no way I could out-wit the host on his own show—I don't control the editing. And if I stormed out of the studio, they'd just cut and edit to make me look like a jerk. So basically, I tried to give snarky answers, with a bit of a smirk, hopefully signaling that I 'got it.'"[29] In today's mass-mediated culture where perception trumps reality, the preservation of reputation and image makes for a critical motivator.

Channel 4's prodigious resources gave Baron Cohen access to a wide, if not yet global, audience. He quickly made use of his new-found profile and begin to build his brand as bamboozler extraordinaire. One feature that distinguished the comedian from his peers was the increasingly prominent position he occupied within British pop culture. His well-documented propensity for mangling the English language (including use of such memorable terms as "techmology," "aminal," "ignoranus," "youf in Asia" [euthanasia], etc.) gifted him the title of master of the malapropism. According to culture watchers, Ali G's speech pattern had become highly infectious. In his article "Why We Is All Now Talkin' Like Ali G," the *Evening Standard*'s Dominic Hayes discussed the spread of exaggerated Caribbean pronunciation combined with "yoofspeak" terms such as "nang" ('good'), "bredren" ('mate'), and "nuff" ('really'): "Teachers have dubbed the phenomenon Jafaican and TV's Ali G would understand it perfectly."[30]

In fact, linguists from London University's Queen Mary College and Lancaster University have recently identified a growing dominance of the dialect which they call "multicultural London English" or "multiracial vernacular" among inner-city London youths. The new form of speech is rapidly replacing Cockney speech and "Estuary English" in the city's working class neighborhoods. The driving force behind the growth of the dialect is the influence of second- and third-generation immigrants who contribute linguistic admixtures from the Caribbean, West Africa, and South Asia. However, the "cool factor" is important as well, as young white Britons attempt to adopt the speech patterns of their minority counterparts. The popularity of rap music and TV shows—Ali G, in particular—has produced a cascade effect in recent years which lends credibility to this new speech pattern.[31]

Ali G's use of Jafaican is double-edged. He is both a medium and mirror of the subculture that gave birth to the language. Baron Cohen certainly did not invent Jafaican, nor was he the first prominent white Briton to employ it; however, his use of the dialect reflects its importance in contemporary youth culture, while simultaneously influencing hordes of youth who connect Jafaican's speech patterns and argot with a particular counterculture, a subculture which is associated with coolness.[32]

His seemingly effortless pranking of politicians certainly garnered laughs, but it was his parody of wiggas ("white niggers") that really struck a chord in Britain—a society struggling to come to terms with profound ethnic diversity, official policies of multiculturalism, and uncertain national identity, a phenomenon explored in greater detail in Chapter 3. In the words of British social theorist Paul Gilroy:

> We are awaiting a more sophisticated and complex political understanding of cultural change, influence and adaptation. In the meantime we are being entertained by Ali G, whose performances provide a satirical Rorschach blot in which even the most neurotic scrutineers of the national psyche can discover their fears and hopes.[33]

Ali G's popularity seemed to know no bounds in Britain. In 1999, only one year after the premiere of *The 11 O'Clock Show* British entertainment magazine *Heat* named Sacha Baron Cohen the fifth hottest star in the world and *GQ* ordained him "comedian of the year." Almost simultaneously, he won "Best Newcomer" at British Comedy Awards and was nominated for "Best Entertainment Performance" by the British Academy of Film and Television Arts (BAFTA). The *Evening Standard* described him as "more remote than the Queen Mother and twice as famous."[34] Perhaps more importantly, Ali's trademark greeting "boyakasha" had entered the vocabulary of British youth (another neologism, "mingin" meaning 'ugly,' has since been included in the Oxford English Dictionary).[35] As Harry Thompson pointed out at the time, Ali G had clearly become a national phenomenon with his finger on the pulse of Britain's confused and often contradictory national identity.

With such kudos, it seemed inevitable that Channel 4 would give him his own show. On 31 March 2000, *Da Ali G Show* premiered with much fanfare. The *Guardian* carped, "It's almost as though Channel 4 didn't need to invest in the obligatory billboard campaign which started last week [since] Ali G had already been talked up, hyped up and marked up to a frightening degree."[36] Realizing that his cover had been blown, Sacha Baron Cohen gave radio and print interviews in his Ali G persona and even appeared in a photo spread with supermodel Naomi Campbell in the glossy men's fashion magazine *Arena Homme Plus*. Channel 4 tried its best to accommodate its rising star by expanding his presence on the network. However, it is likely that the network's executives had already realized their ability to monopolize Baron Cohen's talents was entering its twilight. On the eve of *Da Ali G Show*'s premiere, Kevin Lygo, Head of Arts and Entertainment at Channel 4, remarked, "All he has done are those three-minute interviews, tucked away in a show that transmits at 11 o'clock at night, and suddenly he is written about in the *Sun* and talked about by kids in playgrounds. He's been promoted beyond his audience base, partly because of clever positioning and by using him strategically."[37] Such approbations would soon be commonplace in reference to Baron Cohen's career.

Taking Center Stage: Ali Gets His Own Show

With a full program dedicated to Sacha Baron Cohen's variegated creations, a few changes were in store. Baron Cohen's grade school chum Dan Mazer joined the show as producer and James Bobin came on as its director. While maintaining the location interviews, the new format brought Ali G into the studio with scripted segments, "special reports," and skits such as the controversial drug knowledge game show "Who Wants to Win an Ounce," which mocked the popular "Who Wants to be a Millionaire." A monologue was introduced and the show often included fantasy segments (including one of Ali G as a goatee-laden child in a miniature track suit being told by his teacher that he would spend the rest of his life in Staines and would never be a "gangsta rapper"). Reflecting Ali G's MC fetish, *Da Ali G Show* introduced guest musical performances which Ali would deliberately ruin. Most importantly, Baron Cohen's foreign correspondent character, who had transitioned from the Moldovan Krickler to the Albanian Kristo, was rechristened as the Kazakhstani reporter Borat Karabzhanov (Borat's last name was later changed to Sagdiyev). In less than a month, the Kazakhstani embassy's first secretary Talgat Kaliyev would issue the country's opening salvo in what would become a six-year war of words (see Chapters 4 and 5).

The premiere of *Da Ali G Show* was an instant success, pulling in large numbers of viewers and beating BBC in its time slot. The inaugural episode featured Ali G sharing a joint with disgraced Tory MP Neil Hamilton. Hamilton had reportedly taken bribes from Harrods' owner Mohamed Al-Fayed (who appeared on the subsequent episode) for raising certain issues in Parliament, colloquially known as the "cash-for-questions" scandal. A media personality in his own right, Hamilton subsequently became one of Sacha Baron Cohen's greatest defenders, especially on the issue of racism. The show also featured a jaunt to Cannes where Ali G pitched his hopelessly convoluted porno plots to unsuspecting American film executives. The launch of "Borat's Guide to Britain" series of skits saw the intrepid and always inappropriate Kazakhstani reporter receiving etiquette training from Lady Chelsea—the ex-wife of one of Britain's richest men, Lord Cadogan—before attending a dinner party. After chugging a large glass of white wine, he declared loudly, "It's niiiice!!!" a tagline that would soon be uttered on playgrounds from San Diego to Stockholm. In the brief skit, Borat also talked about his favorite subjects: going to the toilet, having sex, and his dead wife. Years before the release of *Borat: Cultural Learnings of*

America for Make Benefit Glorious Nation of Kazakhstan, the shtick had already reached its maturity.

Episode Two centered around an interview of "Alf," i.e., Mohamed Al-Fayed, who was clearly in on the joke when Ali G asked him if he was rich enough to hire someone to wash his testicles. Al-Fayed graciously offered to lend Ali the services of his own cleaner who possessed a special hoover which "sucks your balls off." Sacha Baron Cohen could barely hold back a smile. In one fell swoop, Al-Fayed had turned Ali G into parody of himself, what Paul Gilroy deems the *Beavis and Butthead syndrome*: "a condition of mass popularity in which the original satirical intentions are misrecognised as affirmation of the object or process they try to subvert or ridicule."[38] Despite the fact that Ali G's interviewees were now in on the joke, they continued to subject themselves to abuse. Explaining this enigma, Gilroy writes:

> The only explanation for their repeated decision to place their celebrity heads on Ali's block is that they mistakenly imagine the language and culture of this country to be far more unified than it is. In other words, they do not appreciate how the problems of communication and translation which made Ali's original interviews so revealing and hilarious have been deepened and augmented as his celebrity has increased.[39]

The next week's guest was Scottish television reporter Gail Porter whose penchant for being photographed semi-nude won her a spot on *FHM*'s 100 Sexiest Women list from 1999 through 2002.[40] Like Ali G, Porter is an icon of British youth's anti-politics. In 1999, *FHM* projected a nude-from-behind picture of Porter onto the exterior of the Houses of Parliament with an accompanying message urging people to "Vote Porter." This stunt occurred at a time when British youth participation in politics was at an all time low. At the end of the 1990s, Britain's "lost generation" of young people were clearly demonstrating themselves to be less interested in serious political issues than the vacuity of modern celebrity culture.[41] According to one author, *fin-de-siècle* British youth were "more likely to be mobile, to live in private rented accommodation and to be separated from enduring personal and social relationships."[42] Consequently, they had become "professionally apathetic" and took a "sod you" attitude towards politicians.[43]

Other marquee guests during the short season included politician Roy Hattersley, BBC presenter John Humphrys, and Anita Roddick, founder of cosmetics giant The Body Shop.[44] Ali also made a trip to America where he visited the sets of the soap opera *The Bold & the Beautiful* and the day-time talk show, *Sally Jessy Raphael*. On the latter program, his accent was called into question by an African-American woman—one of the few times any ever questioned the character's authenticity.[45] The rarity of such an exchange suggests a great deal about contemporary race relations, a topic explored in greater detail in Chapter 3. While it is not surprising that a black person would be the one to question Ali's "blackness," I argue that the venue also contributed to the contestation of Ali's identity. The American tabloid talk show formula creates an environment where projected images are exaggerated and even completely false. In the 1990s, freaks of all sorts parading themselves on *The Jerry Springer Show, Geraldo,* and similar programs became common television fare. Viewers and the in-studio audience were cognizant that the producers used manipulative techniques to provoke absurd behavior, while the guests understood the requirement to "perform" the role assigned to them.[46] This environment naturally produced a discursive free-for-all which stripped away "normal" rules of interrogation which would otherwise govern people's interactions with the "black" Ali G.

Back in the studio, musical guests included Chrissie Hynde of the American alternative band The Pretenders, Fran Healy of Scottish supergroup Travis, Gaz Coombes of Oxford-based Supergrass, and indie rocker Jarvis Cocker of Pulp. The choice of musical guests is interesting given that each performer is a paragon of white, middleclass musical tastes, ranging from the 1980s alt-rock goddess Hynde up through current complaint rock favorite Fran Healy (Ali G famously asked him, "So, Travis—why is you so fucking depressed?"). While Ali G used his mic and turntable to funk up the performances, it was clear that he was catering to Oxbridge rather than Brixton.[47]

Continuing his fabulously successful strategy of promotion beyond his audience base, Baron Cohen released a DVD of the show's highlights, entitled *Ali G, Innit*, in 1999. It quickly became a bestseller. The success of *Da Ali G Show* allowed the comedian to turn out two more compilation videos: *Ali G, Aiii* (2000) and *Ali G: Bling Bling* (2001). Further expanding his fame, the perennially hip Madonna gave Ali G a cameo in her video for the pop single "Music" in 2000. The prologue features Ali as Madonna's chauffeur:

ALI: Is you Madonna?
MADONNA: Are you my driver?
ALI (dubiously): Is you Madonna? Your babylons [breasts] look less big than they do on the telly . . . but I still definitely would.
MADONNA: You wish.
ALI: I do actually.

He is also featured in the intermezzo—both in cartoon form and rapping his own lyrics to Madonna's 1984 hit "Like a Virgin."[48] In 2001, Ali G received top billing at the annual anti-global poverty fundraiser *Comic Relief*. His responsibilities included interviewing world-famous footballer David Beckham and his wife Victoria, also known as Posh Spice. Ali G, decked out in a garish leather track suit emblazoned with "Save Africa" above a map of Italy and Corsica, introduced the couple to the live audience with the words: "Every boy wants to be in his boots and every man wants to be in his missus. Big up for none other than Victoria and David Beckham!" The supercouple, intent on raising money for charity, went along with Ali's salacious humor. However, both were visibly uncomfortable throughout the 40-minute long interview. David Beckham mustered only a few responses, mostly blushing and laughing nervously while his wife made pithy quips on his behalf.

Despite the fact that Ali G responded to a *Guardian* interview question about his favorite books by asking, "Are you calling me a battyboy [homosexual]?," he is a published author. The mass-market paperback *Da Gospel According To Ali G* was released in 2001 in the UK and features Ali G's thoughts and views on the Ten Commandments, education, drugs, violence, and sex. In keeping with Baron Cohen's dogged authenticity as Ali G, the back of the book reads:

YA SEEN HIM ON DA HBO SHOW?
GOOD!
YA SEEN HIM ON DA MOVIE SCREEN?
EVEN BETTA!
NOW STEAL DIS BOOK OR GET YOUR MOM TO BUY IT.
RESPEC!
Ali G

With its glossy photos and gratuitous nudity, *Da Gospel* shares more in common with an issue of *Hustler* than with any of the books of the New Testament. The book includes encomia to McDonalds's and Ali's hero Tupac Shakur, how-to-guides on oral sex and marijuana cultivation, and faux renderings of Ali's schoolwork and a partially-completed application for welfare. Ali's map of the world is especially amusing as it labels the continent of Africa as Jamaica and the East Indies as "Jurassic Park." Like his soon-to-be released motion picture, Ali G's book was long on style and short on substance. Even more unfortunate, *Da Gospel According To Ali G* lacks the political flair which characterizes both the television skits and the film, thus making it simply an encyclopedia dedicated to middle class simulacrum of the gangsta lifestyle.

Drafting off the success of *Da Ali G Show*, the Madonna video, his book, and a string of controversial public appearances including the BBC Radio gaff which many saw simply as pre-premiere propaganda, Sacha Baron Cohen brought Ali G to the big screen. Unlike his scintillating 2006 *Borat* film, Baron Cohen unwisely abandoned the mockumentary style which had made Ali G such a success on Britain's Channel 4. The scenes were scripted in order to support an impossibly facile plot involving Ali G's successful run for Parliament in order to save a Staines community center. The antics at the 22 March 2002 premiere of *Ali G Indahouse* ultimately proved more entertaining than the movie itself.

Sacha Baron Cohen showed up at the Empire Cinema in Leicester Square in full Ali G drag. Sporting a jewel-studded crown and a thirty-foot long velvet cape, he was accompanied by six of his "bitches" clad in cannabis-shaped bikinis. Poking fun at himself for failing to draw attendance from the British royal family, he stated, "The Queen and Charles said no. And Harry said no—probably 'cos him still owe me 20 squid [pounds] for dat eighth."[49] A crowd of protesters jeered Baron Cohen for his depiction of blacks, calling him the "new Al Jolson," an oft-repeated comparison to the Jewish-American father of minstrelsy (black face) that has dogged Baron Cohen's career. Peter Akinti, editor of black male lifestyle magazine *Untold*, who staged the Leicester Square demonstration, told *The Guardian*:

> He's effectively blacked up to take the piss out of a stereotype of young black men that is deeply offensive. . . . He is a white Jewish Cambridge graduate, and he uses the word "nigger" and asks "Is it 'cos I is black?" There's no way you would be able to get away with making similar jokes about the Jewish community—you would be called a racist before the words had left your lips.[50]

Ali G's response was: "Let me just say to all those brothers outside doing the demonstration. Whatever it is you was protesting against I is with you brethren. I is with you."[51] Shades of the coming "battle over Borat" were evident at Leicester Square as Baron Cohen sardonically welcomed condemnation from self-appointed "identity police" of his humor.[52]

Despite its stilted performances and paper-thin plot, *Ali G Indahouse* would go on to become the highest grossing British film of 2002. While the movie was a commercial success in Britain, it opened to reviews ranging from tepid acclaim to excoriating criticism. The *Daily Mail* deemed it the very worst British film ever made.[53] While some attacked the film's purported racism, most of its critics simply thought it lacked humor. In particular, *Ali G Indahouse* suffered from that all-too-familiar malady, difficulty in translating a television success to the big screen. There were other problems as well. Deprived of his improvisational platform, Sacha Baron Cohen struggled to keep the rather shallow Ali interesting. Inevitably, the viewer learns more than he or she needs to about Ali. Sacha Baron Cohen was subsequently condemned for de-masking his creation by making it clear that Ali is a white, middle-class boy from the un-ghetto Staines.

Particular elements of the wannabe pimp's identity had long "hovered in the background of Ali G's insecure patter about himself on the small screen. [These elements] were shrouded in mystery, cleverly sketched out in such a way that we didn't know whether they were real. They, and we, were better off that way."[54] Film historian Richard Howells states, "*Ali G in da House* strongly suggests that Ali G may in fact be white, but that makes his preferred 'street-black' persona all the more interesting. It is something to which he still clings in terms of style, language and outlook." Yet it is now clear that Ali is rather sensitive, and does not at all resemble the gangstas he so wishes to emulate. In the words of Gilroy:

> Ali is not homophobic, macho, aggressive or anti-social. He obeys the speed limit, believes in the healing power of god's green herb and has identified the terminal duplicity of all forms of politricks. He is loyal, decent and honest. When punched by Charles Dance's repellent Deputy Prime Minister, he starts to cry.[55]

In a stroke of marketing genius, Sacha Baron Cohen released "Me Julie," a duo with Jamaican-American rapper Shaggy, in advance of his motion picture. When the movie premiered, the song was number two on the British charts. *Ali G Indahouse* and the "Me Julie" video were recorded in Staines, Jamaica, Los Angeles, and London. A harbinger of things to come, the choice of Staines prompted a massive increase in tourists in the wake of the film's premiere. A Spelthorne Borough Council spokesman told *The Daily Star*, "Ali G has been a huge hit and the council helped him film in Staines last year. I think it's right to use him in tourism brochures. We can use him very positively—he has increased awareness of the town a lot."[56] Nearly the same claim would later be made by the Kazakhstani authorities (though only after an infinitely more complex dynamic had developed).

Channel 4's *Da Ali G Show* was simply the prologue for its bigger and brasher American namesake (to be called *Ali G in da USAiii* in Britain). *Home Box Office* (HBO), the premium American cable channel, picked up the series and aired two six-episode seasons beginning in February 2003. The show also aired on the *Showcase* network in Canada. Each episode was loosely centered on a particular theme allowing each of Baron Cohen's personae to offer their unique take on key issues in American society. The laugh track which had been part of the on-scene interviews for Channel 4 was excised in the American version. Also absent were the musical guests, skits, and most of the in-studio antics. The monologue—an integral part of the Channel 4 version—remained.

In essence, the humor returned to its unscripted and less self-aware roots. These revisions seemingly allowed Baron Cohen to once again take pleasure out of humiliating the politically powerful. Furthermore, the transatlantic shift enabled him to procure the "A-list" guests that characterized his last season on *The 11 O'Clock Show*. These august personalities included Newt Gingrich (Speaker of the US House of Representatives, 1995-1999), Boutros Boutros-Ghali (UN Secretary-General, 1992-1996), Brent Scowcroft (National Security Advisor to Presidents Ford and Bush I), and C. Everett Koop (US Surgeon General, 1981-1989). Simon Weaver welcomed Ali G's reversion from celebrity interviewer to his earlier hoaxer stage. "The anonymous nature of Ali G is of prime importance in this stage, as it would be for any comic character attempting to 'send-up' establishment figures with a certain amount of capital to protect within a particular field."[57] Baron Cohen was able to resurrect his old style simply because he was relatively unknown in the United States. Owing to the country's media diversity, strong generational fractures, and size, Americans tend to be more segregated in their fluency with contemporary popular culture than their British counterparts. Recognizing the possibility that not everyone in America knew him, Ali G recounted his tortured past to his new audience.

> Me woz born in da heart off da Staines ghetto. . . As well as bein unemployed—i iz also got a lot off well important careers. As head of Da West Staines Massive, me control da most peace lovin and violent gang in da hole of Barkshire.[58] Afta happearin on some crap programme dat woz on at 11 a clock or somefin, it werent long before me ad me own show. Dis meant me was able to take a in depf look at a lot off serious issues. . . . I iz now easily da most respekted face on Brittish telly and it iz probably only a matter off time before me get offered me own slot on Channel 5—or hopefully even cable.[59]

The first episode of HBO's version of *Da Ali G Show*, entitled "The Law," opened with Ali G standing in front of a backdrop depicting an instantly recognizable icon of American national identity: Mount Rushmore. While George Washington's visage remained, the faces of Thomas Jefferson, Theodore Roosevelt, and Abraham Lincoln had been replaced by Biggie Smalls (The Notorious B.I.G.), Ali G, and Tupac Shakur, respectively. Within seconds, Ali G invokes the "terrible events of 7/11." Such insensitivity to the still-fresh psychic wounds of 11 September 2001 did not instantly endear him to the larger American viewing audience. Some critics lauded the show, while others lambasted *Da Ali G Show* as "tasteless," "a massive flop," "a spotty venture," and "not nearly funny enough." The *Associated Press'* review bayed "Nice to meet you, Mr. Cohen. Now go home. Please."[60]

Delivering less than a million viewers to HBO, while receiving such mixed reviews, got the show off to a lackluster start. Part of the problem was a predictable transatlantic comedic disconnect. The *Financial Times* explained the juxtaposition of British satirical excess and the response of "irony-free" American audiences as such:

> According to American manners, it's rude to point out someone else's rudeness. And finding fault with one's host is trickier still. But what about when the host gets wildly confrontational, by suggesting a culprit behind a messy washroom, by slipping a porno shot among some family photos for strangers to flip through, by greeting macho cops or rodeo cowboys with man-to-man cheek kisses? In each wince-inducing fracas, Cohen frays the nerves of participant and spectator alike, and gasping laughter is the only means of relief.[61]

In keeping with the inaugural show's theme of law and order, Ali G attended a training session at the Philadelphia Police Academy and interviewed former US Attorneys General Edwin Meese and Richard Thornburgh. He famously asked the latter, "What is legal?" then "What is illegal?" and, finally, "What is barely legal?" Meese was cajoled into doing a rap: "I was Attorney General/My name is Meese/I say go to college and don't carry a piece." Borat went to a dating coach and *Funkyzeit mit Bruno* featured the Austrian journalist at Fashion Week voguing with Paris Hilton before storming the runway and making a mockery of one of the event's shows.

Episode Two's theme was "War," which provided Sacha Baron Cohen the opportunity to engage with the former UN Secretary-General Boutros Boutros-Ghali. Ali hilariously added one or two extra Boutroses to the Secretary-General's name every time he addressed him. Standing in front of UN headquarters, he referred to the "United Nations of Benetton" as the world's "player haters"[62] because of the organization's mission to end "wars, international drug trafficking, and everything else that is a bit of a laugh." Ali forced Boutros-Ghali to explain why Disneyland is not a member of the UN, and got him to curse in the silliest language he spoke (i.e., French). His other victims included General Brent Scowcroft and former CIA Director Robert James Woolsey, Jr. Ali suggests to the former that the US should nuke Canada, taking advantage of the element of surprise. He attempts to glean from the latter "Who shot J.R.?," likely mistaking the *Dallas* character with assassinated American president John F. Kennedy (JFK). The episode also featured an in-studio roundtable on religion including an academic from Georgetown University, a rabbi, a Roman Catholic priest, and a representative of the Atheist Alliance. His uncouth questions included: "Ain't God just like an over-hyped [street magician] David Blaine?;" "Why did Jesus go around with all they reindeers?;" and "Why do you [Jews] chop one of your nuts off?"

Politics was the subject of the third American episode of *Da Ali G Show*. Newt Gingrich, leader of the US Congress' 1990s "Republican Revolution," headlined the show. After being forced to spell his name, Gingrich pedantically explained to Ali why one should not make more money the longer one remains on the welfare rolls. Staying on topic, Bruno polls fashion designers about "trailer trash" or "primitive rubbish people," asking whether or not they buy the clothes shown at fashion shows. From there, Bruno vexed one vacuous victim about major figures in world politics; Bruno's prey ultimately admitted that he considered Osama bin Laden to be "very stylish." The show concluded with Ali discussing drugs with DEA agent Will Glasby. In a memorable exchange, Ali asked the drug enforcement officer about the negative effects of narcotics. Glasby responded that they slow down your brain. Ali then reiterated: "And is there any *negative* effects?" Such comments evocatively tapped into an attitude of nonchalance and anti-intellectualism prevalent among today's youth—an attitude bred by consumerism and nurtured by the mass mediation of celebrity "role models" as diverse as Kate Moss and Snoop Dogg.

Taking on "Art" in his fourth American episode, Sacha Baron Cohen nearly met his match in James Lipton, host of the interview show *Inside the Actor's Studio*. The dean emeritus of the estimable Actors Studio Drama School in New York City refused to brook Ali G's use of derogatory terms for women, telling him, "I don't use words like 'hos' . . . I know it's the vernacular . . . I hate words like 'bitches.'" At nearly every turn, Ali G was bested by the formidable Lipton, though Baron Cohen would later take revenge by revealing on *The Daily Show with Jon Stewart* that Lipton had purportedly shown him pictures of his wife in various states of undress after the interview. The belated and rather petulant response to Lipton's seemingly heartfelt defense of women smacked of sour grapes. Celebrity hair stylist Jonathan Antin, enthusiastically contended with Bruno in a discussion of fashion and world politics agreeing that all evil people (Stalin, Hitler, and Saddam Hussein included) have moustaches, before looking into the camera and foolishly stating: "You motherfuckers in the Middle East, God help you if I ever come over there because I'll take all you cocksuckers out!" The episode was rounded out with a truly humorous interview with Buzz Aldrin.

> ALI: I know this is a sensitive question, but what was it like not being the first man on the moon. Was you ever jealous of Louis Armstrong?
> ALDRIN: It was Neil Armstrong. And no, I was not jealous. He was a very, very qualified person.
> ALI: Whatever. So when you arrived on the moon, was the people there friendly or was they scared of you?
> ALDRIN: There was absolutely no thought of encountering any living being whatsoever.
> ALI: Do you think man will ever walk on the sun?
> ALDRIN: No. The sun is too hot. It is not a good place to go to.
> ALI: What if they went in winter when the sun is cold?
> ALI: Me know you has been axed this a zillion times . . . What do you say to all those conspiracy theorists who come up to you say the moon don't really exist.
> ALDRIN: I don't think there are many people who actually question that the moon really exists.
> ALI: Aiight, you is heard it here! The moon does exist.

Completely unaware of his role in Baron Cohen's farce, Aldrin then tried to explain comedy to Ali G, stating, "Things are funny when you mix the real with the absurd."

In the season's two remaining episodes, Baron Cohen took on the sacred cows of "Science" and "Belief," interviewing American Green Party leader and former presidential candidate Ralph Nader about the environment. Nader complained that scientists have yet figure a way to "put a box on the assholes" of the world's tens of millions of cows to prevent harmful effects to the atmosphere. Ali G asked a thoroughly unamused former US Surgeon General C. Everett Koop why skeletons were involved in so much evil stuff. He also tried to convince former US Secretary of State James Baker of the efficacy of getting either Iran or Iraq to change their name to avoid confusion.

Shortly before the second season began, Baron Cohen demonstrated his gift for self-promotion. Draped in a ridiculous crimson track suit emblazoned with "Professor of Erbology," Ali G gave the class day speech at Harvard University on 9 June 2004. Class Day is the less formal, student-oriented complement to commencement which followed the next day (Baron Cohen wryly commented that UN Secretary General Kofi Annan would have to rewrite his commencement speech since it was basically the same as his). In his address to "da most cleverest students in America," Professor G commended Harvard's "brainboxes" for their memorization of the alphabet from A through X. He sarcastically peppered his inappropriate comments with "You is well happy you is brought your grandparents, innit?" to uncomfortable laughs from his international and multigenerational audience.

Season Two kicked off in the summer of 2004 with a show dedicated to one of Ali's catchphrases, "Respek!" In a fit of irony, Ali opened the show by encouraging his viewers to respect everyone: "animals, children, bitches, spasmos, mingas, lezzes, fatty boombas, and even gaylords." The program included a discussion of bias with respected TV journalist Sam Donaldson who was prompted to rap: "News ain't just for the white man. It's for the bros and sisters, too. . . . Mad props to the hood, yo!" As Bruno, Baron Cohen sent up Pastor Lance Quinn, a self-described "gay converter" from The Bible Church of Little Rock, Arkansas.[63] The painfully earnest cleric told America that watching the NBC comedy *Will & Grace* and "being fabulous" are forbidden (*nicht nicht*), but that eating brunch is ok (*ach ja*). The unspoken message of this exchange hinged on the ambivalent attitudes of Middle America towards gays: celebrating the community's contribution to certain fields (entertainment, style, etc.), while rejecting homosexuality in other realms (equal protection before the law, the morality of gay relationships, etc).

In episode two, Baron Cohen scored one of his most famous interviews with conservative commentator and former presidential candidate Pat Buchanan. Playing along with Ali G, Buchanan condemned Saddam Hussein's use of "BLTs" on the Kurds and affirmed that it was worth going to war over sandwiches. He ended the interview by laughingly admitting to Ali that he "had a little puff" of marijuana before they started shooting. The Pat Buchanan interview would serve as an exception to the standard formula. Buchanan acted like a normal person in his interactions with Ali G, laughing at himself, his interrogator, and the foolishness of the entire exchange. He effectively disarmed Baron Cohen by being funnier than him.

The highlights of "Episode 3: Peace" included Bruno's interview with fashion guru Leon Hall in which he wished that actress Liza Minnelli would get a malignant tumor and that a bomb would fall on her. It also saw the airing of the now infamous "Throw the Jew Down the Well" skit (discussed in detail later). The subsequent show, entitled "Realize," saw Ali G explaining the dangers of terrorists hijacking a train and driving it into the White House to US Immigration and Naturalization Service Commissioner James Ziegler. He also spent some time with Christine Todd Whitman, former New Jersey governor and Environmental Protection Agency administrator, about the "massive" size of whale feces and its effect on global pollution.

The penultimate installment of the show featured a memorable tête-à-tête with the venerable historian, author, and commentator Gore Vidal, as well as a rare in-studio bit on safe-sex educator Sally Epstein. She brought along her larger-than-life-sized genitalia model which produced plenty of laughs. Epstein's appearance echoed that of Mohamed Al Fayed in season one in that it signaled the show had once again become self-aware. The final program featured a poignant segment with curmudgeonly *60 Minutes* contributor Andy Rooney. Rooney pedantically corrected Ali G's grammar throughout the interview, at one point interjecting: "What language are you most comfortable with?" Eventually, Rooney grew tired of Ali G's presence and tried to force him to leave, to which Ali responded, "He's chucking me out 'cos the color of me skin." Rooney simply laughs off the accusations of "racialism." By this point, it was clear that *Da Ali G Show* had run its natural course. Less than a year later, HBO announced that it did not plan to renew *Da Ali G Show* for a third season.

After he had seemingly run out of steam with his Ali G shtick, Baron Cohen turned his focus towards the Hollywood mainstream. The actor lent his vocal talents to the children's film *Madagascar* portraying King Julien, the ruler of a kingdom of partying lemurs. The character, originally scripted for only a few lines, ended up stealing the show with 20 minutes of dialogue. According to director Tom McGrath, "Sacha came in and was playing around with accents—a little Indian, a little French—and then finally he based this character on this odd uncle of his. At least that's what he told us. . . . We were just laughing so much we changed the roles, figuring this guy has to be king of these lemurs. He was so much fun and so inventive and he brought a lot of laughs."[64] However, Baron Cohen was true to form and much of his ad-libbing failed to make the final cut, being deemed "too obscene for the kiddy market."[65]

Building off his budding relationship with Madonna and Guy Ritchie which began with Ali G's cameo in one of the songstress' videos, Sacha Baron Cohen slowly joined the ranks of Hollywood's in-crowd establishing friendships with a handful of major American movie stars after relocating to Los Angeles. Initially, Baron Cohen made contacts through *Friends* star Jennifer Aniston and her then husband Brad Pitt.[66] However, the relationship which propelled Baron Cohen into the American mainstream was the one he developed with comedic actor and *Saturday Night Live* veteran Will Ferrell. In an interview with Charlie Rose, Hollywood's highest-paid actor lavished praise on Baron Cohen and *Borat,* stating, "It is a fiercely brave movie and it is hysterical . . . it's one of the funniest things I have ever seen."[67]

Baron Cohen won a supporting role in Ferrell's 2006 summer blockbuster *Talladega Nights: The Ballad of Ricky Bobby.* The NASCAR-themed film, which challenges *Borat* in its insidious anti-Americanism, featured Baron Cohen as Formula One champ Jean Girard. Girard—played for bigoted laughs—embodies everything that NASCAR is not: he is openly homosexual, a Frenchman, and a connoisseur of the finer things in life (his race-car is sponsored by Perrier and he sips macchiato at the wheel). The character is the polar opposite of Ferrell's ultra-macho, fast food-eating, Wonder Bread car-driving Ricky Bobby, whose triumphalist, almost Manichean, tagline is "If you ain't first, you're last" (alongside other zingers like "I get up in the morning and I piss excellence" and "I'm a big hairy American winning machine!"). Ferrell's farcical *Talladega Nights* is a plebian replay of the Franco-American spat over the Iraq War. The allusion to politics remains muted but evident throughout the film. According to film reviewer Stephen Himes,

> By sticking to the biopic formula, the filmmakers don't risk alienating their audience, nor do they artificially shoehorn a bunch of preachy politics into a wacky comedy. . . . Still, [director/co-writer Adam] McKay and Ferrell seem like they don't want to push too hard; they don't want to offend by bringing [US President George W.] Bush into it. Ferrell blunts the impact of Ricky Bobby by turning the film into a family drama.[68]

Evoking shades of George W. Bush, Ricky Bobby is a Southern good ol' boy who prays to "Baby Jesus" and lives in a world of moral absolutes.[69] After rising to the top of the NASCAR rankings rather unexpectedly, he throws caution to the wind and grows drunk on his own power. His archnemesis Girard—like former French president Jacques Chirac—is a relativist and overly calculated in his decisions on and off the racetrack. The latter's *sangfroid* ultimately wins the day and Ricky Bobby suffers a total mental breakdown with his friends, fans, and even family abandoning him in defeat.

Baron Cohen enjoyed a precipitous increase in his profile with the success of *Talladega Nights*. He put this new found fame to good use by immediately shifting gears from Jean Girard to Borat. Celebrity news programs such as *Entertainment Tonight* began to profile the Briton, predicting that he would soon emerge as the next big thing from across the pond. As Borat's budding fame gained momentum, diplomats in the little-known country of Kazakhstan began to worry that their nation's reputation was about to be irrevocably hijacked by an unpredictable comedian with a penchant for the obscene.

Notes

1. See, for instance, Sandro Monetti, "Why British Stars are Laughing All the Way to America," *Express on Sunday*, 11 March 2007, 49-51; *The Office*, after its run on BBC and BBC America (which gave Gervais an unexpected 2004 Golden Globe win for his role as David Brent and another for "Best Television Comedy"), became a successful overseas franchise with officially-licensed American, French, and Canadian versions, as well as a German doppelganger which was later forced to credit Gervais with its inspiration after purportedly reaching a financial settlement.

2. Sally O'Reilly, "Dead Funny," *Art Monthly* 302 (December 2006-January 2007): 7-9.

3. See House of Commons Hansard Written Comments for 23 July 1996 (pt 10).

4. Dominic English, producer of *The 11 O'Clock Show*, addressed the links between Baron Cohen's comedy and that of Morris stating, "Morris is such a groundbreaking force that there will always be the accusation of plagiarism. But once you've moved the goalposts, other people have to aim for the goal where it is now, not where it was then;" see Jane-Ann Purdy, "Spoof or Dare," *Scotsman*, 15 May 1999, 6.

5. Fur-Q's song "Uzi Lover" parodied Phillip Bailey's song "Easy Lover" with over-the-top sexual references and adulation of violence.

6. Thompson explains, "The Hoax TV genre is a common ingredient of modern TV comedy, for the simple reason that it's quick and cheap. It only takes 10 minutes to confront an MP in the street, pretend to throw up in front of him and film his weary reaction; and it only takes five minutes to dream up the idea. It's no coincidence that many exponents of the Hoax genre have come up through the tiny budgets of cable TV;" see Harry Thompson, "G Force," *Guardian* (London), 27 April 1999, 19.

7. Ironically, Staines is a solidly middle class town in the Spelthorne borough of Surrey and part of the London commuter belt of southeastern England.

8. Thompson, "G Force," 19.

9. See "Harry Thompson: Obituary," *Times*, 9 November 2005.

10. Michael Eboda, "We Can Take Ali G's Humor in Our Stride," *Independent*, 12 January 2000, 4.

11. By the late 1990s, Westwood was in great demand not only as a DJ but also as a consultant to the music industry. According to the *New Statesman*, he represented the pinnacle of Britain's "lucrative . . . complex, multi-leveled business" of hip-hop; Richard Cook, "The White DJ in Black Culture," *New Statesman* 128, no. 4447 (2 August 1999): 18-19; Cook, "The White DJ in Black Culture," 19.

12. Mickey Hess, "Metal Faces, Rap Masks: Identity and Resistance in Hip Hop's Persona Artist," *Popular Music and Society* 28, no. 3 (July 2005): 297–311.

13. Interestingly, Ali G gave an interview to *Rolling Stone* claiming that his viewers would instantly recognize him as the "black Eminem." He argued that he had not yet cracked the music industry due to his "race," stating: "I mean, you got to ask why ain't I as successful a rapper as Eminem. Me tried for years to break into the record industry and you always heard the same things, like, 'You ain't got no riddim.' 'You literally cannot rhyme.' 'You has a terrible voice.' 'You look like a prick.' But we all know the real reason: It's racialism, innit? Tell me, have you ever seen a black man succeed in the world of rap? I rest my case;" see Mark Binelli, "Idiot Power," *Rolling Stone* 918 (20 March 2003): 34-35.

14. Hess, "Metal Faces, Rap Masks," 300.

15. Rachel Garfield, "Ali G: Just Who Does He Think He Is?" *Third Text* 54 (Spring 2001): 63-70.

16. "Profile: Ali G—It's Chillin' What Da Boy Get Away With," *Sunday Times*, 9 January 2000.

17. Britain's Office of Communications (Ofcom) has since taken over these responsibilities.

18. Purdy, "Spoof or Dare," 6.

19. See William Cook, "After Ali: The IOS Profile: Sacha Baron Cohen," *Independent on Sunday*, 22 August 2004, 19.

20. Jay Rayner, "The Observer Profile: Sacha Baron Cohen: Mutha of Invention," *Observer*, 24 February 2002, 27.

21. Boyson had been previously bamboozled by Chris Morris' *Brass Eye*.

22. See John Mullan, "Lost Voices," *Guardian*, 18 June 1999.

23. Sir Teddy Taylor, "Wicked! The Day Ali G Made Me Look a Clown," *Mail on Sunday*, 16 January 2000, 55; Such comments certainly added to the humor, but they also did harm to Sacha Baron Cohen by ripping the veil of secrecy away from his comedic methodology. Sir Teddy meticulously recounted the practices of the Channel 4 production team, ultimately making future victims aware of the threats posed by this track-suited poseur.

24. Miriam E. David, "Sue Lees: An Appreciation," *Gender and Education* 15, no. 1 (March 2003): 3-4.

25. Alex A. Alonso, "Tricked into Silly Interview with Wanna Be Gangster Ali G of Britain," *Streetgangs.com*, 12 March 2002, http://www.streetgangs.com/topics/2002/031202aligshow.html (7 April 2007).

26. Roger Lancaster. Email interview by the author, 21 May 2007.

27. Tony Benn, "How I Tamed Ali G," *Guardian*, 30 March 2000, 17.

28. Sam Schechner, "Respek! How Does Ali G Keep Conning Famous Guests?" *Slate*, 20 September 2004, http://www.slate.com (2 June 2007).

29. Lancaster, personal interview, 2007.

30. Dominic Hayes, "Why We Is All Now Talkin' Like Ali G," *Evening Standard*, 10 April 2006, 3.

31. Derek Kravitz, "Cockney Accent Being Swept Aside in London by New Hip-Hop Inspired Dialect," *Associated Press Newswires*, 13 April 2006.

32. Ali G's other habitus have also influenced British youth culture. According to Twentieth Century Fox's fact sheet hawking Baron Cohen for an Oscar in 2007, doctors have begun to report cases of what has been deemed "Boyakasha Syndrome" after teenagers became afflicted with wrist injuries resulting from imitating Ali G's trademark "fingerclick;" see Twentieth Century Fox, "Sacha Baron Cohen Fact Sheet Awards," Academy of Motion Pictures Arts and Science Web site, 2006, http://www.oscars.org/press/presskit/nomannc/pdf/bios_notes/36_cohen_sacha_baro n_borat.pdf (8 April 2007).

33. Paul Gilroy, "Ali G and the Oscars," *Open Democracy* Web site, 4 April 2002, http://www.opendemocracy.net/arts-Film/article_459.jsp (9 April 2007).

34. Allison Pearson, "Da Importance of Not Being Earnest," *Evening Standard*, 29 March 2000, 15.

35. Twentieth Century Fox, "Sacha Baron Cohen Fact Sheet Awards," Academy of Motion Pictures Arts and Science Web site, 2006. http://www.oscars.org/press/presskit/nomannc/pdf/bios_notes/36_cohen_sacha_baron_borat.pdf (8 April 2007)

36. Michael Collins, "Hold on to Your Hats," *The Guardian*, 27 March 2000, 2.

37. Collins, "Hold on to Your Hats," 2.

38. Paul Gilroy, *After Empire: Melancholia or Convivial Culture* (Oxford: Routledge, 2004), 147.

39. Gilroy, "Ali G and the Oscars."

40. *FHM* or *For Him Magazine* is a leading "lad's mag" in Britain. It is also distributed in 27 other countries.

41. The term was frequently applied to secondary school students by Tony Blair's then-Secretary of State for Education and Employment, David Blunkett.

42. Richard H. Kimberlee, "Why Don't British Young People Vote at General Elections?" *Journal of Youth Studies* 5, no. 1 (March 2002): 85-98.

43. Kimberlee, "Why Don't British Young People Vote at General Elections?" 87.

44. Interestingly, there was some bad blood between Harry Thompson and Hattersley. The latter had cancelled his appearance on *Have I Got News For You* on short notice after several reschedulings; then-producer Thompson responded by filling his spot on the game show with a tub of lard.

45. Ali was able to balance his identity being questioned by one of Sally Jessy Raphael's guests with Sally's closing remarks to him: "Do you know what's good about you? You're you!"

46. See Joshua Gamson, *Freaks Talk Back: Tabloid Talk Shows and Sexual Nonconformity* (Chicago: University of Chicago Press, 1998).

47. Brixton is a tough south London area, and the unofficial capital of the Jamaican and Caribbean community of London

48. Always one to spot a trend-in-the-making, Madonna had reached out to Sacha Baron Cohen earlier in the year via a call to his mobile phone. As he had never spoken with the Queen of Pop, he almost hung up on her thinking it was one of his friends having a laugh; see Dominic Mohan, "Madonna Called But I Thought It Was A Joke," *Sun*, 10 June 2000, 25.

49. Jessica Callan and Eva Simpson, "3am—Reigns Massive," *Mirror*, 21 March 2002, 12. An "eighth" refers to a 3.5 gram bag of marijuana.

50. Paul Kelso, "Race Protest at Ali G's Film Premiere," *Guardian,* 21 March 2002, 7.

51. "Ali G Steps Out in Regal Style," *Reuters News,* 20 March 2002.

52. According to Hilary N. Weaver, identity police are those self-appointed individuals who "divide communities and accuse others of not being [ethnic] enough because they practice the wrong religion, have the wrong politics, use the wrong label for themselves, or do not have the right skin color;" see Hilary N. Weaver, "Indigenous Identity," *American Indian Quarterly* 25, no. 2 (Spring 2001): 240-55.

53. Ali's opus magnum went straight to DVD in the US market. Drafting off the success of *Borat* in 2006, the film gained something of a second life; Gilroy, "Ali G and the Oscars."

54. Michael Clifford, "The Great Pretender . . . Innit?" *Sunday Tribune,* 24 March 2002, 15.

55. Gilroy, "Ali G and the Oscars."

56. Robin Hutchison, "Ali G Pulling 'Em in Staines Massive," *Daily Star,* 1 April 2002, 25.

57. Simon Weaver, "Comprehending Ambivalence: Ali G and Conceptualisations of the 'Other.'" Paper presented at The Connections Conference, University of Bristol, 2005, 3.

58. Interestingly, Staines is not part of Berkshire, but Surrey.

59. Ali G, "About the Show," Home Box Office Web site, http://www.hbo.com/alig/about (14 April 2007).

60. Lynn Elber, "British Comic Lowers the Satire Bar in HBO's 'Da Ali G Show,'" *Associated Press,* 19 February 2003. Retrieved via *Factiva.*

61. Ned Martel, "Booyakasha! Is You Ready for Ali G?" *Financial Times,* 4 April 2003.

62. The Web-based slang dictionary, *Urban Dictionary,* defines a "player hater" as: "someone who dislikes or resents or disapproves of a player (the term is used to criticize people who are jealous or who don't respect successful people)."

63. Many religious figures in the United States claim to have used prayer, "reparative therapy," and other methods to treat homosexual desire. The cartoon series *South Park* famously parodied the notion by sending one of its characters, Butters, to a special re-programming camp to "pray the gay away."

64. John Millar, "Mail Movies: Ali G Has Wild Time in Jungle Romp," *Sunday Mail,* 10 July 2005, 31.

65. Claire Sutherland, "Voice Squad," *Herald-Sun,* 15 September 2005, I5.

66. In fact, Baron Cohen and his girlfriend Isla Fisher were staying at a Hollywood apartment owned by Aniston when she separated from Pitt in early 2005.

67. "Will Ferrell Talks Movies," *Charlie Rose Show,* PBS, 9 November 2006.

68. Stephen Himes, "Review of Talladega Nights," *Flak Magazine,* 18 August 2006, http://www.flakmag.com/film/talladega.html (3 March 2007).

69. Will Ferrell regularly portrayed George W. Bush on *Saturday Night Live* until he left the show in 2002.

Chapter 3
Personae Comicae: The Postmodern Politics behind Ali G, Borat, and Bruno

In 2007, *Time* magazine named the creator of Ali G, Borat, and Bruno as one the world's 100 most important people. Sacha Baron Cohen joined luminaries and heads of state such as global steel magnate Lakshmi Mittal, Queen Elizabeth II, and China's president Hu Jintao. The comedian Roseanne, who penned his entry, wrote: "Sacha Baron Cohen has created uniquely outrageous characters for our uniquely outrageous times."[1] She argues that Baron Cohen's humor also shows "that the world is growing smaller and less tribal." Rather than simply relying on traditional ethnic humor made at the expense of minorities, Baron Cohen's style is based on satire and ridicule of the stereotypes themselves. With the spread of multiculturalism, the advent of globalized media, and increased education about the beliefs and values of minority communities, the general public has come to develop a certain level of sophistication about diversity within ethnic groups. Such understanding provides new opportunities for comedians seeking to interrogate those differences.[2] However, this begs the question, is Baron Cohen exploiting this familiarity with diversity to make himself the object of laughter or is he lampooning the wanna-be blacks, flamboyant gays, or bumbling foreigners he portrays?[3] Regardless of the answer, his humor represents something more than just a series of cultural jibes; it is a form of political satire that both shapes and is shaped by the postmodern politics of today's globalized society. The blurred lines between information and entertainment make his comedic jaunts not only possible, but valuable—even necessary—in a world where youth have been almost totally depoliticized.

Humor, Mass Mediation, and Postmodern Politics

Western society is currently undergoing a massive transformation, analogous to the one which reshaped Europe during the Industrial Revolution.[4] This shift is the result of a confluence of changes occurring in science, technology, economics, culture, and everyday life. Politics, like almost every other aspect of human activity, is being deeply affected by this transformation. The advent of myriad platforms offering ubiquitously available delivery of media content (Internet, satellite radio, 24/7 satellite news channels, etc.) has altered the political landscape and allowed new actors to enter the fray, from citizen-journalists to celebrity bloggers to talk show hosts. This reordering of power has greatly contributed to what might be labeled *post-modern politics*. According to political scientists Lawrence Alfred Powell and Lloyd Waller, in such a milieu "a pivotal source of power and strategic advantage belongs to whoever 'defines the reality'—that is, whoever is in a position to frame the media debates over social issues and determine which interpretations are appropriate to place on the national agenda for public consideration."[5]

Politicians and their supporters have responded to these shifting sands by changing the way they interact with the masses. Rather than relying on centuries-old traditions of political communication (door-to-door canvassing, mobilization through party-controlled literature, and face-to-face meetings with organized interest groups), today's politicians market themselves as products via multiple media channels. (This has, in turn, made voters into users or, more accurately, consumers of such products.) According to political theorists Steven Best and Douglas Kellner: "As new technologies transform every aspect of life, as culture plays a more crucial role in domains from the economy to personal identity, and as capital creates a new global economy and new syntheses of the global and the local abound, politics too takes on new forms and content."[6] Candidate branding, issue framing, manufactured events, and news management are redefining politics for the current era of mass media.[7] Putting these theoretical concepts into straightforward terms: politicians employ the tools of the marketplace to ensure that their image is recognizable, distinct, and attractive; they use discursive manipulation to craft a reality conducive to their policy recommendations; they create pre-packaged pseudo-events which are easily portrayed on the evening news; and they use their influence over journalists and editors to mold reporting and determine the content of the news.[8]

The ebbing divisions between "real" political actors, the media, critics, and entertainers is more evident with each passing year as political candidates build their brand by appearing on the talk show circuit (US Senator and Republican presidential candidate John McCain is a regular guest on several late night talk shows), making movies (Al Gore's fame for his documentary *An Inconvenient Truth* trumps his notoriety as Vice President under Bill Clinton), inviting voters into their homes (David Cameron, Britain's Conservative Party leader, broadcasts even his most mundane activities via webcam), and even subjecting themselves to the iniquities of reality TV (Scottish MP "Gorgeous" George Galloway appeared on Britain's *Celebrity Big Brother* in 2006).[9] In addition to direct engagement with the media, politicians also employ hordes of image consultants, brand marketers, and media shills to hone their public personae. The management of imagery and the manipulation of political perceptions can be described as the heart of postmodern politics.

Tony Blair, Prime Minister of Britain (1997-2007), epitomized both the personalization of politics and the projection of a carefully framed version of multivalent "reality." From the early days of his leadership, Blair's meticulously managed media persona was an integral part of the style and substance of his tenure. In such an environment, traditional issues associated with "power and process" are eschewed in favor of emotive, private, and personal stories and topics.[10] For politicians like Blair, the political must be turned into the popular. "Given the need to produce new subjectivities, political education, rational persuasion, and moral appeals remain of the greatest importance, but they can be very weak opponents of the seductive pleasures of MTV, blockbuster films, the Internet, fashion and advertising, and commodity consumption of all kinds."[11] In such an environment, politicians can not be blamed for resorting to image production as a means to reach "the people." Perhaps the most relevant example of this trend was the transformation of Princess Diana's death into a mass-mediated spectacle, and one which served to solidify Tony Blair's power and popularity (at the expense of Queen Elizabeth and the British Royal Family in general).

The media are an indispensable part of the process of postmodern politicking. As delivery platforms for both entertainment and news, they inevitably conflate the two giving rise to a muddled hybrid known as "infotainment." Human interest stories, personal drama, and lifestyle subjects are valued for the ability to generate ratings, and thus improve the bottom line of the increasingly consolidated transnational media giants and their parent companies such as News Corp., General Electric, Viacom, and the Walt Disney Company. In the English-speaking world, "soft news," i.e., news that is dramatic, personalized, easily understandable, and typically irrelevant to "power and process," has come to account for a plurality of news broadcasting. In the event of certain celebrity misadventures (O. J. Simpson, Paris Hilton, Britney Spears, *et al.*), it often consumes a majority of air time on cable television news networks. In turn, politicians have sought to portray themselves sympathetically, i.e., as a person rather than a politician, and are doing so to ever larger audiences. This has resulted in MPs, presidential candidates, and other public servants discussing fashion (Hillary Clinton), playing musical instruments on stage (Bill Clinton), and clearing brush on the ranch (George W. Bush) in an effort to reach out to their constituencies on a personal rather than political level.

This conflation of politics with entertainment has begun to transform political behavior among the consumers of politics. Instead of participating in the political processes of the "real world," young people often express their political desires in cyberspace and manifest political action in a virtual world. An astounding example of such "YouTube politics" occurred in 2007 when a University of Florida college student was tasered by police as he attempted to question Senator John Kerry (D-Mass.) at an open forum. Rather than coming to his defense or even condemning the police for their draconian tactics, Andrew Meyer's peers reached for their mobile phones so they could record the melee, later posting the videos to the Internet. It was only when they were safely ensconced in front of their computers, that they expressed their revulsion at the violent stifling of free speech on a (liberal) college campus. The proliferation of "hactivism," i.e., using Internet-based attacks against corporations or states in recent years can also be seen part of the virtualization of politics. Cyberspace allows Internet-enabled activists near total anonymity and the ability to conduct attacks from almost anywhere in the world.

This brave new world of globally-linked media platforms, pre-packaged candidates, and YouTube politics has proved an irresistible temptation to an old critic of the system: satirists. While there is nothing new about political satire—it is at least as ancient as politics itself—the contemporary environment has rendered the dividing lines between politics, political theatre, entertainment, and political satire more gossamer than ever. Sacha Baron Cohen has made himself comfortable at the nexus of all four. As a student of history, a lifelong activist for progressive causes, and a member of a religious minority, Baron Cohen is especially well-placed to observe and comment on the humor and tragedy of contemporary political culture.

Fake, but Funny: "News" in the 21st Century

Baron Cohen's humor can be likened to that employed by Comedy Central's premiere "fake news" program *The Daily Show with Jon Stewart*. *The Daily Show* is a Peabody and Emmy Award-winning American satirical television program that delivers news-related comedy and satire. In the tradition of *Saturday Night Live*'s "Weekend Update" and Channel 4's *The 11 O'Clock Show*, the program lampoons politicians for their foibles. However, *The Daily Show*, since Jon Stewart took over as host in 1999, also targets the media itself. Much of Stewart's humor is based on an explicit critique of politics *and* the media by interrogating the press' treatment of politicians, as well as what the politicians actually say and do. According to media specialist Geoffrey Baym, "Like all satire, *The Daily Show* is dialogic in the Bakhtinian sense, the playing of multiple voices against each other in a discursive exchange that forces the original statement into revealing contexts."[12] Stewart gleefully shows montages of *CNN*, *FOX News*, and *MSNBC* parroting White House talking points and engaging in inane banter about trivialities which ultimately distract from, rather than contribute to, civic participation. Stewart is unabashed in his loathing of certain formats that have come to dominate in the current news environment. He famously appeared on CNN's moderated debate show *Crossfire* in 2004 and condemned cable news media for "hurting America." He told the program's two hosts, Paul Begala and Tucker Carlson, "You're part of [the politicians'] strategies. You are partisan—what do you call it—hacks. . . . I am here to confront you, because we need help from the media and they're hurting us. . . . You have a responsibility to the public discourse, and you fail miserably."[13]

Baron Cohen and Stewart both engage in what political scientist Jamie Warner calls "political culture jamming" in an effort to interrupt the cultivated political messages of politicians. Such humor is built upon a postmodern political aesthetic that confronts the structure of our image-based society in an attempt to "undermine it from within . . . by way of image itself, and planning the implosion of the logic of simulacrum by dint of ever greater doses of simulacra."[14] Akin to the *Daily Show*'s farce, Baron Cohen's style is meant to reach out to what political scientist Matthew Baum refers to as "a politically inattentive public" that only gets its information through "soft news."[15] However, the key difference is that Stewart seeks to inform while lampooning, while Baron Cohen seems content to simply ridicule. Though, as cultural studies professor Chris Rojek points out, "A careful reading of Ali G reveals that the comedy operates to deflate cant and humbug, whether articulated by racists and sexists or by those elected to serve as our moral guardians."[16] However, Baron Cohen never makes these criticisms explicit. He leaves it up to the viewer to draw his or her own conclusions.

In this regard his comedic project is similar to that of the Yes Men, a loosely affiliated group of agitprop anti-capitalists who declare their mission to be: "Impersonating big-time criminals in order to publicly humiliate them. Targets are leaders and big corporations who put profits ahead of everything else." They have infiltrated corporate conferences and international governance summits posing as academics and subject-matter experts, even appearing on *BBC World* in character. The group's ostensible ringleaders, Andy Bichlbaum and Mike Bonanno, argue that their project is a complement to journalism since it allows reporters to cover troubling issues in the corporate world which would otherwise remain below the radar. While the film *The Yes Men* (2003) recorded some of their antiglobalization activism, their primary goal is to embarrass corporate giants and international governmental organizations through mainstream press coverage of their antics. Unlike Baron Cohen who claims to work for fake news programs and networks such as the fictional Belarus, the Yes Men claim to represent genuine organizations such as the National Petroleum Council, the World Trade Organization, McDonald's, ExxonMobil, Dow Chemical, and the US Department of Housing and Urban Development. Their various stunts have included presentations about a human-flesh based fuel, promotion of legal vote-selling in democracies, and the recycling of human feces into food for the Third World.

Baron Cohen's deep use of personae to gird his humor also provides striking parallels to the methodology of *Daily Show* veteran Stephen Colbert. The latter's *The Colbert Report* follows *The Daily Show* on Comedy Central, thus providing a full hour of "fake news" combined with genuine political commentary.[17] *New York Times* columnist Maureen Dowd described the concept as follows: "A fake news show, 'The Daily Show,' spawned a fake commentator, Colbert, who makes his own fake reality defending the fake reality of a real president, and has government officials on who know the joke but are still willing to be mocked by someone fake."[18] *The Colbert Report* is, in effect, a 30-minute full-dress parody of Bill O'Reilly's *The O'Reilly Factor* which airs on *FOX News*.[19]

Bill O'Reilly makes an easy target as he is the highest rated host on cable news, an unrepentant populist, a champion of ultra-traditional values, and a magnet for controversy and criticism.[20] According to the *New Yorker,* "Stephen Colbert has obviously made a close study of O'Reilly's mannerisms and opinions . . . [Colbert] often uses his fake right-wing persona to score points for the left."[21] Viewers of such comedy, i.e., Baron Cohen as Ali G and Colbert as O'Reilly's doppelganger, are, of course, in on the joke. In other words, it is nearly impossible to take the humor at face value. Speaking of Baron Cohen, Roger Lancaster, one of Ali's victims and a professor of cultural studies at George Mason University, states, "In the sense that he calls attention to the artifice of his performance, in the act of performing, this could be dubbed 'postmodern.'" In watching Ali, we know he is a sham because he reminds us incessantly.

However, unlike Sacha Baron Cohen who has never come face to face with a "real" Ali G, Bruno, or Borat (at least on screen), Colbert has actually faced down his own alter-ego's mirror image, O'Reilly. In January 2007, Colbert had O'Reilly as a guest on his show where he asked O'Reilly about the purported "culture war" that O'Reilly so frequently invokes, including in the title of his most recent book, *Culture Warrior* (2006). O'Reilly responded, "It's between secular progressives like yourself and traditionalists like me." Colbert—a Sunday school teacher and practicing Roman Catholic—instantly retorted, "I am not a secular progressive. I am a deeply religious man who will do everything you say."

While Baron Cohen makes clear distinctions between himself and his various personae, the line between Colbert the Character and Colbert the Man is a bit murkier and even more postmodern. This stems from Colbert's well-documented religiosity, which is hard to disentangle from his character's rabid Catholic proselytizing and Christian chest-thumping. He is known to recite the Nicene Creed from time to time, but also once declared:

> If you non-Catholic Christians are upset, well just have your Pope issue a response. Oh, that's right, you don't have a Pope. Because your faith is defective. Sorry, Catholicism is clearly superior. Don't believe me? Name one Protestant denomination that could afford a $660 million sexual abuse settlement. I think the Lord has spoken on this one.

Is this Stephen Colbert speaking or his character? Is it both? For the viewer, teasing out who is who while watching *The Colbert Report* is often a complicated undertaking.

Political Pantomime: Ali G, Ethnic Ambiguity, and Contested Identity

Through the instrument of his Ali G persona, Sacha Baron Cohen takes direct aim at the identity politics of our time. Rather than attacking multiculturalism outright, he insidiously attempts to undermine the pervading notions associated with political correctness. His satire takes aim at those among the white, upper class who equate respect for "diversity" with the toleration of abominable behavior of "tribal youths." Many of his victims fail to contest such behavior even in its most grotesque forms (calling women "bitches," veneration of guns, etc.) for fear of being seen as "intolerant" toward minorities. In the words of Jane Freebury:

> It takes a brave man to dive into the muddy waters of identity politics, with its ethnic, culture and gender issues, and swim clear to the other side. But I think Ali G somehow does it, and that's despite the weight of his heavy golden neck chains and pendants and the depths of cheerful poor taste to which he plunges. He manages to have a go at feminists, gays, rappers, asylum seekers, the British establishment including the Queen, and the bleeding-heart liberals (is that everyone covered?), and still come through the other side unscathed.[22]

Simultaneously, he targets those politicians who are so disconnected from those whom they govern that they lack the tools to combat outrageous ignorance, racism, and sexism when confronted by these societal ills. Bringing together a penchant for mimicry with a strong normative orientation towards politics (and specifically identity politics), Baron Cohen has emerged as a *force majeure* in contemporary British culture.

I do not bestow these laurels simply because Ali G, Bruno, and Borat have attained seminal roles in pop culture. Baron Cohen both embodies and shapes cultural awareness in postmodern Britain; in effect, he is the prodigal son of the country's cultural studies movement. This school of thought began its history with the foundation of the Birmingham Centre for Contemporary Cultural Studies in 1964. The Jamaican-born theorist Stuart Hall was the center's director and its leading luminary during the early years. Cultural studies grew in strength and resonance during Prime Minister Margaret Thatcher's tenure by providing a plausible explanation for the marked shift of working class loyalties from Labour to the Conservative Party. At its root, cultural studies is concerned with the relationship between cultural praxes and power. However, the discipline is deeply normative in its orientation, supporting a progressive political project and condemning the domination of the existing system by elites on both the left and the right. Many of the field's scholars, in fact, came from colonial backgrounds, and felt themselves precluded from access to the mainstream of the British Left establishment.[23]

During the 1980s, the focus of British cultural studies broadened to include many sub-groups: punks, women, blacks, gays, Muslims, etc. Each group's "rituals" were interrogated for symbols of resistance to the dominant, i.e., white, upper class English system. With this shift, traditional cultural studies scholars like Hall and E. P. Thompson were joined by postcolonial theorists such as Homi Bhabha, Gayatri Chakravorty Spivak, and Kwame Anthony Appiah among others in their investigation of the power of coding and decoding of cultural symbols. In describing the transitory shift in cultural studies from its origins to the current state of the field, Marxist scholar Esther Leslie notes: "There has been a transformation of Cultural Studies from something interested in resistance in the popular to something interested only in consumption and the ways in which culture is a motor of capitalism, rather than its brake."[24]

Baron Cohen is a manifestation of what I call the post-cultural studies generation, i.e., those who came of age in early 1990s Britain. By this time, the original earnestness of cultural studies had been undermined by its overemphasis on "niche cultures." Symbols of the Other were now all open to academic scrutiny. The consumption of these totems, as Leslie notes above, had become more important than their reasons behind their consumption. Baron Cohen—as Ali G, Bruno, and Borat—is obsessed with consumption in all its forms. Consequently, Baron Cohen's criticism of globalized capitalist excess is muted, if not totally absent. In Baron Cohen's mutant form of cultural studies, consumption is resistance. His performance of others' rituals is a unique form of postmodern politics which simultaneously critiques cultural studies while concurrently pushing its agenda in the only way he knows how: lampooning its enemies, i.e., white elitists.

As a Cambridge student in the early 1990s, Sacha Baron Cohen experienced the viral spread of political correctness (PC) from across the Atlantic. While British universities were only experiencing the "the thin end of the wedge" during the early 1990s, the PC revolution was clearly under way.[25] As the decade progressed, he repeatedly demonstrated his disdain for sacred cows by portraying a "shvitzing" Hassidic rapper to pimping Catholic girls to the head of the Grand Orange Lodge of Ireland. Inherent in much of Baron Cohen's humor is a "reactionary, nihilistic backlash" against political correctness—a political correctness which has been perpetuated by "notions of a sacrosanct multiculturalism."[26] His humor rails against the buttoned-up elites of British society who project their respect for multiculturalism, but are so tone-deaf to the realities of everyday diversity in Britain that they are unable to sniff out an obvious imposter like Ali G. According to postmodern thinker Mark Lipovetsky, "Baron Cohen perfomatively reveals a paradoxical connection between political correctness and xenophobia."[27] By playing the fool, Ali G is able to demonstrate how multiculturalism sustains and complexifies existing bigotries.[28] According to Chris Rojek, "Cohen plays Ali G cleverly, sometimes dangerously, pricking at both racial stereotyping and the sanctimony of political correctness. The comedy lies not only in Ali G's strident sincerity but also in the jaw-dropping credulity of the powerful, often rich, people he interviews who take Ali G at face value."[29]

Baron Cohen, in a rare out-of-character appearance, defended his interviews-*cum*-ethnic pantomime as attempts at "showing how separate these people are from the society they govern, and that's a very worrying thing, that they believe that an Ali G could exist."[30] Baron Cohen's Ali G persona functions as a trope for turning his politically powerful guests into visibly flawed characters oblivious to the reality around them. According to Dan Friedman, Ali is able to "deny the foundations of authority without ever appearing to have a clue."[31] Baron Cohen refers to these "successful, powerful white men who rule the country" as "legitimate targets" for ridicule, especially when they are accommodating someone as silly as Ali G.[32]

Baron Cohen's personae all exploit the intrinsically postmodern tension between fear and attraction to the "unclassifiable" other. The sociologist Zygmunt Bauman describes these dual competing orientations as *proteophobia* and *proteophilia*. In particular, Ali G exploits this complex interplay of loathing and curiosity with aplomb as he forces politicians, cultural elites, and the super-wealthy to manage the unclassifiable Ali within their own social spaces.[33] Ali G's protean identity, which transitions through a stunning array of British ethnicities but remains perniciously indefinable, triggers a crisis in nearly every interview. According to Bauman, "Unreliability means erratic behavior which defies probabilities and makes calculation based on knowledge of rules useless."[34] In some cases, they try to befriend and constantly show deference to his warped worldview (proteophilia). Though, as Bauman points out, the end goal of the interviewee is always to preserve the stranger's (i.e., Ali's) "strangeness," though one might take some amusement from the exchange.[35] In other situations, Ali's interviewees react in horror to his incongruous appearance and allotropic babble, producing a situation where the guest enters into a deep state of anxiety (proteophobia). Here, an attempt is typically made either to "recycle" or "dispose" of the stranger within the extant social spaces of society.[36] Regardless, both of these responses are evidence of Bauman's idea that the modern nation-state is built on the principle that all strangers within the confines of the polity must be "dealt with."[37] It should be stated that Ali G often proves a hard subject to quarantine or exile after an interview has begun; this was born out in his last interview with the irascible Andy Rooney who literally ejected Ali from his office. These reactions often (though not always) break down along political lines with leftists tending towards proteophilia and social conservatives demonstrating proteophobia.[38]

Paul Gilroy employs Bauman's conceptual tools to discuss the peculiarity of Baron Cohen's humor, making allusions to Voltaire's Candide and Montesquieu's Usbek.[39] Like these cultural interrogators of the past, Gilroy argues that Ali G is undertaking a "daring act of patriotic love" by teaching Britons about themselves.[40] He does this through a performance which evinces both love and hate for that which is strange, foreign, or just difficult to comprehend. Simon Weaver points out that Ali G is a valuable trope for understanding emergent British hybrid culture, and that his resounding popularity represents a proteophilic response on a mass—even national—scale.[41] In his analysis of the proteophobia engendered by Baron Cohen's parody, Gilroy states, "For those angry people, the betrayal that Ali G represented was the culmination of a larger process of dilution and mongrelization in which the protective purity of largely racial cultures was being lost, leaving them vulnerable to unprotected encounters with difference that can only involve risk, fear, and jeopardy."[42] In both cases, it is readily apparent that responses to Ali G's "subversive, cross-racial-dressing liminality" represent an important litmus test for identity in 21st century Britain.[43]

Baron Cohen has long made a study of black culture, mores, and values. Even in his teens, he was drawn to blackness, as performances with his breakdance troupe known as Black on White proved. It was during this period that Baron Cohen began his attempts at earnest mimicry of the "street codes of blackness" for comic effect, a praxis which would later serve to fortify his Ali G persona.[44] His youthful mimicry of African American B-boys (breakdancers) gave way to a more intellectual investigation of the politics of race and ethnicity in his college years. Furthermore, coming of age in late 1980s Britain, Baron Cohen witnessed the ascendance of identity politics in the political sphere. According to Best and Kellner:

> Perhaps the dominant form of politics today, known as "identity politics" refers to a politics in which individuals construct their cultural and political consciousness through engaging in struggles or associations that advance the interests of the groups with which they associate . . . for example, with the black, gay and lesbian, or with whatever community from which one gains their identity and sense of self and belonging. . . . In identity politics, individuals define themselves primarily as belonging to a given group, marked as "oppressed" and therefore as outside the dominant white male, heterosexual, capitalist culture.[45]

Each of Baron Cohen's three characters represents a critique of identity politics in the postmodern West. Concurrently, his comedy highlights the fact that such issues are quite important to British youth, especially when compared to the traditional Left-Right, Tory-Labour issues of their parents' generation. Political sociologist Richard Kimberlee argues, "Young people's interest in environmental and identity politics has led them to develop an interest in single issue groups and protest politics. . . . Concern with lifestyle and non-materialistic values appears to be a central feature of young people's involvement in contemporary political life." As such, Ali G (and, to a lesser extent, Bruno and Borat) politically engage British youth in a more visceral and vibrant way than do traditional party politics.

Ali G negotiates the pitfalls of identity politics most directly by presenting a character that purposefully confuses *objective* and *subjective* aspects of identity. One's subjective identity is based on self-conception, while one's objective identity is forged by others' perceptions. Biological or social factors strongly inform the latter. The man parading as Ali G is obviously white, and therefore his objective identity should be whiteness. Baron Cohen's purported "whiteness" in the context of modern Britain is, however, somewhat problematic. As cultural studies professor Jon Stratton has pointed out, Jews are not necessarily considered "white" in Britain (whereas this is a given in the Anglo-Celtic settler societies of Australia and the United States).[46] Calling upon his own experiences as a British-Jewish transplant to Australia, Stratton argues that Jews in Britain have the choice to either "come out" as Jewish or "pass" as white.[47] Baron Cohen's early career certainly involved his own coming out as Jewish after a prolonged public discussion of the racial and ethnic origins of the "man behind the mask" of Ali G. In modern societies, one is a Jew because one claims to be. After the initial ambiguity over Baron Cohen's real identity, this question was permanently settled by Baron Cohen's own affirmation of his Jewishness.[48]

Once he was "outed" as a Jew, Baron Cohen's ethnic transvestism as Ali G became both a political issue and challenge to the very notion of identity in modern Britain.[49] Political philosopher Akeel Bilgrami argues, "It is neither routine nor plausible, at least in a political sense, to conceive of yourself as something you manifestly are not."[50] Yet, Ali steadfastly refers to himself as black and invariably perceives slights (real and imagined) as emanating from his "blackness." Baron Cohen has effectively used a fabricated subjective identity to engender a false but accepted objective identity. In the words of Stratton, "we live in a time which ostensibly privileges the cultural over the racial."[51] Consequently, the praxes of multiculturalism not only permit, but, in some cases, encourage the purposeful crossing and blurring of the boundaries between races and ethnicities. The key is genuineness. According to Howe, Ali G is convincing because Baron Cohen's caricature goes beyond simple mockery; "Baron Cohen . . . wraps himself around the culture of conflicting groups in society and looks at them through the prism of race. . . . He is absolutely authentic in his parody of black street kids."[52]

Ali (Baron Cohen) employs blackness not simply as an inherited marker of race or kinship, but also as a political tool making each and every interaction, from police management of an environmental protest to his ejection from Andy Rooney's office, into a political statement.[53] Rachel Garfield describes this postmodern phenomenon as a paradigmatic example of the "politics of appearance" in which racial constructs are challenged by actors who do not fit the outward mold, but nonetheless complexify the debate over "blackness" and "whiteness."[54] Thus, Baron Cohen, through the mechanism of Ali G, brings into question the entire notion of the black/white binary which pervades Western culture. He accomplishes this through his playful exploitation of the tension between what is seen versus what is perceived.[55]

In his essay "'Is It Because I Is Black?' Race, Humor and the Polysemiology of Ali G," Richard Howells argues that race has become a taboo subject in contemporary Western society. "Just as with sex in Victorian times, race is not nowadays mentioned in polite company. Indeed, it is rarely discussed freely at all. And just like with Victorian sex, one suspects there is a marked gap between public pronouncement and private practice."[56] Baron Cohen's Ali G shtick exemplifies while subtly critiquing this phenomenon. According to Howells, "anyone can see that Ali G is clearly not black. Sacha Baron Cohen is white; he does not 'black up' (that is to say darken his face with stage make-up) to play this character. He simply adopts the (exaggerated) dress, manner and style of a certain kind of black person."[57] Exchanges with comedic foils are funny because Ali G is convinced that he is black. According to Dan Friedman, a media critic and friend of Sacha Baron Cohen,

> This delusion that he is a black gangsta rapper allows him to skate blithely through the register of normal social markers of 'blackness'—language, name, family set up, music, livelihood, location—and treat his own anomalous situation as exemplary for gangstahood. Moreover, and here the comedy takes on an entirely new dimension, despite his gross inauthenticity, he often manages to pass—in real life. As if playing some part in a vast cultural studies experiment, most of the people he interviews accept that he is, in fact, black.[58]

As communications theorist Susanne Mühleisen argues, "The stubborn insistence on being black despite any physical evidence of an African or Caribbean heritage has furthermore an element of self-parody and travesty—this relies on the dichotomy of behavior versus appearance—and leaves his interviewees and the audience confused about the ethnic signifiers he is playing with."[59] This purposeful confusion about Ali's true identity is both a source of humor and a political move on the part of Baron Cohen.[60]

The ethnically ambiguous Ali G—whose style is dominated by his tacky, yellow track suit, urban skull cap, preposterous array of jewelry, and idiosyncratic argot—is protected by a multilayered patina which few of his victims are willing to challenge. He is interesting because he is simultaneously white and black, a form of hybridity which makes him the perfect postmodern hero.[61] "[Ali G] contributes to the dissolution of ethnic barriers that seem impermeable if judgment is based solely on paternity-related considerations."[62] Sacha Baron Cohen uses language rather than skin color to blur ethnic borders.[63] The success of Ali G's racial trespassing would be hard to replicate outside of contemporary British society, a place where subjective identity production most strongly impacts objection identity reception. Howells states, "In an increasingly multi-cultural Britain, it is becoming all the more clear that race and identity are not the same thing. Race is given; identity is not."[64] This was made abundantly clear when multiple groups (Greeks, Sikhs, Jews, Welsh, Indians, Scots, Bangladeshis, Pakistanis, and blacks) tried to claim Ali G as their own before his "true" identity was revealed.[65] Yet, according to Garfield, Ali G fails to represent anyone's likeness. "His popularity undermines the conventions of 'representational politics' and moves the conversation away from who has the right to speak for whom into the realms of the failure of representation to really represent."[66]

Ali G's Exposure of the Vagaries of 21st Century "Britishness"

Identity in Britain is an especially thorny problem. As Canadian journalist Mark Steyn has pointed out, "Britishness" is the original multi-ethnic identity.[67] Such notions were echoed in 2001 by Robin Cook, Britain's then foreign secretary, when he affirmed, "The British are not a race, but a gathering of countless different races and communities, the vast majority of which were not indigenous to these islands."[68] While many outside the country conflate Britishness with Englishness, British national identity is, in fact, built on a fragile coalition of commonality amongst Welsh, Scots, Irish, and English—the latter being a hodge-podge of Celts, Angles, Saxons, Danes, and French. (It is also worth remembering that the royal family itself is "English-by-adoption.")

In the post-World War II era, decolonization and the demands of the labor market precipitated massive immigration of former colonial subjects into the UK. Initially, the vast majority of newcomers were South Asians and Afro-Caribbeans; over time, these communities became integral parts of British society. In recent decades, sizeable numbers of labor migrants and asylum seekers from all over the world have flocked to Britain, introducing large numbers of Poles, Arabs, and Chinese into an already kaleidoscopic society. Further complicating the situation, regional identification within England itself also functions as an important society division with strong north-south allegiances, as well as a growing perception that cosmopolitan, polyglot London exists apart from the rest of the country.[69] For all intents and purposes, such complexity precludes an ethno-nationalist approach to identity.

Britain—like its former settler colonies, the US, Canada, and Australia—ascribes to civic nationalism, rather than the "blood nationalism" (*jus sanguinis*) associated with traditional nation-states where a single ethnic group dominates the political, economic, social, and cultural life of the country.[70] Civic nationalism is not dependent on blood, place of birth, or attachment to any particular soil. Instead, a given society is voluntarily bound by principles that transcend ethno-religious backgrounds and individual interests, uniting a people together as citizens, which in turn confers political legitimacy upon the state in which they live. Respect for some level of diversity—religious, ethnic, cultural, and socio-economic—is a constituent part of any such project. The ideology of multiculturalism takes this notion a step further, supporting the idea that modern societies should embrace and include multiple, distinct cultural groups, and endow each with equal social status. Such measures are not universally accepted as necessary components of civic nationalism; yet, in modern Britain, multiculturalism has become inextricably linked to the larger national identity project.[71] However, it should be stated that significant segments of the population argue instead for a multi-ethnic Britain united by a common culture—an approach which gained ground in the latter years of Blair's prime ministership.[72]

Paradoxically, such policies have failed to achieve social unity in the country and have resulted in "self-segregating communities" leading "separate but parallel lives."[73] Throughout Great Britain, lower class whites live apart from their wealthier counterparts, while both communities are spatially and culturally separated from the various communities of South Asian Muslims, Hindus, and Sikhs, who in turn are increasingly distancing themselves from one another. Similarly, newer Eastern European, Turkish, and African immigrants tend to recreate their own communities in England which, again, stand apart from those of Britons whose ancestors were born in England, Scotland, or Wales. Increasingly, many Britons have grown critical of their government's policies on multiculturalism. The anxiety stems principally from three sources: 1) popular fear associated with bans on traditional cultural practices associated with Christmas, eating of pork, etc.; 2) difficulties in crafting a national narrative for a society comprised of conquerors (white

Britons) and conquered (South Asians, West Africans, descendents of West Indian slaves, etc.); and 3) the incompatibility of protecting certain societal praxes which are antithetical to Britain's liberal, pro-woman, religiously tolerant culture.[74]

In the waning days of Tony Blair's reign, "New Labour" distanced itself from its long-held support of unquestioned multiculturalism, and tentatively embraced a policy of putting the "Great" back in "Britain."[75] According to the *Economist*, "The government now believes that Britain has struck the wrong balance between the tolerance of cultural diversity and the need for minority communities to integrate with wider society."[76] Such a policy shift may spell disaster for Britain's "real" Ali Gs as the country shifts away from placing "tribal youth culture," imported Islamic mores, and Scottish Highlander traditions on the same plateau with "standard" markers of Britishness, and towards making "non-negotiable" British values (i.e., belief in the law, freedom of speech, equal opportunities, and respect for one's neighbor) sacrosanct. Despite this *volte-face*, Britain is—and will likely remain for the foreseeable future—a country where people of radically different backgrounds and motivations live side-by-side, often in shocking ignorance of one another.

It is this milieu that made Ali G a hit in his homeland. Paul Gilroy opines, "I'm sure that Ali G's highly educated creators knew that a sense of what it meant to be English was at stake in the timeliness of their joke," since much of the humor is built upon the "country's incomplete transition to cultural diversity and plurality."[77] Ali G has proved to be a powerful symbol and frequent cudgel in the debate over Britishness and minority identity within Britain. Chris Myant, spokesman for the government's Commission for Racial Equality, used Ali's post-imperial, racial ambiguity as a referent to elucidate the generational differences in defining Englishness, stating that "young English people have an understanding of a very different identity. My children don't have the baggage of the empire . . . there are parts of the baggage of being English we have to get rid of, but none of us can determine what the future of Englishness will be." Despite Myant's claims that Ali proves that England has moved beyond empire, Baron Cohen has been known to wryly touch upon the complicated themes of Britain's imperial history, including one exchange with an Orangeman in Northern Ireland who asserted his Britishness only to have Ali G ask: "Is you here on holiday?"

Curiously, a number of scholars and cultural commentators, especially those outside of the UK, have increasingly come to identify Ali G as an intrinsically British figure. In their article on celebrations of Britishness in Australia, Sara Wills and Kate Darian-Smith lament the spuriousness of such "authentic" representations of contemporary British culture by pointing to the marked absence of Ali G.[78] Along with the failure to include Baron Cohen's post-British straw man, the authors identify an absence of references to symbols of post-war Indian and Asian migration to Britain. Without Ali, Indians, and Afro-Caribbeans, they conclude that Gilroy's famous maxim "there ain't no black in the Union Jack" is even truer abroad than at home.[79] In his recent obituary for Tony Blair's decade of leadership, *Guardian* columnist Gary Younge pointed out that Ali G's "emergence as a comic force" is an important symbol that "Britain without non-white people" has become unimaginable. Neo-conservative American commentator Steve Sailer, while bemoaning the existence of the poseur from Staines, nevertheless accepts his centrality to contemporary British identity: "While Ali G, as promised, wholly assimilated into English culture, it was not the England that gave us Shakespeare and Locke, but the lowest common denominator Cool Britannia of council estate chavs from the working class."[80]

Just as Ali's exotic, polytropic Britishness has become a symbol of the changing face of modern Britain, he has also emerged as a lightning rod for defining Asian—and more specifically Muslim—identity within the country. In his essay "Between Lord Ahmed and Ali G: Which Future for British Muslims?," Philip Lewis, the inter-faith advisor to the Anglican Bishop of Bradford, suggests that the "ghetto fabulous" Ali G reflects the lifestyle choices of a substantial number of hereditary Muslim males in Britain. "The social reality encapsulated in the figure of 'Ali G' is part cause, part response to disturbing figures on educational under-achievement in these communities."[81] In the words of Rojek, "Celebrities simultaneously embody social types and provide role models."[82] Ali G has shone an often unwelcome spotlight on this aspect of Muslim youth culture in Britain, while undoubtedly influencing its spread among certain sections of the community.

A Muse on a Mission: Bruno, Attacking Artifice, and Evincing Homophobia

While Ali G is used to expose the foibles of politicians, Bruno's targets are a bit more diverse. One the one hand, he lampoons fashion gurus, style junkies, and "party people" who take themselves and their pursuits too seriously. Baron Cohen's flamboyant Austrian fashion critic and (self-declared) part-time muse for "Chrysler" serves as a mechanism for drawing out the ignoble side of his subjects. For instance, at New York's prestigious Fashion Week, Bruno coaxed a fashion groupie to agree that all unstylish people should be put on trains and sent off to camps. Since bringing *Da Ali G Show* to the US, Baron Cohen also used the character to target a new quarry: homophobes. Like Ali and Borat, Bruno is obsessed with sex; however, his preference for those of the male gender has occasionally prompted virulent—bordering on violent—reactions in supposedly tolerant America.

In the Bruno sketches, we see Sacha Baron Cohen at his bitchiest, as he only thinly veils his disgust for his subjects. Speaking of his Bruno persona, Baron Cohen states, "We're interviewing the most pretentious and superficial people, and Bruno is the most pretentious, superficial person that anyone's met, and so they let their guard down . . . the kind of people that we tend to target with Bruno tend to be superficial, tend to have a value system that I don't really respect."[83] This is painfully evident when Bruno interviews fellow fashionistas. He uses devilishly obsequious questions to butter up his subjects before delving into truly horrific analogies, syllogisms, and gedankenexperiments. In one episode, he postulates that World War II could have been prevented only if house music had been around in the 1930s, evoking strong support from one of his interviewees. In another skit, he encouraged one of his subjects to refer to *Lord of the Rings* director Peter Jackson as a "fashion terrorist," and to his sloppy appearance at the Oscars as a "mini 9/11."

Like Ali G and Borat before him, Bruno possesses his own idiolect, replete with faux Deutschlish (German-English pidgin) terms for a variety of concepts, including *Poopenschaft* ('rectum'), *Scheißendummführer* ('shitting dumb leader'), *Schantineux* ('a dirty animal'), and *Schwanzenstück* ('penis'). He also employs genuine German words such as *entschuldigung* ('excuse me'), *nicht* ('not'), and *jetzt* ('now') in his skits. Bruno is a self-appointed constable in the transnational *Fashionpolizei*. His personal mantra is as follows: "My name ist Bruno, one name—like Madonna, und I'm on a mission: to reveal the true beauty of fashion. After all, fashion saves a lot more lives than doctors, right?"[84] Similarly inane and insensitive comments pepper Bruno's pantomime.

Bruno regularly makes reference to the Jewish Holocaust in his comedy—a trend which has earned him surprisingly little criticism when compared to the fiery condemnations made of Borat for similar breaches. Austrian diplomats, unlike their Kazakhstani counterparts (as discussed in the next chapter), can barely be bothered with the character or his Nazi fetish. When confronted with a question about Baron Cohen's next movie project which targeted his country, an Austrian Foreign Ministry official responded, "Bruno who?"[85] Despite being the birthplace of Hitler, Austrians seem to have moved on from worrying about historical stereotypes, especially in light of media attention surrounding the government's recent imprisonment of the British historian and Holocaust-denier David Irving.[86] While Viennese diplomats may not be taking much notice, the same cannot be said for the country's tourism industry.

> Panic is now spreading among Austria's tourism marketers, who fear that the gay fashionista, Bruno, will trigger images of a country brimful of Nazis instead of the advertised mountains, blue lakes and pretty girls in Dirndl folk costumes. If Borat's success is indicative, they are justifiably terrified. Bruno's air-headed adoration of Adolf Hitler could well remind prospective visitors that Austria still has a number of unresolved issues with its Nazi past, not to mention an active and rather successful rightist party.[87]

Bruno purportedly works for the fictional Austrian TV station *Österreichischer Jungen Rundfunk* ('Austrian Youth [or Boy] Broadcast'), whose name mocks Austrian national broadcaster ORF (*Österreichischer Rundfunk*). When pressed, he confesses it is really "Austrian Gay TV." Such an admission has lead to threats of physical violence on multiple occasions, e.g., when Bruno was interviewing testosterone-driven jocks during Spring Break in Daytona Beach, Florida.

Just as Ali G creates hilarious dissonance by employing "youfspeak" when interviewing speakers of Upper Received Pronunciation, i.e., the Queen's English, Bruno sparks proteophobia by assuming everyone is gay or bisexual. According to journalist Kaizaad Kotwal, "His subjects don't find that funny and this makes their homophobia come through in spades."[88] At an Arkansas pro-America rally (read gun show), a rabidly anti-Semitic libertarian defended Bruno's right to homosexual intercourse behind closed doors before exploding and telling him not to be "so fucking gay." Bruno's most well-known exploit involved joining the University of Alabama's cheerleading squad in "the gayest part of America" (i.e., the southern state of Alabama). His impromptu performance in front of the Crimson Tide's

fans ended in a pathetic scene with elements in the crowd cursing and calling him a faggot. Baron Cohen recounted the event in an interview:

> Bruno is the subject of a lot of homophobia. The main difference be-
> tween playing Borat and Bruno is that it is a lot more dangerous doing
> Bruno, because there is so much homophobia. So for example, when I
> was doing Bruno at the Alabama, Mississippi football game a few years
> ago, 60,000 people in the crowd started chanting faggot, and started
> throwing stuff at me, taunting me, spitting at me, threatening to kill me.
> Those kinds of situations are a lot more common when you are playing a
> gay character. It is almost as if homophobia is one of the last forms of
> prejudice that really is tolerated.[89]

Bruno was the *Da Ali G Show*'s most underutilized character. It is therefore
no surprise that Baron Cohen has waited the longest to unleash a feature-
length movie starring the Austrian reporter. At the time of writing, it is unclear what sort of chord the prospective Bruno movie, tentatively being
marketed as the "Fabulous Fashionista Film," will strike. However, with his
campy style and a built-in fan base, Baron Cohen's Bruno is likely to probe
new depths of unorthodox humor. Given Sacha Baron Cohen's late 2007
announcement that he was permanently retiring Ali G and Borat, there is
now an added allure to the Bruno character as the only surviving vestige
from Baron Cohen's first decade of performance art.

"Reportings" of a Culture Warrior: Borat, Anti-Semitism, and Miming Misogyny

Sacha Baron Cohen owes his career to the bumbling and bigoted reporter
now known as Borat. As discussed earlier, it was the videotape of Baron
Cohen in foreigner-drag which won him a spot on *The 11 O'Clock Show*.
And it was the critical and commercial success of *Borat* which gave the ac-
tor/comedian international celebrity. While the character has gone through
several iterations, the core has remained remarkably consistent. Regardless
of his origins (which shifted from Moldova to Albania and finally to Kazakhstan), Sacha Baron Cohen's most original creation has proved himself
able to draw humor from multiple sources with his inane, obscene, and racist questions. While the various issues surrounding the politicization of Borat will be explored in subsequent chapters, it is worth pausing for a moment
to locate Borat within the overall schema of Sacha Baron Cohen's humor.

Borat is a chimera of Islamo-Arabic foreignness with a colorful Soviet
gloss. Peter Bradshaw writes, "it is clear that 'Kazakhstan' is a joke card-
board country, a post-Soviet neverland picked at random, as cheerfully as
Robert De Niro and Dustin Hoffman, the spin doctors in the political satire
Wag the Dog, once picked 'Albania' for their divisionary hoax war."[90] Borat
bears no resemblance to modern (or pre-modern) Kazakhs either in-country
or in diaspora. His Ba'ath party moustache, two-meter frame, and Semitic
features elicit nothing reminiscent of the Kazakhs, who tend to be stocky,
beardless, and Asiatic in appearance (owing to their Turco-Mongol heritage). Likewise, the musical accompaniment to the Borat skits seems to be
drawn right out of a 1980s Turkish kilim shop and in no way resembles traditional Kazakh melodies.[91]

Borat regularly uses Polish expressions, e.g., *jak się masz* ('how are you?'), *dzień dobry* ('good day'), and *dziękuję* ('thank you').[92] He adds to these genuine catchphrases with a mixture of Hebrew and idiosyncratic nonsense. He has never uttered a word of Kazakh or Russian (the two predominate languages used in Kazakhstan) in his skits or the movie. The strings of Cyrillic lettering which adorned *Da Ali G Show* were pure gibberish; "Kazakh Television Presents:" is rendered as *'Zshch Lfyaflryeft'ylshch'g'* and "Borat's Guide to America" as *'Pshv Ishchkfef L F'ykshlsh.'* He also fails to represent Kazakhstan in other ways. According to Borat, Kazakhstan's key features include the largest man-made box, the second biggest goat, and the inexplicable absence of an Olympic swim team. Further pushing the envelope, Kazakhstan is supposedly a place where dowries are paid in bulk quantities of insecticide and wine is derived from fermented horse urine (none of these things, of course, are true).

Despite Baron Cohen's ludicrous rendering of Kazakhstan, there are some aspects of the post-Soviet everyman (*homo post-sovieticus*) in Borat that ring true: his naïveté, his obsession with the differences between America and his home country, and his bad suit. Slavist Nancy Condee argues that Borat "helps Americans make sense of the former Soviet Union, the ex-socialist expanse from Brest to Vladivostok" with his "outrageous set of fantasy distortions based in part on our Cold War tropes."[93] Mark Lipovetsky and Daniil Leiderman describe Borat as a "Second World trickster" that personifies the lingering prejudices of the West towards the Soviet bloc, combined with newer biases framed by interactions with economic immigrants from transitioning societies. "The combination of his values, his combination of naivety and cynicism, his honest love/envy for America and still more his honest rejection of anything smelling of 'political correctness' appears to be most suitable to the image of the Second, post-communist, World and its representatives."[94]

Borat could have easily (and probably should have) hailed from Georgia, Armenia, Yakutsk, or Bulgaria. While Borat's Kazakhness (*Kazakshilik*) rings false, the character himself is surprisingly genuine. Borat's authenticity also comes from his localization of identity and constant affirmation of a small set of cultural attributes. Baron Cohen is careful to maintain consistency in Borat's narrative; he is always from Almaty, he is always a widow, he is always a reporter, etc. His moustache is real and takes six weeks to grow. The highly-focused localization is buttressed by the reliable—though fabricated—"cultural" attributes of the Borat persona: an overactive libido, anti-Semitism, conviviality tempered with bouts of depression, etc. Borat's juxtaposed localness and foreignness are crucial signifiers of authenticity for his skits—how else could he get a big-game hunter to admit on camera that he had killed a Pere David Deer, a critically endangered species which has been extinct in the wild for over 100 years.

Armed with these tools, Borat was able to step out of Ali G's shadow as the luster of the gangsta-rapper began to fade in the wake of his poorly reviewed movie and over-exposure in Britain. Without the pursuit of "authenticity," Borat might be just another forgettable parody rather than the cultural lightning rod he has become. Borat's most dramatic act of global self-promotion came with the MTV Europe music awards in 2005. It was the scent of danger, in fact, that drew MTV executives to Borat; according to MTV Europe president Brent Hansen, the risks entailed in using such a controversial choice as Borat adds to the attractiveness of the MTV Europe brand.[95] According to the *New York Times,* Baron Cohen uses Borat to "head straight for the most sensitive areas of politically incorrect global culture, and for the first time will be doing so for a mass audience, far beyond the sophisticated niche of HBO."[96]

Initially Borat functioned as a trope for playfully mocking the English's reserve, patience, and good humor. However, when Baron Cohen took *Da Ali G Show* to America, the Kazakhstani journalist unveiled a new repertoire of tactics which were specifically geared towards American "common folk". For Baron Cohen, the Borat persona was especially helpful in tearing down the myths of racial tolerance in the southern United States. According to the comedian, "The interesting thing about Borat is that people really let down their guard with him, because they're in a room with someone who seems to have these outrageous opinions. . . . They sometimes feel much more relaxed about letting their own outrageous, politically-incorrect, prejudiced opinions come out."[97] In one segment, he exposes a "Southern Gentleman's" racism by feigning ignorance about slavery. As Baron Cohen recounts:

> We were in a private gentlemen's club in Jackson, Miss. And all the serving staff were black. There's this unsaid racism; there's still segregation there. I can't remember the actual line, but I asked if he had slaves, and he said, "Slavery's over now." And I go, "Yeah, that's right." He goes, "It's good." And I go, "Good for them!" He goes, "Yeah, good for them. Bad for us."[98]

After reviewing the segment in question, it is obvious that Borat actually put these words in the man's mouth; however, it is clear these sentiments were just below the surface of the discussion. In another skit, Borat gets a Texan to divulge his anti-Semitic feelings: "They were so bad in Germany, controlling the money and everything that the Germans said we are going to have a final solution and kill them all."[99] The man then agrees with Borat's notion that hunting clubs should be able to kill big game and Jews in equal numbers.

Perhaps Borat's most audacious act occurred in an Arizona bar where he performed a Country & Western tune of his own creation entitled "So My Country Can Be Free," but popularly known as "Throw the Jew Down the Well." The ditty opens by declaring that Kazakhstan has a problem: the Jew. In broken English, the lyrics describe Jewish avarice, before advancing a genocidal solution to the country's (non-existent) economic woes, to wit, throwing the Jew down the proverbial well. Borat then cautions his listeners on the Jew's horns and sharp teeth, but promises a big "par-tee" if the threat is successfully dispensed with. The lyrics evoke the hoary anti-Semitism of pre-modern Europe. To the ergotism-addled minds of medieval peasants, descendents of the Israelites were, at best, "Christ-killers," and at worst, necromancers, anthropophagi, and children of Satan. While Baron Cohen's American audience is clearly more refined than its 12th century European equivalent, it is clear that comedian believes they are just as malleable, and equally prone to ethno-religious hatred. Before it is over, Borat has the patrons enthusiastically singing the refrain, "Throw the Jew down the well." In this sketch, we see Borat/Baron Cohen at his most insidious, slyly probing the depths of humanity's foulness and somewhat sullying his own soul in the process.

The skit resulted in an investigation by Britain's Office of Communications (Ofcom). Ofcom eventually decided that *Da Ali G Show* had not violated television standards in a ruling that stated, "When such hard-edged comedy is concerned, it is very difficult to censure a characterization if its purpose is to use the very attitudes which it intends to mock."[100] The sketch also drew criticism from the Jewish community, including censure from Abe Foxman of the Anti-Defamation League who stated, "While we understand this scene was an attempt to show how easily a group of ordinary people can be encouraged to join in an anti-Semitic chorus, we are concerned that the irony may have been lost on some of the audience, or worst still that they simply accepted Borat's statements about Jews at face value."[101] Despite such condemnation, Baron Cohen agreed to join the Board of Guardians of British Jews as Chairman of the Arts and Culture division in late 2004. This distinction, however, did not temper his humor. The *Borat* movie included references to Jews as cockroaches and nightmarish effigies of devilish Jews.

In the wake of the "Throw the Jew down the Well" controversy, Baron Cohen's star rose precipitously in the US. Video clips of the sketch quickly spread throughout cyberspace and ranked as the number one comedy download on the site iFilm for several weeks. Baron Cohen's supporters defended the segment by arguing that the skit was a "dramatic demonstration of how racism feeds on dumb conformity, as much as rabid bigotry."[102] Quentin Schaffer, a spokesperson for HBO, said that critics are missing the point. "Through his alter-egos, he delivers an obvious satire that exposes people's ignorance and prejudice in much the way 'All in the Family' did years ago."[103] This is the defining character of Baron Cohen's humor; he baldly does and says things that no one in polite society should countenance. Two of his personae (Bruno and Borat) create seductively neutral zones of discourse where anything goes, whereas his keystone character Ali G forces his guests to either tolerate his ridiculous notions or waste time correcting him, a fool's errand for most. The audience is meant to laugh at violations of social norms, both ludic and artificial (those perpetrated by Baron Cohen's personae) and authentic and sad (those of his guests).

A key aspect of the Borat farce is its mimed misogyny. In one episode of *Da Ali G Show*, Borat goes house-hunting only to find (much to his dismay) that cages are not standard in the American boudoir. Perplexed, he asks the real estate agent, "Why they [i.e., women] do not run away?!?" In another, he famously declared his amazement at the American democratic system where "women can vote, but horse cannot!" During his pre-release marketing of *Borat,* Baron Cohen ratcheted up the character's disdain for the distaff by introducing a hitherto unused cultural trope from the Muslim world, i.e., refusing to shake hands with women. In the film itself, he informs the Veteran Feminists of America that a Kazakhstani doctor has proven that women's brains are smaller than men's, a revelation to which they respond with horror. Such humor has been ill-received among many of his fans and even some of his former friends who see the unrepentant misogyny as simply unfunny if not cruel. While the misogyny seamlessly dovetails with the rest of the "backward foreigner" repertoire, it flies in the face of Baron Cohen's otherwise leftist political project.[104] It is also curious that

Baron Cohen has never had to face the sort of public condemnation for his anti-woman comedic practices that he has experienced with his treatment of Gypsies, Jews, blacks, etc.

In Ali G, Baron Cohen has locked onto a powerful and, some might even argue, important mimesis. Mimesis is defined as the "stylizing of reality in which the ordinary features of our world are brought into focus by a certain exaggeration."[105] This is the beating heart of satire. The battle over Borat, however, presented new challenges and opportunities for Baron Cohen. Borat is built on what Huhn describes as a "transfigured mimesis" which "performs not as re-production but rather as production, and indeed a production upon an excessive mistakenness."[106] Through his subreption of *Kazakshilik*, he insulted a whole nation. After being threatened with legal action for his parody, Baron Cohen's response was to turn up the volume rather than shy away from controversy. That decision proved to have ramifications which will far outlast the comedian's career.

Notes

1. Roseanne, "The *TIME* 100: Sacha Baron Cohen," *Time* 169, 20 (14 May 2007): 143.

2. Alleen Pace Nilsen and Don L. F. Nilsen, "Just How Ethnic is Ethnic Humor?" *Canadian Ethnic Studies* 38, no. 1 (2006): 131-139

3. See Rachel Garfield, "Ali G: Just Who Does He Think He Is?" *Third Text* 54 (Spring 2001): 63-70.

4. This process builds on the advances of late modernity, and disproportionately affected Europe and North America during the second half of the 20th century. Since the 1980s, however, the transformation has become a global phenomenon and is felt in Lagos as much as in Los Angeles (if more acutely).

5. Lawrence Alfred Powell and Lloyd Waller, "Politics as Unusual," *Communication World* 24, no. 2 (March/April 2007): 20-23.

6. Steven Best and Douglas Kellner, "Dawns, Twilights, and Transitions: Postmodern Theories, Politics, and Challenges," *Democracy & Nature: The International Journal of Inclusive Democracy* 7, no. 1 (March 2001): 101-117.

7. See Lance Bennett, *News: The Politics of Illusion*, Seventh ed., New York: Longman, 2007.

8. A classic example of this phenomenon is the Bush administration's "No Child Left Behind Policy," which naturally puts opposition forces in danger of being accused of "wanting to leave children behind."

9. See http://www.webcameron.org.uk/.

10. Bennett, *Politics of Illusion*, 40-41.

11. Best and Kellner, "Dawns, Twilights, and Transitions," 110.

12. Geoffrey Baym, "*The Daily Show*: Discursive Integration and the Reinvention of Political Journalism," *Political Communication* 22, no. 3 (July 2005): 259–276.

13. Transcript of "Jon Stewart's America," *CNN Crossfire*. Aired 15 October 2004, 16:30 EST.

14. Jamie Warner, "Political Culture Jamming: The Dissident Humor of 'The Daily Show With Jon Stewart,'" *Popular Communication* 5, no. 1 (2007): 17-36.

15. Matthew A. Baum, "Sex, Lies, and War: How Soft News Brings Foreign Policy to the Inattentive Public," *The American Political Science Review* 96, no. 1. (March 2002): 91-109.

16. Chris Rojek, *Celebrity* (London: Reaktion Books, 2001), 24.

17. Both *The Daily Show* and *The Colbert Report* feature in-depth interviews with politicians, academics, and activists in the last segment of their respective programs. In fact, "real news" is regularly made during these segments, such as declarations of presidential campaigns, admissions of political missteps, etc.

18. Maureen Dowd, "America's Anchors," *Rolling Stone* 1013 (16 November 2006): 52-139.

19. *The Colbert Report's* stage, segments, program pacing, graphics, and other dramatic features mimic *The O'Reilly Factor*, in addition to Colbert's own parody of O'Reilly's persona.

20. See, for instance, John Colapinto, "Mad Dog," *Rolling Stone* 956 (2 September 2004): 104-111.

21. Nicholas Lemann, "Fear Factor," *New Yorker* 82, no. 6 (27 March 2006): 32-37.

22. Jane Freebury, "Ali G Ready to Save the World," *Canberra Times* (20 July 2002), 13.

23. Ziauddin Sardar and Barin Van Loon, *Introducing Cultural Studies* (Cambridge, Icon Books Ltd., 1999), 40.

24. Esther Leslie, "Modernism and Cultural Studies: Address to Modernist Studies Association," Birmingham (26 September 2003), http://www.militant esthetix.co.uk/polemix/moderncs.htm (14 September 2007).

25. Frank Ellis, "Political Correctness in Britain: A Blueprint for Decline," *Academic Questions* 7, no. 5 (Fall 1994): 77-101.

26. Ali Nobil Ahmad, "Ali G—Just Who Do *We* Think He Is? A Response to Rachel Garfield," *Third Text* 56 (Autumn 2001): 79-81; Tristram Hunt, "Why Britain is Great," *New Statesman* 134, no. 4751 (1 August 2005): 12-14.

27. Mark Lipovetsky and Daniil Leiderman, "Angel, Avenger, or Trickster?: The 'Second-World Man' as the Other and the Self," in Stephen Hutchings (ed), *Screening Intercultural Dialogue: Russia and its Other(s) on Film* (London: Palgrave, forthcoming).

28. See Nancy Condee, "Borat: Putting the Id Back in Identity Politics," *Slavic Review* 66, no. 1 (Spring 2008): 84-87.

29. Chris Rojek, *Celebrity* (London: Reaktion Books, 2001), 24. Though in defense of his victims, Ali speaks an idiolect that frequently seems to prevent many of his victims from comprehending just how vulgar and/or vacuous his questions and comments truly are.

30. Jim Windolf, "Ali G for Real," *Vanity Fair* 528 (August 2004): 178-192.

31. Dan Friedman, "Genuine Authentic Gangsta Flava," *Zeek: A Jewish Journal of Thought and Culture* (April 2003): 1-4, http://www.zeek.net/.

32. Sacha Baron Cohen, "Two Cents," *Broadcasting & Cable*, 134, no. 29 (19 July 2004): 40; Ali Nobil Ahmad argues that despite his ostensible critique of Britain's "Establishment," Baron Cohen is very much part of England's white elite. According to Ahmad, the Ali G shtick is little more than "a black cultural freak show for the white middle classes [which] belongs to the violent history of white appropriation;" Ahmad, "Ali G," 81.

33. Weaver, "Comprehending Ambivalence," 1.

34. Zygmunt Bauman, *Postmodern Ethics* (Oxford: Blackwell, 1993), 162.

35. Bauman, *Postmodern Ethics*, 166.

36. Bauman, *Postmodern Ethics*, 164-5.

37. See Jon Stratton, *Coming Out Jewish: Constructing Ambivalent Identities* (London and New York: Routledge, 2000), 35-36.

38. Ironically, feminists react similarly to right-wingers when confronted with Ali G's misogyny; Simon Weaver, "Comprehending Ambivalence," 10.

39. Both are the protagonists of satirical works of an earlier age. Candide, of the eponymously named 1759 novella, travels through Europe, America, and the Ottoman Empire exposing the peccadilloes and more serious maladies of 18th century

European culture. Usbek, the fictional author of Charles-Louis de Secondat's *Persian Letters* (1721), abandons his seraglio for an extended stay in Paris. From Europe, he corresponds with friends back home on certain lurid and laughable aspects of Western Civilization.

40. Paul Gilroy, *After Empire: Melancholia or Convivial Culture* (Oxford: Routledge, 2004), 149.

41. Weaver, "Comprehending Ambivalence."

42. Gilroy, *After Empire,* 146.

43. Ahmad, "Ali G," 79.

44. See Garfield, "Ali G," 63-64.

45. Best and Kellner, "Dawns, Twilights, and Transitions," 112.

46. In the United States, racial division between the white "self" and the African-American "other" have effectively "whitened" Jews over the past century, a process which has had a similar effect on other ethnic groups such as Irish, Italians, and Greeks. In Australia, Ashkenazi Jews have traditionally been grouped with other Western European immigrants, rather than "ethnics" from the Eastern Mediterranean (Lebanese, Greeks, etc.), though this is not always the case.

47. Stratton defines 'coming out' as "the practice of publicly acknowledging that which need not be acknowledged in that particular society, precisely because a person can, and has, passed;" Stratton, *Coming Out Jewish*, 12. In Europe, Jews have historically represented the paradigmatic internal Other, while the Muslim (whether Arab, Turkish, or Tatar) has long been constructed as the consummate external Other (though the Muslim now functions as an internal other as well). While many Jews may appear as "white" in terms of appearance, once their identity as Jews is made public, they have historically been perceived as "non-white" in many European societies.

48. Conveniently, Sacha Baron Cohen has actually defined how he views Jewishness. In his senior thesis, he wrote, "The principal criteria . . . to define a persona as Jewish are: self-definition; definition by significant others (such as political elites, teachers or peer groups); and having one or both parents who define themselves or are defined by 'significant others' as Jewish" (1993: 4).

49. See Werner Sollors, *Beyond Ethnicity: Consent and Descent in American Culture* (New York: Oxford University Press, 1986).

50. Akeel Bilgrami, "Notes Toward the Definition of 'Identity,'" *Daedalus* 135, no. 4 (Fall 2006): 5-16.

51. Stratton, *Coming Out Jewish*, 17.

52. Darcus Howe, "Ali G is a Great Act," *New Statesman* 129, no. 4469 (17 January 2000): 12.

53. Susanne Mühleisen, "What Makes an Accent Funny, and Why? Black British Englishes and Humor Televised" in Susanne Reichl and Mark Stein, *Cheeky Fictions: Laughter and the Postcolonial* (Amsterdam: Rodopi, 2005), 240.

54. Garfield, "Ali G," 63.

55. Garfield, "Ali G," 63-64.

56. Richard Howells, "'Is It Because I Is Black?': Race, Humor and the Polysemiology of Ali G," *Historical Journal of Film, Radio and Television* 26, no. 2 (June 2006): 155–177.

57. Howells, "'Is It Because I Is Black?'" 159.

58. Friedman, "Genuine Authentic Gangsta Flava," 2.

59. Mühleisen, "What Makes an Accent Funny," 239.

60. Garfield, "Ali G," 70.

61. Anoop Nayak, "After Race: Ethnography, Race and Post-Race Theory," *Ethnic and Racial Studies* 29, no. 3 (May 2006): 411-430; for more on hybridity, see Homi K. Bhabha, *The Location of Culture* (London: Routledge, 1994).

62. Mühleisen, "What Makes an Accent Funny," 240.

63. Mühleisen, "What Makes an Accent Funny," 240.

64. Howells, "'Is It Because I Is Black?'" 171.

65. See Friedman, "Genuine Authentic Gangsta Flava."

66. Garfield, "Ali G," 70. In their essay "Borat the Trickster: Folklore and the Media, Folklore in the Media," Natalie Kononenko and Svitlana Kukharenko argue that such antics, when directed at societal elites, are far from postmodern. Instead, it is simply a reprise of the common folkloric tropes of the "trickster" and the "clever fool," which are found in Native American, Slavic, and other mythologies. "Borat combines qualities of both the animal trickster and the clever fool. Preoccupied with bodily functions like the animal trickster, he is also oblivious to social norms and misunderstands the directives of those in authority, like the clever fool. Also like the clever fool, he exposes the flaws and inconsistencies of the American system, which he is ostensibly studying and presenting to his countrymen as a model worthy of emulation;" Natalie Kononenko and Svitlana Kukharenko, "Borat the Trickster: Folklore and the Media, Folklore in the Media," *Slavic Review* 66, no. 1 (Spring 2008): 9-10.

67. Quoted in John O'Sullivan, "The Real British Disease," *New Criterion* 24, no. 1, (September 2005): 16-23.

68. Robin Cook, "Robin Cook's Chicken Tikka Masala Speech: Extracts from a Speech by the Foreign Secretary to the Social Market Foundation in London," *Guardian Unlimited*, 19 April 2001.

69. Cook, in the speech referenced above, noted: "Today's London is a perfect hub of the globe. It is home to over 30 ethnic communities of at least 10,000 residents each. In this city tonight, over 300 languages will be spoken by families over their evening meal at home."

70. However, it should be noted that Britain, unlike its former settler colonies, is not a society where virtually everyone's ancestors were immigrants. Britons, as Scots, Welsh, and English, can claim a primordial attachment to the soil of the British Isles, and membership in the extended kin network upon which Scottishness, Welshness, and Englishness are based. The preeminent interwar theorist of nationalism Hans Kohn divided Europe into two camps: the blood-based, ethno-nationalists east of the Rhine and the liberal-democratic, statist nationalists west of the Rhine; see Hans Kohn, *The Idea of Nationalism: A Study in its Origins and Background* (New York: Macmillan, 1944).

71. This is true in Canada as well. Increasingly, the United States' northern neighbour has come to define itself in opposition to the "melting pot" paradigm which characterizes the immigrant experience south of the border.

72. See O'Sullivan, "The Real British Disease."

73. Varun Uberoi, "Social Unity in Britain," *Journal of Ethnic and Migration Studies* 33, no. 1 (January 2007): 141-157.

74. See O'Sullivan, "The Real British Disease."

75. See Peter Preston, "Freedom from 'Britain': A Comment on Recent Elite-Sponsored Political Cultural Identities," *British Journal of Politics and International Relations* 9, no. 1 (February 2007): 158–164.

76. "The Uncomfortable Politics of Identity," *Economist* 381, No. 8500 (21 October 2006): 68.

77. Gilroy, *After Empire*, 145.

78. Sara Wills and Kate Darian-Smith, "Beefeaters, Bobbies, and a New Varangian Guard? Negotiating Forms of 'Britishness' in Suburban Australia," *History of Intellectual Culture* 4, no. 1 (2004): 1-18.

79. Paul Gilroy's *There Ain't No Black In the Union Jack: The Cultural Politics of Race and Nation* exposed British racism in the 1980s and critiqued inherent biases within British cultural studies. I can, however, offer a paradoxical counter-example to this phenomenon. In 2007, I attended an annual Irish festival in a historically

Irish-American area in central New Jersey. Among the obviously pirated DVDs on sale at one stand, *Ali G Innit?* sat uncomfortably next to Chieftains concerts, *RTE* series, *Waking Ned Divine,* and other "standard" Irish fare. I asked the Irishman selling the DVDs why he had included it. He responded, "Everybody in Ireland loves him. He's the most popular comedian in the country."

80. Steve Sailer, "21st Century Polish Jokes," *American Conservative,* 4 December 2006, http://www.isteve.com/Film_Borat.htm (14 August 2007); while there exists a widely-held misconception that the term is an acronym derived from "Council House And Violent," 'chav' is actually etymologically linked to the Romani word for child (*chavi*). It refers to the youthful peasant underclass of contemporary Britain. Chavs are readily identifiable by purposefully bold displays of bad taste in their wardrobe choices, aggressive and ungrammatical speech, and violent—sometimes criminal—behavior. For more on the chav subculture, see Robert A. Saunders, "Happy Slapping: Transatlantic Contagion or Home-grown, Mass-mediated Nihilism?" *Static* 1, no. 1 (October 2005): 1-11.

81. Philip Lewis, "Between Lord Ahmed and Ali G: Which Future for British Muslims," in Wasif A. R. Shahid and P. Sjoerd van Koningsveld, eds., *Religious Freedom and the Neutrality of the State: The Position of Islam in the European Union* (Leuven: Peeters, 2002), 135.

82. Rojek, *Celebrity,* 16.

83. Windolf, "Ali G for Real," 192.

84. See Bruno's MySpace page at http://profile.myspace.com/index.cfm?fuse action=user.viewprofile&friendid=185712923.

85. "British Comedian Cohen Sets His Sights on Austria," *Reuters News,* 30 October 2006.

86. Irving pleaded guilty and recanted some of his statements. He was released after spending 13 months in jail. Upon his return to England, he reaffirmed his views that the Holocaust is a myth. He has been banned from ever returning to Austria.

87. "Austrians Fear the Return of Borat," *Austria Today,* 29 November 2006.

88. Kaizaad Kotwal, "Booyakasha!" *Gay People's Chronicle,* 16 March 2007, http://www.gaypeopleschronicle.com/stories07/march/0316074.htm (18 October 2007).

89. "Meet the Real Sacha Baron Cohen, *NPR,* 4 January 2007.

90. Peter Bradshaw, "Bear-Baiting in Bushville," *Guardian,* 27 October 2006, 7. Director Barry Levinson's *Wag the Dog* (1997) depicted the misadventures of an American presidential administration covering up their boss's sexual misconduct with a fake war in the Balkan country. Coincidentally, the film was released just weeks before the Monica Lewinsky scandal broke and US President Bill Clinton's missile strikes on Sudan and Afghanistan.

91. Lucy Kelaart, "Inside Story: 'Is It Cos I Is Kazakh?'" *Guardian,* 11 April 2003, 7.

92. These phrases, however, are spelled phonetically on the Borat web site, e.g., 'Jagshemash,' perhaps purposefully obscuring their origins.

93. Nancy Condee, "Learnings of Borat for Make Benefit Cultural Studies," *Pittsburgh Post-Gazette,* 12 November 2006, H6.

94. Lipovetsky and Leiderman, "Angel, Avenger, or Trickster?"

95. Lars Brandle, "New Ingredients Spice Up MTV Europe Show," *Billboard,* 19 November 2005.

96. Sharon Waxman, "Equal-Opportunity Offender Plays Anti-Semitism for Laughs," *New York Times,* The Arts, 7 September 2006, E1.

97. "Ali G Crosses the Ditch," *Press* (Christchurch, New Zealand), 31 August 2004, 9.

98. Virginia Heffernan, "The Cheerful Confessions of Ali G, Borat and Bruno," *New York Times,* Sec. E, Col. 1, The Arts/Cultural Desk, 15 July 2004, 1.

99. Nicole Lampert, "Ali G Star's 'Anti-Semitic' Song Starts a TV Storm," *Daily Mail* (London), 20 August 2004, 36.

100. See Doreen Carvajal, "Kazakh Officials Don't See Spoof's Humor," *International Herald Tribune*, 15 December 2005.

101. Lampert, "Ali G Star's 'Anti-Semitic' Song."

102. William Cook, "After Ali: The IOS Profile: Sacha Baron Cohen," *Independent on Sunday* (London), 22 August 2004, 19.

103. Liel Leibovitz, "Did Ali G Go Too Far?" *The Jewish Week*, 13 August 2004, http://www.thejewishweek.com/news/newscontent.php3?artid=9732 (12 June 2006).

104. See Dickie Wallace, "Hyperrealizing 'Borat' with the Map of the European 'Other,'" *Slavic Review* 66, no. 1 (Spring 2008): 35-49.

105. Michael Davis, *The Poetry of Philosophy* (South Bend, IN: St Augustine's Press, 1999), 3.

106. Tom Huhn, "Heidegger, Adorno, and Mimesis," *Dialogue and Universalism* 11-12 (November-December 2003): 43-52.

Part II
The Battle over Borat

Chapter 4
Defining and Defending Kazakhstan:
The Battle over Borat Begins

Kazakhstan has long been aware of Baron Cohen's Borat persona. Within a few weeks of the premiere of *Da Ali G Show* in Britain, the Kazakhstani government demanded that Borat be unequivocally banned. The response was jeered by the British press as quasi-totalitarian, and was unhelpful to the country's international image. After a brief flurry of condemnation, Kazakhstani political elites resigned themselves to counteractive measures hoping that Borat would eventually go away. He did not. In 2005, MTV's decision to have him host its European music awards proved an unforgivable outrage to Astana.[1] No longer content to use its local embassy officials in the UK and the US to condemn Baron Cohen and distance the Kazakh nation from his grotesque renderings of their national identity, the government of Kazakhstan formally threatened Baron Cohen with legal action. The government's comments deepened the prejudice among many Western cognoscenti that Kazakhstan was a paranoid, anti-democratic nation, unworthy of the praise lavished upon it by its friends amongst the security community and multinational corporation set.[2] However, for others in the West, it was a shock to learn that Kazakhstan was a real country intent on defining and defending itself against Sacha Baron Cohen. In this chapter, I provide a brief introduction to Kazakhstan's history, culture, and evolving national identity in order to lay a foundation for understanding its muscular reaction to the Boratistan parody.

The "Undiscovered" Country: Kazakhstan before Borat

Kazakhstan is a massive, landlocked central Asian republic of some 15 million people. It is the ninth largest country in the world, roughly the size of Western Europe or four times the size of Texas, and covers three time zones. The country is situated between western Siberia and South Asia, and has a continental climate with hot summers and cold winters. Its defining geographic feature is the steppe, a vast plain similar to the American prairie. The Kazakhs steppe rises to meet the Tian Shan Mountains in the southeast and the Altai mountain range in the northeast. In the west, the country sits on the Aral and Caspian Seas, and is hemmed in by the Volga River. In the north, Kazakhstan shares the world's longest continuous border with Russia.[3] Technically speaking, Kazakhstan is a Eurasian state as roughly 5% of its geography lies west of the Ural River, which divides Europe from Asia. The country possesses extensive natural resources including petroleum, natural gas, coal, gold, and uranium.

The country's population is a mixture of ethnic Kazakhs, Russians, Ukrainians, and 100 other minorities; collectively, the country's citizens can be referred to as Kazakhstanis. Ethnic Kazakhs, who account for a slim majority of the population, are a product of co-mingling between the Mongol-Turkic hordes who conquered Inner Asia in the 13th century, and the various Turkic and Indo-European tribes native to the region. Like all Turkic peoples, the Kazakhs originated in the Altai Mountains.[4] The term "Kazakh" comes from a Turkic word for 'adventurer' or 'independent,' and is thought to share its etymology with "Cossack." The similarity of pronunciation often leads to confusion, especially given that Cossacks represent a sizeable presence within Kazakhstan. While 'Kazakh' is an ethnic category, 'Cossack' is a social classification, referring to Slavic-speaking, semi-nomadic peoples of the southern Eurasian steppes who adopted many aspects of Tatar culture, including a strong military orientation.[5]

The Kazakhs—like the other Turkic peoples of Inner Asia—began to embrace Islam shortly after the Arab conquests which followed the death of the Prophet Muhammad (c. 570-632). However, this was an uneven process due to the physical geography of the Kazakh steppe. On the edge of the Silk Road, the centuries-old trade route which linked the Eastern Mediterranean and China, the Kazakh lands were always peripheral to the larger Muslim world.[6] Yet, Arab merchants did settle in the oases and small towns of what is today southern Kazakhstan. There they began to seek converts among the indigenous population. However, most Kazakhs had only the most rudimentary understanding of the religion during its first millennium and ranked as Muslims in name only. According to one commentator, "Religion in Kazakhstan never prevailed over other forms of social consciousness . . . and no single confession had a direct impact on the social, economic and political aspects of the state's evolution."[7]

As a nomadic and predominantly illiterate people, the austere interpretation of Islam associated with the Arab world never took hold among the Kazakhs. Instead, the practice of the religion was characterized by syncretism with older shamanistic beliefs known as Tengrism (still practiced by some of the Kazakhs' Mongol cousins in Russia), as well as certain aspects of animal and ancestor worship. For centuries, the Kazakh steppe represented a self-contained world with little regard for cities or urban life. *Adat*, traditional customary law which dates back to at least the 13th century, continued to trump *sharia* law into the modern era. Ironically, it was the influence of the Russians that resulted in the final Islamicization of the Kazakh nomads. Catherine the Great thought sedentary, observant Muslims would be easier to rule than "wild" pagans. Under Russian direction, Tatar missionaries, mullahs, and merchants were brought in from southern Russia and given elite status.[8] Local Muslim organizations were supported, generous loans were made for those who agreed to take up farming, and Christian proselytization was officially discouraged. In concert, these factors precipitated a certain level of homogenization of Islamic practices across the Kazakh population and finished the process of conversion from paganism to Sunni Islam.

The Kazakhs began to emerge as a separate ethnic group during the 15th century under the rule of the khans Janibek and Kirai. Political cohesion among the recently developed ethnos followed with the influential reign of Qasim (1511-23).[9] Ultimately, this political union would distinguish the Kazakhs from the Uzbeks, who were remarkably similar in terms of language, economy, and culture to the Kazakhs.[10] During the next century, central authority slowly broke down. In this power vacuum, the Kazakhs organized themselves into extended familial networks known as hordes or *jüzes*: the Great Horde (*Ulu Jüz*) in the southeast of the country, the Middle Horde (*Orta Jüz*) in the northeast and central parts of the country and the Lesser Horde (*Kişi Jüz*) in western Kazakhstan.[11] Despite this division, the Kazakhs maintained a surprising level of cultural cohesion across the three hordes, while simultaneously avoiding reincorporation into the Uzbek polity.

The territory of the Kazakh steppe was methodically incorporated into the Russian state after a request of protection was made by Kazakh clan leaders fearful of incursions on their ancestral lands by various enemies.[12] This initiated a 300-year process of Russian immigration into the country and a steady process of Russification of the ethnic Kazakhs. From 1720 until 1830, the Russians and the Kazakhs made a series of agreements that were intended to protect the Kazakh hordes from invasion, but the true aim of tsarist authorities was to incorporate the lands of the Kazakhs into the Romanov Empire. Russian expansion into the region closely followed the model of eastward expansion established under the reign of Ivan IV, whereby the first stage of imperialism involved "unofficial" conquest by paramilitary bands of Cossacks followed by official incorporation into the tsarist empire.[13] As the Sovietologist Aurel Braun states, "Historically, [Kazakhstan's] border with Russia was not a barrier to the movement of people. This has long influenced Russian attitudes. The vagueness of the border facilitated settlement in Kazakhstan, particularly in Soviet times, as industrialization and urbanization increased."[14]

The steppe lands of the Kazakhs proved to be a primary destination of new Russian settlers after the abolition of serfdom on 3 March 1861, when countless Slavs were freed from their bonds of labor while concurrently being dispossessed of their right to the lands where their families had resided for generations.[15] The socio-economic turmoil wrought by the end of feudalism initiated a massive migration of Slavs to the east with the northern Kazakh steppe as a major destination after its official opening to settlement in 1896. Concurrently, St. Petersburg restricted land ownership among the pastoral Kazakhs. "Each Kazakh head of household was allotted 40 acres of property. All remaining land was expropriated, thus denying the nomads the use of their traditional pasturelands."[16] The predictable result was economic misery for most Kazakhs. Between 1906 and 1912, more than a half-million Russian farms were established in Kazakhstan under the direction of Russian Prime Minster Pëtr Stolypin, forever disrupting the traditional Kazakh way of life based on seasonal migration and nomadic herding.

In 1916, the Kazakhs, who had been pressed into state service despite previous guarantees against such actions, rebelled against the Russian state. After an initial flurry of Kazakh-on-European violence, the tide turned in favor of the Russians, with tens of thousands of Kazakhs being slaughtered.[17] Many fled to Mongolia or China to avoid violent reprisals by the army and local Russian and Cossack populations. During the period between the February and October Revolutions of 1917, Kazakh elites attempted to create an autonomous republic within the new framework of a liberal-democratic Russian state. However, the burgeoning Kazakh nationalist movement, which coalesced under the banner of the Alash Orda political party, failed to prevent to the reestablishment of colonial rule in the region.[18] With the Bolshevik's consolidation of power in Central Asia, there came a sharp diminution of Kazakh interests in favor of the Slavic settlers. The forced collectivization of Kazakhstan in the 1920s and 1930s significantly reduced the ratio of Kazakhs to Slavs as massive famines further depleted the indigenous population. According to official statistics, 1.5 million Kazakhs and 80 percent of the republic's livestock died; however, actual numbers may have been much higher. The actions of the state also permanently destroyed the traditional lifestyle of the pastoralist Kazakhs through prohibition of annual migrations, confiscation of livestock, etc.

Despite the hardships of the interwar period, the Kazakhs emerged as a model for Sovietization during the 1930s, as once marginalized elements of Kazakh society (e.g., lower-class Kazakhs who lacked sizeable herds or flocks and access to good grazing land) embraced nascent industrialization. With their rapid inclusion into the ranks of the working class, the Kazakh cadres became a peripheral embodiment of the new Soviet Man *(homo Sovieticus)*.[19] This was in part due to the fact that collectivization and sedentarization completely debased traditional society, leaving most with no other option than to embrace the new world order imposed by Moscow.[20] The early Stalinist manifestation of a "trusted" relationship between the Kazakhs and the Kremlin allowed for the creation of a large Kazakh proto-state in the form of the Kazakh Soviet Socialist Republic (SSR).[21] In 1936, Kazakhstan, hitherto an autonomous part of the Russian Federated Soviet Socialist Republic, gained republican status endowing it with many of the attributes of a sovereign state.[22]

World War II precipitated massive influxes of non-natives as wartime evacuation and, more ominously, ethnic cleansing further altered the ratio of Kazakhs to non-Kazakhs in favor of the latter. During the Great Patriotic War (as WWII was known in the Soviet Union), the Soviet premier Joseph Stalin ordered the deportations of eight nations in their entirety: the Volga Germans, Crimean Tatars, Kalmyks, Chechens, Ingush, Balkars, Karachai, and Meskhetian Turks.[23] The deportees were rounded up, herded into railroad cattle cars, and transported mostly to Kazakhstan, but also to other parts of Soviet Asia. Most estimates indicate that close to two-fifths of the affected populations perished. Other peoples shipped to Kazakhstan included "political unreliables" from the occupied countries of Poland, Estonia, Latvia, and Lithuania, as well as the resident minority populations of Koreans, Bulgarians, and Greeks.[24] Perversely, the Soviet propaganda machine later lauded Kazakhstan as the "planet of a hundred nationalities" after using it as a "human dumping grounds."[25]

In the wake of Joseph Stalin's death, his successor Nikita Khrushchev's "Virgin Lands" campaign attracted large numbers of agricultural settlers to the Kazakh SSR from the European parts of the Soviet Union. Khrushchev's grandiose plan to develop superfarms for corn and other grains on the Ka-

Ali G Publicity Photo (Home Box Office, Inc.)

Ali G Making Harvard's Class Day Speech (Jon Chase/Harvard News Office)

Almaty's Republic Square at Night (Vlad Gorshkov)

World War II Monument in Central Almaty (Robert A. Saunders)

Soviet Mural in Kokshetau, KZ (Robert A. Saunders)

President Nursultan Nazarbayev (R. D. Ward, Department of Defense)

Zenkov Cathedral, Almaty (M. Fino)

Homo Kazakhstanus? (M. Fino)

Young Kazakhstan (M. Fino)

zakh steppe was a complete disaster, ultimately triggering further desertification in the region. This was to be the last major influx of non-Kazakhs to the country, and by the 1970s Europeans had begun a slow process of emigration from the republic (which would turn into a flood in the 1990s). Republic-wide advances in health care, nutrition, education, and general welfare combined with the comparatively high birth rate of autochthonous Kazakhs reversed the long decline in the Kazakh population.[26] Kazakhstan was the scene of rare ethnic clashes in 1986. Following the replacement of the long-serving General Secretary of the Communist Party Dinmukhamud Konayev (an ethnic Kazakh and strong promoter of indigenization of the party ranks in Kazakhstan) with a non-Kazakh, riots broke out pitting Kazakhs against Russians and other European residents of the republic.[27] Though the *Jeltoqsan* ("December') riots were quashed, Soviet Premier Mikhail Gorbachev prevented Kazakhstan's new general secretary, Gennady Kolbin, from conducting a massive purge of the party ranks and prominent nationalist figures. As a result, many date the unrest as the beginning of the end for the Soviet Union.[28] As the decade closed, Kolbin was replaced by the ethnic Kazakh Nursultan Nazarbayev who saw the country through its independence and still rules today.

Who are the Kazakhs?

The Kazakhs represent the most thoroughly Russified peoples of Central Asia. This dubious distinction results from of a number of factors including their long relationship with tsarist Russia, Russia's control of education and the formation of economic elites, massive influxes of Russians and Ukrainians over the centuries, and catastrophic disruptions of traditional social structures under the Romanov tsars and the Soviet commissars. This unique and complex combination of historical factors provides a stark contrast between the Republic of Kazakhstan and the other four Central Asian Republics (Kyrgyzstan, Tajikistan, Turkmenistan, and Uzbekistan) where the period of imperial subjugation was much shorter. As a predominately non-literate and historically nomadic people, the Kazakhs were significantly more susceptible to Russification during the 19th and 20th centuries than their sedentary and more literate counterparts in Central Asia. The religious, educational, cultural, and societal infrastructures of the Tajiks and Uzbeks, who tended to reside in long-settled urban areas along the old Silk Road (Samarkand, Khiva, Bukhara, Kokand, etc.) were much better able to withstand the pressures of tsarist and later Bolshevik policies of Russification.[29] The Kazakhs, whose itinerant lifestyle prevented meaningful engagement in a national project until well into the 20th century, had few of the tools to contest Russian-dominated policies for the creation of Kazakh identity. When an educated elite emerged in the mid-1800s, it was strongly influenced by Russian language education, affected Russian cultural norms, and economically-oriented towards sustaining Russia's colonial policies.[30]

I do not mean to imply that the Kazakhs lacked a strong sense of self. Their cultural or "ethnic" identity was extremely vibrant, but typically based on family lineage, clan affiliation, and membership in their *jüz*, rather than a "national" identity.[31] At the turn of the century, there was a palpable increase in nationalist activity among a nascent bourgeoisie culminating in the previously-mentioned Alash movement. Although many of the institutional precursors for national mobilization identified by Karl Deutsch, Ernst Gellner, Miroslav Hroch, Anthony Smith, Benedict Anderson, and other scholars of nationalism began to develop in the first two decades of the 20th century, they were diluted first by pan-Turkism (which promoted the creation of a vast Turkic federation from Istanbul to Ürümqi under Turkish hegemony) and then short-circuited by the Bolshevik consolidation of power in the wake of the Russian Civil War.[32]

Defining Kazakhs remained a sticky issue well into the Soviet era. Arguably, the Kazakhs, who were known as the Kirghiz until the early Soviet period, were ethnically indistinguishable from the denizens of modern-day Kyrgyzstan until the Leninist-Stalinist regime made an *ex post facto* division of the two based on political expediency and physical geography during the period of national delimitation (1924-1936).[33] With the Stalinist-era delimitation of nations, the Kazakh *jüzes* were permanently grouped together as a single "nation." Despite possession of their own republic after 1936, the Kazakhs—more than any other "autonomous nationality"—constructed their national identity through the optic of the Russian language. Similarly, Kazakhstan identity was constructed against a backdrop of Russian identity. Kazakhs effectively defined themselves by denying attributes affiliated with Russianness.[34] These tendencies arguably retarded a full-fledged embrace of "Kazakhness" during most of the 20th century. Paradoxically, the yoke of Russian (and later Soviet) rule solidified a sense of Kazakhness, principally through the delineation of a piece of territory named after the Kazakh people, as well as through new forms of political institutionalization.[35] The majority of ethnic Kazakh elites during the Soviet period were Russian-speakers, Russophiles, and Russian *Kulturträgers* ('culture bearers').[36] As I will discuss later, this trend has been subdued since independence in 1991, but remains important. As such, defining Kazakhness after independence proved more complicated than was the case for defining "Georgianness" in Georgia, "Estonianness" in Estonia, etc. This problem is compounded by the country's close relationship with Russia, and many Russians' views of the Kazakh steppe as part of what historically constitutes the "traditional" Russian state.

Like all the non-Russian Soviet republics, the post-Stalinist period saw the resurgence of *korenizatsiya* in Kazakhstan. The process, which derives its title from the Russian word for 'putting down roots,' promoted the ethnic population of a given republic (also called the titular majority) within the public sector.[37] Thus, in Kazakhstan, ethnic Kazakhs steadily took control of more leadership roles in the party, academia, science, and industry at the expense of their Russian (and other "non-indigenous") counterparts. This was the second wave korenizatsiya in Kazakhstan. In the 1920s, the Kazakhs had benefited the Soviet Union's "Affirmative Action Empire," as the rosters of factories and firms in the country swelled with recently-trained ethnic Kazakhs.[38] The policy was initially a Leninist stratagem for securing support amongst the national elites of the various non-Russian territories of the nascent Bolshevik regime. In the 1930s, Stalin reversed many of the gains made by indigenous elites, and placed Russians in many positions of power in the provinces. After Stalin's death in 1953, the process of 'rooting' indigenes began again. According to historian and former president of the Kazakh Political Sciences Association Nurbulat Masanov:

From the 1960s to the 1980s, one could observe an obvious tendency in
Kazakhstan toward formation of the general social stereotype that Kazakhs had a natural legal right to a dominant position in Kazakhstan's territory: to occupy the highest posts; to receive higher education; to advance their values in civic consciousness; to defend their culture,
language, traditions, and history. Thus Kazakhs, quite appropriately, have
a privileged claim to self-realization, in all respects, in Kazakhstan's territory.[39]

In particular, Konayev's reign (1964-86) saw the Kazakhs taking an ever
more active role in shaping their own destiny within the larger framework of
the USSR. With the deepening of Gorbachev's policy triad of economic
uskorenie ('acceleration'), *perestroika* ('restructuring'), *glasnost* ('open-
ness'), further opportunities for nativization of power presented themselves.
Gorbachev's final policy plank—*demokratizatsiya* ('democratization')—
fueled this ongoing process as the decade came to a close.[40] Kazakhs and
other titular nationalities began the active promotion of their own language
within their respective republics in the waning years of Soviet rule, a
process known as the "linguistic revolutions." In 1989, the Russian language
was rendered the "language of inter-ethnic communication," while Kazakh
was promoted to the status of the "official state language" of the Kazakh
Soviet Socialist Republic, becoming requisite for high level officials in
firms and government, a policy which remains in effect today.[41]

The modest attempts at promoting the "Kazakh Way" under late Soviet
rule gave way to a full-fledged "Kazakhization" in the wake of independence, as the "entire ideological basis necessary for creating an ethnocratic
state was developed."[42] While the Nazarbayev regime has been careful to
protect the physical and economic safety of the country's European population, his reign has seen Kazakhstan turned into a nationalizing state. According to Rogers Brubaker, a nationalizing state is one that is involved in a
"compensatory" project aimed at elevating the interests of the indigenous
nationality above the interests of other nationalities.[43] Such projects typically occur in a milieu where the titular nationality has historically been
oppressed by another nationality, usually an imperial invader. During the
first half of the 20th century, Poland and Czechoslovakia represented para-
digms of this process, as they sought to expunge German influence in the
wake of their independence from the Teutonic empires of the Hohenzollern
and Habsburg dynasties. In effect, the state's goal was to eradicate all legacies of imperialism, especially those which previously confined the majority
nationality to positions of weakness. Much of this transformation occurs at a
symbolic level (statues, street names, etc.) through the replacement of imperial symbols with native ones.

Such was the case in post-independence Kazakhstan with So-
viet/Russian conquerors being displaced by indigenous heroes such as
Zhambyl and Abay.[44] In the words of President Nazarbayev:

Our native tongue acquired the status of a state language. The historical
names of localities are returning; the good names of renowned sons of
Kazakhstan have been restored, and their anniversaries are commemo-
rated. In preserving this national distinctiveness, much has been done in

the past several years. We have carefully restored everything that was
lost: half-forgotten traditions, historic rights, culture, language, belief.[45]

State-supported revisionist history and pseudo-science have also proliferated
to right the wrongs (real and imagined) of the Russo-Soviet past and buttress
territorial sovereignty moving forward. Spurred on by Nazarbayev's seemingly boundless ability to extol the virtues of the Kazakhs, pride in one's
ancestors has been subsidized by the state.[46] Kazakhstan's political elite—
like their counterparts in other former Soviet states—understand the neces-
sity of filling the void left by the collapse of the USSR. According to Kazakhstan expert Martha Brill Olcott, "In the wake of the collapse of a universal communist ideology, the task of creating an inclusive national
identity is a particularly difficult one, to which Kazakhstan's leaders have
devoted considerable energies."[47] With independence, a new sense of civic
identity based on *Kazakshilik* ('Kazakhness') is developing, albeit slowly,
with the support of the political elite within and outside of the Nazarbayev
administration, although *shezhire* (familial linkages) still tend to trump
bonds based on national fraternity.[48] In the words of historian Edward
Schatz, post-Soviet Kazakhstan has "a Kazakh face" and Kazakhs are sin-
gled out for "linguistic, demographic, political and cultural redress."[49]

Despite the physical difference between ethnic Kazakhs and their Slavic
and German counterparts, outright racism has never been a part of this process. The primary mechanism for achieving the Kazakhization of the state
has been promotion via shezhire and clan ties, thus guaranteeing a predomi-
nance of ethnic Kazakhs as Russians, Ukrainians, Germans, and other minorities lack the networking linkages necessary to compete for high level
positions with the state apparatus. Rather than explicit promotion based on
ethnicity (as is common in Latvia, Estonia, and other post-Soviet nationali-
zation states), informal ties accomplish the same goal without incurring international condemnation or local outrage. As Schatz points out, the Nazarbayev administration has proved itself to be adept at "manipulating the
discursive field, managing the producers of knowledge, and carefully crafting images of state and society for popular consumption" both at home and
abroad.[50] While informal Kazakhization has intensified since independence,
this policy was initially cultivated under Konayev in the 1970s.[51] Language
has continued to play an important role as well; according to Olcott, language proficiency in Kazakh has emerged as "a ready tool for political exclusion" of non-Kazakhs, in particular, the Russians, who many ethnic Kazakhs see as having been pampered under Soviet rule.[52] However, such tools
are used infrequently or intermittently in post-independence Kazakhstan.

Ethnic Kazakhs now command most if not all of the top spots in state-
run enterprises and most other organizations as well. The titular majority
similarly accounted for over three-fourths of the country's political elite by
the end of the last century.[53] However, Russians still figure prominently in
the middle class and occupy many middle management positions. As Braun
states:

> Despite attempts at indigenization—according preferential treatment to
> Kazakh speakers, usually ethnic Kazakhs—of the economy and the polity,
> the Russian minority in Kazakhstan, for the time being, remains relatively
> comfortable. In large part, this is because such indigenization has been
> limited. The economic payoff for speaking Kazakh remains low, and

there has not been much movement to try and assimilate even Russophone Kazakhs. Ethnic Russians, therefore, feel little compulsion to learn Kazakh and no immediate risk to their position.[54]

Political Kazakhization of the state has not provoked excessive ire among the non-indigenes because it has occurred at a pace which is roughly equal to the changing demographic situation in the country. After the collapse of the Soviet Union in late 1991, many Russians, Germans and other non-natives quit Central Asia for their respective "ethnic homelands" or third countries such as the US, Canada, and Australia. Since independence, the European population of Kazakhstan has dropped by over 2.5 million, a phenomenon which has prompted a major demographic shift. In 1989, Europeans were a plurality at 49.7% of the population; today, they are just under 30% of the population.[55]

Though much less important in terms of total numbers, roughly 500,000 ethnic Kazakhs have immigrated to Kazakhstan since 1991. Many Kazakhs living in exile repatriated to their ancestral homeland with promises of preferential treatment (Kazakhstan is the only Central Asian country to have more of its titular majority repatriating than emigrating).[56] The state continues to provide economic assistance and land to *Oralmandar*, i.e., Kazakh returnees from Mongolia, China, and Afghanistan (though no such measures are provided to returnees from within the borders of the old Soviet Union).[57] This program, in conjunction with the 1990s exodus of Slavs and Germans, has resulted in majority status for the titular nationality for the first time in the history of the republic in its Soviet or independent manifestations. As of 2006, ethnic Kazakhs represented nearly 60% of the population.[58] Perhaps even more importantly, there has been a demographic transformation within the country which has diluted long-standing ethnic divisions. Russians once dominated the country's northern tier; however, since the capital was relocated to the north-central city of Astana (formerly Aqmola, and Tselinograd during Soviet times), ethnic Kazakhs have settled there in significant numbers. New economic opportunities for Kazakhs in other formerly-"Russian" cities has also occurred since the mid-1990s. Collectively, these phenomena have dampened local efforts for devolution of power, while also quieting the voices of Russian irredentists operating abroad.

Who are the Kazakhstanis?

While it has hopefully become clear who the Kazakhs are, another question remains: who are the Kazakhstanis? While mainstream English language media tend to refer to all citizens of Kazakhstan as 'Kazakhs,' a technically more precise to term for the country's citizens is *Kazakhstani*.[59] The term—a neologism coined originally in Russian as *Kazakhstanets* meaning 'a person from Kazakhstan'—carries no ethnic connotations. A tidy analogy can be drawn with Iran. Just like Kazakhstan, slightly more than half of the population are members of the majority population (in the case of Iran, Persian). While it is acceptable to refer to an ethnic Persian as such, it would be silly to call an Azeri Turk, a Kurd, or an Arab a *Persian*, they are *Iranians*, an identifier derived from the name of the state in which they live.

While 'Kazakhstani' has failed to achieve universal usage, the term it-self does have semantic value since it promotes civic cohesion and remains outside of the discourse of implied ethnic loyalties. Despite this, many non-Kazakhs self-identify as Kazakh-Russians, Kazakh-Germans, etc. in a lin-guistic inversion of the American immigrant mode of identification with ancestral country of origin. Kazakhstani identity, or what I call *Kazakstan-shilik*, is based on what Schatz describes as a "phantasmic amalgam" of peoples who reside in the heart of the Eurasian super-continent and who represent an organic mixing of multiple civilizations.[60] Even in today's world of transnational loyalties and cultural mélange, such an identity seems impossibly contrived. Yet, it continues to gain ground among those born after Gorbachev's rise to power.

While some have been quick to label Kazakhstan a nationalizing state, this is an oversimplification. President Nazarbayev's administration cer-tainly speaks of its commitment to a form of civic nationalism loosely-based on American, British, and Latin American models. However, ethnification of the levers of power has proceeded at a steady rate, though such policies are comparatively tepid when contrasted with the nationalizing policies of the Baltic States and even other Central Republics. Eurasian specialist Cen-giz Surucu describes this Janus-faced policy as "an all-inclusive territorial citizenship combined with a 'remedial ethno-nationalism' of the indigenous ethnic group."[61] He adds that this situation creates an ambiguous discursive space, which naturally promotes a struggle for hegemony amongst the coun-try's elites. Consequently, the gap between Kazakh national identity (based on ethnos) and Kazakhstani civic loyalty (Kazakstanshilik) continues to complicate the evolution of identity in this young state. Regardless, many Kazakhstanis are proud of their efforts at creating a diverse, but not neces-sarily divided society in Inner Asia. According to Braun:

> Kazakhstan is still in the process of developing a national identity. Despite nationalist rhetoric, it remains, in certain respects, a multi-cultural state. Cultural and linguistic diversity is not only demanded by the Russian mi-nority but is also strongly encouraged by Russophone Kazakhs. Nearly two-thirds of urban Kazakhs speak Russian as their daily language.[62]

As such, Kazakstanshilik is inclusive of non-ethnic Kazakhs; however, the dominant paradigm guiding the construction of identity is and will remain inextricably linked to the culture of the steppe.

Nazarbayev himself is the driving force behind the "Kazakhization of civic consciousness."[63] According to Masanov, "President Nazarbaev has unambiguously formulated the idea that Kazakh culture ought to be an inte-grating factor for all the peoples of Kazakhstan."[64] This truth is underlined by statements such as the following by the Kazakhstani president:

> With respect to the integrating role of Kazakh culture, this is genuine pragmatism; it is not some kind of nationalist exercise. . . . This is the cul-ture of the majority of the country. This is a culture that possesses the en-tire array of institutional instruments. It is a culture that has been geneti-cally formed in this particular territory and, to a great extent, has predetermined the character of historical development of Kazakhstan the state. . . . Therefore, it is no paradox nor is there anything politically incor-

rect in the assertion of the integrating role of Kazakh culture. We need to say this directly and without any ambiguity.[65]

Despite such unambiguous rhetoric about the ethnic component of national identity in his country, Nazarbayev deserves kudos for keeping Kazakhstan from coming apart at the seams. Unlike most of his colleagues governing other newly independent, post-Soviet states, Nazarbayev was denied two immediate sources of legitimacy: mono-ethnic nationalism and anti-Russian populism.[66] Unlike other states where the titular population enjoyed an overwhelming majority such as Azerbaijan and Uzbekistan, Kazakhstan could ill-afford to ignore the voices of Russians and the country's dozens of other demographically relevant minorities. Nor could the government engage in the sort of disenfranchisement of Russophone minorities which Estonia and Latvia undertook in the 1990s, for fear of angering Kazakhstan's powerful northern neighbor Russia.[67]

Pleasing, or more accurately, not angering, both Russians and Russia were important parts of Nazarbayev's policy platform. Recognizing the integral role played by Russians, Ukrainians, and Germans in the Kazakhstani economy, Nazarbayev worked to stanch the flow of Europeans out of his country. He did this partly by taming the angrier voices among the Kazakh nationalists in the country's south. His policies ultimately tempered ethnic Kazakh revanchism and won him the backing of many ethnic Europeans. Never one to pass up an opportunity, Nazarbayev simultaneously employed the tools of the state, political manipulation, and subsidies of folk groups to fracture (non-Kazakh) Soviet identity into its component parts. During the 1990s, the Russian-speaking "Europeans" (*Evropeitsy*), who had coalesced into a single group under Soviet rule, slowly gravitated back to their ethnic groups (Russians, Ukrainians, Germans, Poles, etc.). Nazarbayev's multi-pronged strategy, described by some as "soft authoritarianism," has both obviated unwanted challenges to his rule and produced an intrinsically stable polity.[68]

Since 1991, the Kazakh political, cultural, and economic elites have labored to develop a robust cultural repertoire which is both grounded in (pre-Russian) history and forward-looking. Kazakhs are meant to be proud of their steppe warrior heritage, nomadic culture, and relationship with nature. However, they are also encouraged to view themselves as well-educated, tech savvy, secular capitalists with an eye to both the east (China and India) and west (Europe). Despite this program, the Kazakh cultural identity remains "formless and inchoate and could devolve into more elemental forms of identity. . . . It is far from clear whether the current environment can facilitate the creation of a shared identity among the Kazakhs themselves, one sufficient to serve as an ideological glue to keep together a stable polity."[69] Thanks to its massive fossil fuel reserves, its well-educated populace, and a salubrious location at the crossroads of East Asia, Europe, and the Indian sub-continent, Kazakhstan is poised to emerge as a globally-oriented society during the second half of the 21st century.

While Nazarbayev successfully avoided ethnic confrontation, Kazakhstan continues to confront the realities of building a new identity. Central Asian specialist Olivier Roy is overly pessimistic, questioning the very viability of national identity in Kazakhstan (and other Central Asian republics) where nationalism *per se* is absent and the trappings of nationhood have been forced upon the polity by a colonial power.[70] When one considers the concurrent challenge of combating the effects of globalization, the dangers of cultural dilution run very high.[71] Even the English language poses dangers as many Russophone Kazakhs and the country's various minorities choose it as a second language over Kazakh, which is still seen as lacking any cachet beyond the borders of the republic.[72] Kazakhstan's weak national identity (resulting from centuries of Russification and the after-effects of Soviet "internationalism") provide few protections against the insidious influence of globalism.

In the Kazakhstani discourse, there is a perceived danger of exchanging Soviet-era "mankurtism," i.e., loss of Kazakh identity due to Stalinism, for a globalized form of the disease. Kyrgyz novelist Chingiz Aitmatov's late-Soviet masterpiece *The Day Lasts More than a Hundred Years* (1980) recounts a Turkic fable of a slave-race known as the Mankurts. After enduring an incomprehensibly painful ritual which claimed the lives of nine out of ten initiates, these mindless vessels lacked any memory of their past and heeded their masters' every wish.

> The *mankurt* did not know who he had been, whence and from what tribe he had come, did not know his name, could not remember his childhood, father or mother—in short, he could not recognize himself as a human being . . . for a *mankurt* was merely the outer covering, the skin of the former man.[73]

The tale is framed as an allegory for the Kazakhs who lost their identity during the painful years of collectivization, sedentarization, and famine, becoming urbanized *Homo Sovietici* who shunned or did not remember their Muslim beliefs, traditional folkways, and the importance of the community. As is common in many orally-based societies, a Kazakh is not a Kazakh unless he can recite his ancestors going back seven generations; the mankurt cannot even identify his mother.[74] The term has gained wide usage across post-Soviet space to describe members of the various nationalities of the old USSR who have abandoned (or never embraced) their heritage cultures (Lithuanian, Chukchi, Uzbek, etc.). It is also used to refer to Russians who were robbed of their national identity *qua* Russians by Sovietization, which erased the ingrained values of church, *mir* ('village'), and countryside making them into so-called "rootless" cosmopolitans.

Mankurtism (*mankurtizatsiya*) is an especially derogative term in Kazakhstan due to the high percentage of ethnic Kazakhs who do not speak their own language compared to the titular majority populations of other former Soviet republics.[75] According to sociologist Ana Barfield:

> Of the heavily Russified Kazakhs, it was precisely the social stratum that would have carried the national revival—the professionals and the intelligentsia—that was the most thoroughly Europeanized, with an often very poor knowledge of the Kazakh language, sometimes even accompanied by a relatively disparaging attitude towards indigenous Kazakh culture and way of life. Rather than lead the national revival and revert to using their native tongue, it was this social group—now often referred to by the derogatory term *mankurt*, meaning a person who has lost his roots—that was in many cases the most averse to letting go of Soviet ideals and abandoning Russian as part of the rejection of all things Soviet.[76]

It is not only the Russified elites that suffer taunts of mankurtizatsiya. Oral-mandar, who generally speak Kazakh as their mother-tongue and often have only a nominal command of their former host country's language (Mongolian, Mandarin, Pashto, etc.), deride the lack of fluency of the Kazakhstani Kazakhs whom they encounter upon repatriation to Kazakhstan. Returnees from Russia and other "near abroad" countries of the former Soviet Union tend to be most prone to attacks as mankurts for their thoroughly Russified mannerisms and speech.[77] As a purported Kazakhstani (though one which does not speak Kazakh, or Russian for that matter), knows little (correct) information about his homeland, and is only concerned with "sexy time," Borat is the ultimate mankurt, and a painful image for Kazakhstanis of all stripes.

Never having possessed a true nation-state, the ethnic Kazakhs now have an opportunity—perhaps even a duty—to promote a "genuine rebirth and essential development" of a ethnically-based Kazakh national culture.[78] Despite Nazarbayev's willingness to promote the Kazakh culture as primus inter pares among the various cultures of his people, there has been a palpable reticence towards the over-ethnification of the country's national identity, opting instead for half measures which, in many cases, have fallen flat.[79] Even the attachment to universal proficiency in the Kazakh language has lessened as of late.[80] As cultural theorist Stuart Hall has pointed out, "national identities are unfinished products that require constant ideological work."[81] Yet, considering the level of ambiguity about who Kazakhstanis are supposed to be, it is increasingly apparent that Kazakhstan's elites are working without a blueprint. Schatz argues that "Eurasianness"—Nazarbayev's central mechanism for crafting the new Kazakhstani identity outside of ethnicity—has failed to take root (though such efforts have seemingly kept the constituent ethnic groups from descending into conflict).[82] Though as Surucu points out, Kazakhstan—the "cradle of the idea of Eurasianism"—has a long and storied history of internationalism which has not erased its people's sense of self.[83]

My own research amongst upwardly mobile Kazakhstani minorities (Russians, Ukrainians, etc.) suggests, however, that an evolving sense of global citizenship is developing in which ethnicity, while not a trivial aspect of one's identity, does not erect barriers to success in the country. In effect, ethnicity is being de-politicized among the younger generations of Kazakhstanis. While Nazarbayev's attempt at promoting an "overarching, civic-secular identity for all ethnicities and denominations" has not been rejected outright, the situation remains fragile.[84] Local socio-economic issues, as well as transborder influences constantly threaten the country's inter-ethnic fraternity. Likewise, Kazakhstan's embrace of globalization tempers the ability of its people to construct their own sense of self in the post-independence milieu. With this in mind, Kazakhstan's political elite can ill afford the encroachments of the subject of this narrative, namely Sacha Baron Cohen, on its turf.

Nazarbayev's Soviet/post-Soviet modus operandi naturally leans towards fiats and threats to achieve action; as the political scientist Pål Kolstø states, "Nazarbaev's pronounced opinions on a subject are in a sense final. They are not open to overt criticism or disagreement in the public debate."[85] Today it is Sacha Baron Cohen, rather than Kazakhstan's meek domestic opposition, on the receiving end of presidential opprobrium. Countries which define their national identity through civic affiliation have a more difficult time than their counterparts that can fall back on the crutch of nationality.[86] Kazakhstan—a multi-cultural state by its constitutional construction with a nearly equal number of titulars and ethnic minorities—thus operates at a disadvantage when compared to its more homogenous neighbors. As such, the fear that alternative narrators (ethno-nationalists, Soviet nostalgics, or Western buffoons alike) may derail the fragile state of identity is ever present.

The Birth of Borat: Kazakhstan's Unwanted Interloper in Its Identity Production

How do we explain the visceral reaction of Kazakhstanis to the Borat pantomime from the average Kazakhstani diasporan all the way up to the president's office? While many countries would have nervously laughed off the flawed mimesis, Astana opted for a very public conflict within weeks of the premiere of *Da Ali G Show* in Britain. I contend that the answer stems from two distinct, yet tangentially-linked factors: 1) the fragile state of Kazakhstani national identity; and 2) the importance of marketing the country's global brand in the postmodern political system. Baron Cohen has inadvertently harmed the first and helped the second through his portrayal of the bumbling reporter from Almaty. I will discuss the first in the remainder of this chapter and explore the second in the subsequent chapter.

From the onset, the relationship between Sacha Baron Cohen and the government of Kazakhstan was a stormy one. In 2000, *Da Ali G Show* premiered on Channel 4 in the UK with Baron Cohen's Balkanesque reporter now going by the name Borat Karabzhanov and claiming to be a representative of the fictitious "Kazakhstan Broadcasting Corporation." Outraged by this travesty, Kazakhstan demanded the show be banned. Talgat Kaliyev, an embassy official in the UK, went on record with his views on *Da Ali G Show* and Borat:

> It is treating my country as if it was somewhere on the edge of the earth. It is a surreal situation. We are a secular state, a member of the OSCE [Organization for Security and Co-operation in Europe], we have a commitment to human rights. They just took a map and looked for a country they did not know . . . [however] we evaluate the humor with full respect. . . . This is a free country. But the picture of this Kazakhstani guy has nothing in common with real experience.[87]

He condemned the caricature of Kazakhs as ridiculous, stating that Borat looked like an Arab or a Turk, but nothing like a "real" Kazakh. His comments smack of Kazakh-centrism since he seemingly did not consider the possibility that a non-Kazakh Kazakhstani might be represented in the form of "Borat," e.g., one of the country's many Uzbeks, Meskhetian Turks, Chechens, or—dare I say it—Jews. Kaliyev further stated:

> We can take a joke like anyone else. But this has gone too far—it's a form of racism. . . . My country is a young country, so you have to under-

stand that we are sensitive to such matters. We do not like the behavior, the manners of this character. He has no idea how to behave in society, asking such questions as he does. We are a secular, modern state, not a state of such barbarians. If this were in a newspaper, this would not be so bad because people might forget it the next day. But this is broadcast to a huge audience.[88]

Kaliyev went on to argue that the show could seriously damage the perception of the approximately 1,500 Kazakhstani expatriates living in Great Britain. He was especially incensed by Borat's callous attitudes towards animals (e.g., Borat's claim that dog-hunting is Kazakhstan's national sport) since Kazakhs have a genuine love of nature, stating: "The horse, for example, is treated as a saint."[89] While the author would agree that the horse is much revered in Kazakhstan, it is also a major feature in the country's diet, often served as *shashlik* (shish kabob)—a curious end for such a "saintly" creature.

The Kazakhstani government's response, while understandable, placed the relatively new country in the spotlight. Here was a two-bit comedian with an obviously satirical shtick triggering a diplomatic crisis. With Cold War media frames still deeply embedded in the Western press, it was perhaps predictable that the British press would have a field day with the controversy.[90] *The Independent* took the opportunity to visit the Kazakhstani embassy to investigate the source of the hullabaloo.

> The Kazakhstani embassy is a pokey diplomatic hidey-hole just a stone's throw from London's Victoria & Albert Museum. Its interior is in keeping with the travails of a former Soviet republic trying to make it in the modern world: a little stuffy and outmoded in the manner of a Seventies hard-currency hotel, but also home to a palpable sense of optimism. The chandeliers and leather sofas are pure communist kitsch, and the boardroom-esque table looks like it was pilfered from some ransacked party HQ, but the Kazakh flag—a sky-blue affair also featuring a gold insignia—is draped proudly under a picture of this eight-year-old country's sole president to date: Nursultan Nazarbayev, a man whose name is often coupled to worrying phrases such as "a firm grip."[91]

Such coverage has a decisively counter-productive effect vis-à-vis the intentions of the diplomatic corps. Rather than reversing negative stereotypes generated out of thin air by Sacha Baron Cohen, the media attention affirmed and/or reinforced generic perceptions of the country as a Sovietesque, tin-pot dictatorship. The notion that Borat would or could be banned was taken as incontrovertible evidence that the Kazakhstani government was still suffering a post-totalitarian hangover (Britain's *Telegraph* carried the headline "Ban Borat, Say Offended Kazakhs"). As the face of Kazakhstan's statecraft, Kaliyev himself even came under scrutiny; "In person, the embassy's First Secretary (his calling card says 'Second Secretary,' but it's scribbled out and corrected) . . . is an impossibly dour, deep-voiced man who seems reluctant to display anything in the way of humor—which only makes his outrage seem more seismic."[92] In trying to defend his country, he was alternatively portrayed as a blustering buffoon or an iniquitous enemy of free speech.

Other media voices were somewhat more sympathetic. In a column for the *Daily Mirror,* Victor Lewis-Smith likened such comedic parody to an act of terrorism: "It detonates without warning, is devastatingly effective and causes maximum chaos for minimum effort. And sometimes, innocent bystanders get hurt."[93] And in the case of Kazakhstan, there is a special irony added to this symbolic violence. "For years their country has been roundly ignored by British television, and now that one of their 'citizens' has finally made it on to the box, he's a caricature who behaves like a well-meaning fool."[94] In the words of another journalist, "a quick flit through the country's history proves that it was rather insensitive to pick on Kazakhstan in the first place: oppression, genocide and countless other grisly horrors have helped define the Kazakhs' recent history. Inaccurate British character comedy is probably the last thing they needed."[95]

The imbroglio did ultimately trigger some actual journalism on the part of the British press. In April 2000, the *Sun,* Britain's most widely-read tabloid and the largest circulation English-language newspaper in the world, ran an informative piece on the "real" Kazakhstan. The article included items on the country's weather, sport, cuisine, and customs; however, there were a number of dodgy and even misleading bits of information to tickle the funny bone, including such pithy gems as: "The Kazakhs grow a massive amount of cannabis" and "most Kazakhs in the capital Astana don't bother with the beach—the nearest one is 500 miles away. But they can still get a glowing tan thanks to all the radioactivity." After reading the *Sun*'s "The Bizarre (Very) Rough Guide to Kazakhstan," it is likely that First Secretary Kaliyev probably wished that the British press would have continued to ignore his country.

Similarly, the premiere of the Anglo-American version of *Da Ali G Show* two years later prompted Britain's leading liberal quality newspaper the *Guardian* to interview Kazakhstanis in Britain about their homeland, Borat, and the parody. Most responded genially, suggesting the joke was on foolish Britons and Americans who fell for Baron Cohen's ruse. A 25-year old Kazakh woman stated, "It lays bare the American attitude towards foreigners: strong accents, loud voices, stupidity, male chauvinism." The article was also occasion for a bit more detail about Kazakhstan to trickle into the mainstream media. The *Guardian* commented that Kazakhstan is a country where "cab drivers quote Pushkin, and a trip to the opera is a cheap and popular night out" though it informed its audience that bride kidnapping is still customary in certain rural areas.[96] The resumption of Borat's ramblings also invited short "infotainment" pieces on the real Kazakhstan that were somewhat more reliable than the *Sun*'s unhelpful "rough guide."

While the first season of *Da Ali G Show* had been generally confined to the British Isles, the next installment of the program, which aired in 2003, was broadcast across the United States via the premium cable channel HBO. As Borat's horizons expanded, the Kazakhstani governmental response kept pace with new defenders of Kazakhstan emerging to combat Baron Cohen's ravings. However, with the spoof now becoming a transatlantic phenomenon, the intensity of Kazakhstan's angst was increased exponentially. With the *Da Ali G Show*'s airing in the US, Sacha Baron Cohen's post-Soviet Boratian parody began to inch its way into cyberspace. A Web site for the character was launched and video clips began to circulate via the Internet. Web-based reports on the parody began to reach Kazakhstanis in their own country and it began to dawn on them that they were increasingly in danger of becoming a laughingstock in the West.[97]

With the advent of the internet, media products are now constantly re-produced and transmitted with little regard for their original authorship or country of origin, thus creating new challenges for the victims of negative media representation. Via the borat.kz (later borat.tv) web site, Borat evolved into a global commodity—available for download regardless of location.[98] Sites such as *YouTube* allowed almost anyone anywhere to visit Sacha Baron Cohen's "Boratistan," Kazakhstan's deformed doppelganger which exists in cyberspace, on television, and in Baron Cohen's brain.[99] Even more disconcerting is that, due to the horizontal structure of the inter-net, the official site of Kazakhstan (government.kz) is roughly equal in terms of bytes and ease of use to find and navigate as Borat's cyber-based parodies of Kazakhstan and its people. As such, cyberspace is reflective of the new dangers posed to states by the lowered barriers to influence in the contemporary international environment. Just as the Peace of Westphalia introduced a new era of diplomatic opportunities and challenges for political elites in 1648, the introduction of global networks of communication in the past 50 years has remade the realities of power and influence.

By the time the third season of *Da Ali G Show* ran in 2004 (HBO's Sea-son II), Kaliyev's quixotic campaign against the Boratian onslaught was now being assisted by the talents of Roman Vassilenko, the press attaché for Kazakhstan's embassy to the United States and Canada.[100] Rather than echoing the borderline hysteria of his British counterpart, Vassilenko pur-sued a calculated approach beginning with an op-ed in the influential con-gressional newspaper *The Hill*, in which he expressed "strong objections" to the portrayal. Vassilenko, whose diplomatic skills should have earned him the National Hero of Kazakhstan medal, emerged as Borat's alter ego, deftly bobbing and parrying in response to Borat's barbs.

Roman Vassilenko viewed the Boratistan parody not simply as an ob-stacle, but also as an opportunity for marketing his country to an ever-widening audience. Neither spiteful nor mewling, his style was character-ized by attention to detail, austere patience, and careful selection of the tim-ing and manner of his response. Rather than attempting to censor, jam, or shut down Borat, Vassilenko used each and every press opportunity to en-gage in counter-programming (a somewhat un-Sovietesque strategy). Usu-ally sporting a slight smirk, the charismatic press secretary diligently in-formed the American press that: *chram* is not the Kazakh word for 'male genitalia;' women are not kept in cages; gypsy-catching is not a remuner-ated profession; "Throw the Jew Down the Well" is not a folk song; and so on. Once he had dashed the litany of falsehoods, he would then utilize his soapbox to drop a positive tidbit about his homeland such as its hosting of an international interfaith conference, positive statistics about women's edu-cation, etc. By providing anecdotal antidotes to dozens of Borat's misrepre-sentations about his country, Vassilenko was not only debunking Baron Cohen's misinformation, he was also building a cogent narrative about the "real" Kazakhstan. His diligence and professional manner even earned him a profile in *New Yorker* magazine in 2004, entitled "Department of Foreign Relations: The Borat Doctrine."

While Vassilenko's cool-headed diplomacy slowly began to temper Ka-liyev's earlier invective, there were still loose cannons in the government. As season three of *Da Ali G Show* was winding down, Yerzhan Ashyk-bayev, a senior foreign ministry official in Kazakhstan, began worrying aloud that the show could lead to a rise in sex tourism to his country, commenting, "We have to react or everyone would think Kazakhstan is like the grotesque portrayal of that man."[101] A little more than a year later, Ashykbayev would do something almost unheard of in foreign policy circles and it would forever change Kazakhstan's national image.

A New Posture: The Battle over Borat Heats Up

From the first days of *Da Ali G Show* in Britain, Astana regularly disavowed itself from the Boratistan parody, but generally tolerated Baron Cohen's pantomime until late 2005. The change in policy came when MTV Europe invited Borat to host its international music awards program from Lisbon, Portugal. The production, which was seen across the Continent and was made available, in part, over the Internet, included Borat's arrival on an Air Kazakh prop plane piloted by a one-eyed drunkard, a performance by the Astana Dancing Heroes doing their rendition of the (fictional) "Official Government Dance of Kazak," and a raft of offensive comments that made Kazakhstanis look like a nation of bigoted wife-beaters. Patience and blithe disregard rapidly gave way to a war of words in late 2005 with the globalization of Borat through the pervasive, influential, and deterritorialized medium of MTV. Previously confined to a narrow slice of the Anglophone West, Borat was foisted onto a pan-European audience with a vengeance. The Kazakhstani response was rapid and unequivocal: cease and desist or face legal sanctions. In a well-covered press conference, Ashykbayev stated:

> We do not rule out that Mr. Cohen is serving someone's political order designed to present Kazakhstan and its people in a derogatory way.[102] We reserve the right to any legal action to prevent new pranks of the kind. We view Mr. Cohen's behavior at the MTV Europe Music Awards as utterly unacceptable, being a concoction of bad taste and ill manners which is completely incompatible with ethics and civilized behavior.[103]

Baron Cohen fearlessly replied in character, issuing a response as Borat via his "official" web site borat.kz. Against the backdrop of a Kazakh flag and dueling pistols, Borat exhorted: "In response to Mr. Ashykbayev's comments, I'd like to state I have no connection with Mr. Cohen and fully support my government's decision to sue this Jew." He went on to add:

> Since the 2003 Tuleyakiv reforms, Kazakhstan is as civilized as any other country in the world. Women can now travel on inside of bus, homosexuals no longer have to wear blue hats, and the age of consent has been raised to eight years old. Please captain of industry, I invite you to come to Kazakhstan where we have incredible natural resources, hard working labor, and some of the cleanest prostitutes in all of Central Asia. *Dziękuję*. Good-bye.[104]

Borat's own press event received nearly as much coverage as Ashykbayev's official rant.

Soon, the media was discussing the strange situation in which a mass-mediated persona was doing battle with a national government. Shortly after Borat's internet-based retort, Kazakhstan upped the ante and took down his site which had hitherto been hosted on Kazakhstani servers, thus forcing relocation to the .tv domain. Nurlan Isin, President of the Association of Kazakh IT Companies, told Reuters "We've done this so he can't badmouth Kazakhstan under the .kz domain name. . . . He can go and do whatever he wants at other domains." The official reason for the removal was "administrator registration under a false name."[105] Reporters without Borders joined the fray on the side of Baron Cohen, condemning the Kazakh response as censorship, and further expressed concerns about "the politicization of the administration of domain names."[106] KazNIC, the country's administrator for domain names, did little to blunt this criticism, stating, "This is a political matter;" though the organization's spokesperson could not say who was behind the decision.[107] The *International Herald Tribune* indicated that the association received complaints from both the government and President Nursultan Nazarbayev's personal security service, which accused the borat.kz web site of impugning the "international image of Kazakhstan" and that the site was registered by a non-resident of the country intent on "unconscientious usage."[108]

Major media outlets quickly took notice of the intensifying spat—a trend which only added to the robustness of Borat's mass-mediated personality and authenticity as a "Kazakhstani." *Good Morning America,* one of the top-rated American morning news programs, framed the quarrel in harsh terms with *GMA* news anchor Robin Roberts introducing a 16 November 2005 segment on the controversy by stating, "Now to an international standoff that has the world's ninth largest country threatening to sue a comedian. The country, Kazakhstan, which used to have more than a thousand nuclear warheads. And the comedian is a guy named Sacha Baron Cohen who's very thankful those warheads are now out of commission."[109] While a nuclear retaliation for Baron Cohen's satirical jibes was not in the cards, the war of words proved to be fierce. In the segment, Vassilenko lamented MTV's choice of Borat as host of MTV Europe's Video Music Awards given his parody of Kazakhstan as a land of the "Stone Age" misogynists and anti-Semites.[110] The *Good Morning America* segment then presented a montage of images representing Kazakhstan's breathtaking scenery, striking modernity, and burgeoning industrial capacity as ABC News correspondent Jake Tapper commented on Kazakhstan's desire that such images, rather than Borat's buffoonery, stick in the minds of Americans.

Every year, the Kazakhstani government pours millions into its global marketing campaign hoping to convince the West that it is pluralistic, stable, prosperous, and open to investment (i.e., not just another 'Stan). Sacha Baron Cohen, however, presented the country as a primitive, quasi-fascist state with a failed economic system and lacking in modern transportation. As for the Kazakh people, the government line (and one which meshes well with my own observations and ethnographic research) is that they are welcoming, well-mannered, family-centric, tolerant, and optimistic. According to one government spokesperson,

> You have to remember that we are a nomad people. And the first law of nomad people is, if you have a guest in your house, you should never ask him where he came from, what his name is, what he is doing here. You must give him a meal first, then ask him questions. That is a law. So, national characteristics are hospitality and tolerance.[111]

External commentators agree. Vladimir Socor, a senior fellow at the Jamestown Foundation, states, "Kazakhstan is—remarkably, after the Soviet repression of ethnicity and faith—an Asian model of ethnic and religious tolerance, with various groups, houses of worship, and languages mingling without incident."[112] Not surprisingly, Borat's anti-black, anti-Gypsy, anti-Semitic, and misogynistic worldview struck Kazakhstan as particularly offensive.

One week after the condemnation of Borat and subsequent media storm, Kazakhstan took out a four-page advertising insert in the *New York Times* touting its democracy, oil production, unique culture, and the power of its women. It also hired two Western public relations firms to help improve its global image.[113] The insert entitled "Kazakhstan in the 21st Century" was "aimed at systematically countering the sexist, anti-Semitic "facts" about the country Borat shares on his Borat In USA segments on the Ali G show."[114] Kazakhstan also received further serendipitous free (positive) press as well, including a 16 November 2005 article in the *Independent* entitled "Kazakhstan—What you won't learn from Borat: 50 things you may not have known." The piece included bits on the country's size, natural resources, athletics program, economic situation, the Baikonur Cosmodrome, and the real lyrics to the national anthem (Borat's *Da Ali G Show* version is gibberish mixed with Hebrew). Hits on the Kazakhstan US Embassy's web site also tripled after the controversy.[115]

Despite Borat's being saddled with the title of "anti-ambassador of Kazakhstan," the "Unofficial Borat Homepage" suggested that the commercial linking of travel sites for Kazakhstan to Borat searches on Google helped to "put Kazakhstan on the map."[116] Subsequently, Kazakhstan began a wider media blitz including color-spreads in prominent foreign policy journals and other print publications. The advertising blitz grew in advance of President Nursultan Nazarbayev's late summer visit the US with the airing "'educational TV spots and print ads about the real Kazakhstan."[117]

Baron Cohen assisted Astana's message-jamming effort in his own bizarre way by providing a venue in cyberspace for "Kazakhstanis against Borat." Stopborat.com, a site linked from Ali G's web site, boyakasha.co.uk, appeared during the controversy selling ten different t-shirts which condemned Borat's portrayal of Kazakhstanis. The slogans, which appear above a photo of Borat with a red circle-slash over his face, include: "Borat is wrong! We have way much culture;" "Do not believe Borat. Kazakh people like the Jew;" and "Kazakhstan is not stupid country." The web site was flanked on the right with (genuine) scenes of traditional Kazakh villagers, hunters, musicians, folk performers, and merchants all stating their dislike of this "funnyman." On the left, an oft-used photo of President Nazarbayev ceremonially opening a new oil pipeline was framed by text extolling the virtues of Kazakhstan including the following invitation: "We ask all western peoples to come and see our country and see the advancement of our society. We have a good reputation in the region and don't need to be made look like a country who has horse and cart on the highway instead of truck and car (maybe you would see that only in Uzbekstan [sic])."

The site also listed a few little known facts about Kazakhstan including that it is *not* part of the "axis of evil." The web site demanded an apology from Queen Elizabeth II and a state visit by Prince Charles and Camilla

Parker-Bowles. While no royal apologies were issued by Buckingham Palace, the new British ambassador to Kazakhstan Paul Brummel did clarify in early 2006 that Baron Cohen was mocking Britons and not Kazakhstanis with his satirical humor. Speaking to members of the Kazakhstani press, he stated, "We should think more about how vague ideas of the British are about what Kazakhstan is and how little they know about it. It is our common task: for me as a diplomat and for you as journalists to show to the British and to the Western community what Kazakhstan is in 2006 and how much it is different from how Borat is presenting it."[118]

Unfortunately for Astana, the Borat persona had become synonymous with Kazakhstan by 2005 (at least for many younger Westerners). An eBay search using the term "Kazakhstan" invariably returned products related to Borat, e.g., a t-shirt displaying a pyramid topped by the golden eagle (*berkut*) and yellow sun which adorn the republic's flag. Inside the pyramid were the following items (in descending order): GOD, MAN, HORSE, DOG, WOMAN, RAT, KARSULI.[119] The eBay listing advertised the product as follows: "This design is based on the hierarchy of society in Kazakhstan presented by Borat from "Da Ali G Show" in the episode 'Guide to Politics.'" Above the pyramid in bold capital letters was the word "KAZAKHSTAN."[120] Borat's nonsense also made it into one of the top 100 Google hits for "Kazakhstan," though this has ceased to be the case by the time of writing. After the MTV tiff, the Kazakhstan's brand confusion vis-à-vis Borat only got worse, peaking in the immediate aftermath of *Borat: Cultural Learnings of America for Make Benefit Glorious Nation of Kazakhstan.*

In its extreme reaction to the Borat characterization of the Kazakhstani people, Astana breathed life into Baron Cohen's shtick which was flagging by 2005. Baron Cohen—no stranger to courting controversy to increase his own profile—may have, in fact, anticipated the over-reaction on the part of the Kazakhstani government in an effort to jumpstart his forthcoming motion picture's marketing campaign, or perhaps he just got lucky. In any case, it was clear that 2006 would see more Americans with Kazakhstan on their lips than ever before. In the ensuing chapter, I will explore how Kazakhstan's political elite turned the tables on Sacha Baron Cohen and made Borat an asset rather than a liability to their country.

Notes

1. In the tradition of international relations writing, I use "Astana," the capital of Kazakhstan, to refer to the country's political establishment.

2. Michael Andersen, "TV Comedian's Satire Falls Flat in Almaty," *Index on Censorship*, 1 December 2005, http://www.indexonline.org/en/news/articles/2005/4/kazakhstan-tv-comedian-s-satire-falls-flat-i.shtml (12 January 2006); see also Edward Schatz, "Transnational Image Making and Soft Authoritarian Kazakhstan," *Slavic Review* 66, no. 1 (Spring 2008): 50-62.

3. The US-Canadian border is slightly longer when including the Alaskan-Canadian border.

4. The Turkic peoples occupy a generally contiguous zone of territory from the southeastern Balkan Peninsula across Asia Minor and Central Asia into western China and the southern parts of Asiatic Russia. Small pockets of Turkic-speakers live in the Crimean Peninsula, Iran, and northeastern Siberia. In addition to the Ka-

zakhs, the Turkic linguistic community includes Turks, Azeris, Uzbeks, Uyghurs, Turkmen, Tatars, and two dozen other small groups.

5. Under tsarist rule, the Christian Orthodox Cossacks were granted a wide array of privileges compared to their serf counterparts and Muslim neighbors. Eventually, they came to be employed as a reactionary force within the empire putting down rebellions and engaging in pogroms against Jews during times of economic and political strife.

6. Prior to the advent of Islam, a number of other religions flourished in the caravanserais of the trans-Asiatic trade routes, including Christianity, Judaism, Manicheism, Zoroastrianism, and Buddhism.

7. Alexandra George, *Journey into Kazakhstan: The True Face of the Nazarbayev Regime* (Lanham, MD: University Press of America, 2001), 4.

8. See Robert D. Crews, *For Prophet and Tsar: Islam and Empire in Russia and Central Asia* (Cambridge, MA: Harvard University Press, 2006).

9. Svat Soucek, *The History of Inner Asia* (Cambridge: Cambridge University Press, 2000), 164.

10. Martha Brill Olcott, *The Kazakhs* (Stanford: Hoover Institution Press, 1987), 9.

11. The hordes are so named for their age, not their size. The Greater (or Elder) Horde is associated with wealth, the Middle with knowledge, and the Lesser (or Junior) with warcraft; see Sally N. Cummings, *Kazakhstan: Power and the Elite* (New York: I.B. Tauris, 2005), 20-21.

12. The Lesser and Middle Hordes were reacting to incursions by the Mongol Oirats (Jungars) who began invading the Kazakh steppe in the 16th century. The Great Horde, the last Kazakhs to fall under tsarist suzerainty, sought Russian protection against the northward expansion of the Khanate of Kokand in the 19th century.

13. The first Slavic settlers were Cossacks who established border garrisons in the Kazakh towns of Oral and Atyrau in the 1600s.

14. Aurel Braun, "All Quiet on the Russian Front?" in *The New European Diasporas: National Minorities and Conflict in Eastern Europe*, edited by Michael Mandelbaum (New York: Council on Foreign Relations Press, 2000), 93.

15. Here, I refer to Eastern Slavs, i.e., "Great" Russians, "Little" Russians, and "White" Russians. In the 19th century, these peoples were more linked by common loyalties to their faith (Eastern Orthodoxy) and sovereign (the tsar) than they were divided by minimal linguistic differences between the spoken languages of Russian, Ukrainian, and Belarusian.

16. Martha Brill Olcott, "The Emergence of National Identity in Kazakhstan," *Canadian Review of Studies in Nationalism* 8 (Fall 1981): 285-300.

17. While the Kazakhs were not sent to the front to fight, they were conscripted into work units engaged in menial labor such as ditch-digging. Their low status and poor treatment vis-à-vis other tsarist subjects further enflamed tensions.

18. Alash is the mythical progenitor of all Kazakhs. Each of his three sons (Uisun, Aktol, and Alshin) purportedly founded the three jüzes (Greater, Middle, and Lesser, respectively).

19. See Matt Payne, "The Forge of the Kazakh Proletariat? The Turksib, Nativization, and Industrialization during Stalin's First Five-Year Plan," in Ronald G. Suny and Terry Martin, *A State of Nations: Empire and Nation-Making in the Age of Lenin and Stalin* (Oxford: Oxford University Press, 2001).

20. Concurrently, massive state investment into the region occurred. The building of the Turksib railroad and other industrialization projects proved alluring to many displaced and disinherited young Kazakhs.

21. The ultimate testament to this was the fact that Kazakhstan shared the rare distinction of having a portion of the USSR's nuclear arsenal stationed on its territory. Overall, however, the nuclearization of the republic is seen as exceptionally detrimental. Semipalatinsk in the northeastern corner of the country was chosen as

the Soviet Union's nuclear program. As a result of the nearly 500 nuclear tests conducted in the area, Kazakhstanis still suffer long-term health problems including cancer, childhood leukemia, and birth defects, as well as the after-effects of environmental degradation.

22. When the USSR disintegrated in 1991, Kazakhstan, like the 14 other Soviet republics, gained full independence.

23. Stalin, an ethnic Georgian, allowed his personal prejudices to color his political decisions during this process. His policies disproportionately targeted other Caucasian nationalities; see Alexander M. Nekrich, *The Punished People: The Deportation and Fate of Soviet Minorities at the End of the Second World War* (New York: W.W. Norton, 1978).

24. The ethnic homelands of these peoples were all classified as enemy states of the USSR during World War II.

25. Robert Conquest, *The Nation Killers: The Soviet Deportation of Nationalities* (London: Macmillan, 1970).

26. As a percentage of the overall population, the Kazakhs bottomed out around 1960 when they constituted around 30 percent of the republic.

27. The office of general secretary represented the highest political position in the country.

28. See William P. Rivers, "Attitudes towards Incipient Mankurtism among Kazakhstani College Students," *Language Policy* 1, no. 2 (May 2002): 159–174.

29. The Tajiks, unlike most other Central Asians, are not of Turkic stock. Instead, they are closely-related to the Indo-European Persians in both ethnicity and language.

30. See Olcott, "The Emergence of National Identity."

31. Kathleen Collins defines 'clan' as "an informal organization built on an extensive network of kin and fictive, or perceived and imagined, kinship relations. The kinship units of Central Asian societies in many ways embody a non-Western, more expansive and fluid notion of kinship;" see Kathleen Collins, *Clan Politics and Regime Transition in Central Asia* (Cambridge: Cambridge University Press, 2006), 25.

32. See Karl Deutsch, *Nationalism and Social Communication: An Inquiry into the Foundations of Nationality* (Cambridge: The Technology Press of the Massachusetts Institute of Technology, 1953); Ernst Gellner, *Nations and Nationalism* (Ithaca, NY: Cornell University Press, 1983); Miroslav Hroch, *Social Preconditions of National Revival in Europe: A Comparative Analysis of the Social Composition of Patriotic Groups among the Smaller European Nations* (Cambridge: Cambridge University Press, 1985); Anthony Smith, *National Identity* (Reno: University of Nevada Press, 1991); Benedict Anderson, *Imagined Communities: Reflections on the Origin and Spread of Nationalism* (London: Verso, 1991).

33. The process of splitting the two was finalized in 1925; however, Kazakhstan's acquisition of union status in 1936 provided an important coda in the process; see Francine Hirsch, *Empire of Nations: Ethnographic Knowledge and the Making of the Soviet Union* (Ithaca and London: Cornell University Press, 2005), 281. For more on the national delimitation of Soviet Central Asia, see Olivier Roy, *The New Central Asia: The Creation of Nations* (New York: New York University Press, 2000), 59-65 and Steven Sabol, "The Creation of Soviet Central Asia: The 1924 National Delimitation," *Central Asian Survey* 14, no. 2 (June 1995): 225-241.

34. This form of identity construction has been labelled "negative identity." Two cogent examples include Canadian identity and, ironically, Russian identity. Canadian identity is dependent on distinguishing Canadianness from Americanness (that is the identity of US citizens), while Russian identity is strongly shaped by distinguishing Russianness from Western Civilization; see Lev Gudkov, *Negativnaya Identichnost* (Moscow: Novoe Literaturnoe Obozrenie, 2004).

35. See Cummings, *Kazakhstan,* 21 and Ronald Suny, "Making Minorities: The Politics of National Boundaries in the Soviet Experience," in *The Construction of*

Minorities: Cases for Comparison across Time and around the World, edited by André Burguière and Raymond Grew (Ann Arbor: University of Michigan Press, 2001).

36. As Gerald Holton states, Kulturträger carries a double meaning: both carrier and pillar of *Kultur*, i.e., 'high culture' as opposed to popular or mass culture. Kulturträgers are usually educated members of the bourgeoisie; however, in Soviet society, middle- and upper-level bureaucrats and managers functioned as an ersatz bourgeoisie; see Gerald Holton, "Einstein and the Cultural Roots of Modern Science," *Daedalus* 127, no. 1 (Winter 1998): 1-44.

37. Kazakhs represented the only "titular majority" among the 15 Soviet republics that could not claim majority status. From the 1950s until the mid-1980s, ethnic Kazakhs accounted for a minority in their own republic. It was only shortly before independence that they gained a slim plurality over the Russians.

38. Terry Martin, *The Affirmative Action Empire: Nations and Nationalism in the Soviet Union, 1923-1939* (Ithaca and London: Cornell University Press, 2001), 148.

39. Nurbulat Masanov, "Perceptions of Ethnic and All-National Identity in Kazakhstan," M.E.S. Series No. 51: *The Nationalities Question in Post-Soviet Kazakhstan, Institute of Developing Economies* (Chiba: IDE-Jetro, 2002).

40. Democratization for Gorbachev meant multi-candidate elections, not multi-party elections. Regardless, the shift allowed for an influx of new voices and approaches to politics within an ever more accommodating political environment.

41. See Erlan Karin and Andrei Chebotarev, "The Policy of Kazakhization in State and Government Institutions in Kazakhstan," M.E.S. Series No. 51: *The Nationalities Question in Post-Soviet Kazakhstan, Institute of Developing Economies* (Chiba: IDE-Jetro, 2002). It is worth noting that nearly two decades later, only half of the country's ethnic Kazakhs possess fluency in their ancestral tongue, with the remainder using Russian at home and in much of their daily lives; see Luke O'Callaghan, "War of Words: Language Policy in Post Independence Kazakhstan," *Nebula* 1, no. 3 (December 2004 – January 2005): 197-216.

42. See Karin and Chebotarev, "The Policy of Kazakhization."

43. Rogers Brubaker, *Nationalism Reframed: Nationhood and the National Question in the New Europe* (Cambridge: Cambridge University Press, 1996), 5-6.

44. Zhambyl Zhabayev (1846-1945) was a traditional folksinger (*akyn*) and Abay Ibrahim Qunanbayuli (1845-1904) was a poet and philosopher.

45. Nursultan Nazarbaev, speech at the World Kurultai of Kazakhs, 1992. Quoted in Karin and Chebotarev, "The Policy of Kazakhization."

46. For instance, Nazarbayev waxed poetic in a 1992 speech, "We are the children of the majestic mountains and the boundless steppes. Here, hundreds and hundreds of generations of Kazakhs were born, gained strength, and reached manhood. These boundless spaces are our cradle, our inheritance, our legacy."

47. Martha Brill Olcott, *Kazakhstan: Unfulfilled Promise* (Washington, DC: Carnegie Endowment for International Peace, 2002), 60.

48. Saulesh Yessenova, "'Routes and Roots' of Kazakh Identity: Urban Migration in Postsocialist Kazakhstan," *The Russian Review* 64 (October 2005): 661–79.

49. Edward Schatz, "The Politics of Multiple Identities: Lineage and Ethnicity in Kazakhstan," *Europe-Asia Studies* 52, no. 3 (May 2000): 489-506.

50 Schatz, "Transnational Image Making and Soft Authoritarian Kazakhstan," 51.

51. George, *Journey into Kazakhstan*, 13.

52. Olcott, *Kazakhstan*, 180.

53. Cummings, *Kazakhstan*, 99.

54. Braun, "All Quiet," 112.

55. Soviet census data from 1989 and "Demograficheskaya situatsiya v Respublike Kazakhstan v 2006g." *Agenstvo Respubliki Kazakhstan po statistike* Web site,

January 2007, http://www.stat.kz/index.php?lang=rus&uin=1176791556&chapter= 1176791809 (21 June 2007). In my definition of Europeans, I include Russians, Ukrainians, Germans, Belarusians, and Poles. While Tatars are arguably a European population, I have not included them in this figure.

56. See Ana Barfield, "Sculpting the Nation: A Comparative Look at the Impact of Past Legacies on the Emerging National Identities in Central Asia," B.A. Thesis, Department of Sociology, Princeton University (April 2004).

57. The government defines an 'Oralman' as: "A person of native nationality expelled outside the boundaries of his/her ethnic motherland and deprived of citizenship owing to acts of massive political repression, unlawful requisition, forced collectivization and other inhuman actions, voluntarily migrating to the Republic of Kazakhstan in the company of his/her descendents with an intention of establishing permanent residence;" cited in Diener, 2005.

58. "Demograficheskaya situatsiya," 2007.

59. A good example is the country's premiere athlete, Olympic cyclist Alexander Vinokourov, who, despite his blond hair and Nordic features, is labeled a 'Kazakh' (rather than 'Kazakhstani') in roughly nine out of ten occasions.

60. Schatz, "The Politics of Multiple Identities," 491.

61. Cengiz Surucu, "Modernity, Nationalism, Resistance: Identity Politics in Post-Soviet Kazakhstan," *Central Asian Survey* 21, no. 4 (December 2002): 385-402.

62. Braun, "All Quiet," 110.

63. Karin and Chebotarev, "The Policy of Kazakhization."

64. Masanov, "Perceptions of Ethnic and All-National Identity," 2002.

65. Nursultan Nazarbayev, *V potoke istorii* (Almaty: Atamura, 1999).

66. See Cummings, *Kazakhstan,* 2.

67. The Baltic States of Lithuania, Latvia, and Estonia enjoyed a high level of protection from the tender mercies of Moscow because of their geographic location, economic importance to the West, and their historical legacies which included interwar independence.

68. See Schatz, "Transnational Image Making and Soft Authoritarian Kazakhstan."

69. Olcott, *Kazakhstan,* 223.

70. Olivier Roy, *The New Central Asia: The Creation of Nations* (New York: New York University Press, 2000), viii-xi.

71. Olcott, *Kazakhstan,* 222.

72. See William P. Rivers, "Attitudes towards Incipient Mankurtism among Kazakhstani College Students," *Language Policy* 1, no. 2 (May 2002): 159–174.

73. Chingiz Aitmatov, *The Day Lasts More than a Hundred Years.* Translated by John French (Bloomington: Indiana University Press, 1988), 126-133.

74. The act known as *zhety ata* ('seven fathers') is, in part, a prophylaxis against endogamy; see Saulesh Yessenova, "'Knowing the Road That Leads You Home:' Family, Genealogy, and Migration in Post-Socialist Kazakhstan," *The Silk Road Newsletter* 1, no. 2 (December 2003), http://silkroadfoundation.org/. Amongst Kyrgyz, the Kazakhs' highland cousins, the standard is ten generations; see Collins, 2006.

75. See Bhavna Dave, "National Revival in Kazakhstan: Language Shift and Identity Change," *Post-Soviet Affairs* 12, no. 1 (1996): 51–72.

76. Barfield, "Sculpting the Nation," 37.

77. The term 'near abroad' carries mildly imperialistic overtones as it describes those countries that were previously under Russian and/or Soviet suzerainty, but which now comprise the Newly Independent States (NIS): Estonia, Latvia, Lithuania, Belarus, Ukraine, Moldova, Azerbaijan, Armenia, Georgia, Kazakhstan, Uzbekistan, Kyrgyzstan, Turkmenistan, and Tajikistan; see Alexander C. Diener, "Ka-

zakhstan's Kin State Diaspora: Settlement Planning and the Oralman Dilemma," *Europe-Asia Studies* 57, no. 2 (March 2005): 327-348.

78. David Laitin, *Identity in Formation: Russian-Speaking Populations in the Near Abroad* (Ithaca, NY: Cornell University Press, 1998), 98.

79. This can be partially ascribed to Nazarbayev's own tendency to issue mixed messages. Despite his lauding of the greatness of Kazakh culture, he is a strong advocate of cultural globalization. In an interview with author Christopher Robbins, he stated, "I tell young people here that they should be citizens of the world and that for them there should only be one nationality—humankind;" Christopher Robbins, *In Search of Kazakhstan: The Land that Disappeared* (London: Profile Books, 2007), 114.

80. Luke O'Callaghan, "War of Words: Language Policy in Post Independence Kazakhstan," *Nebula* 1, no. 3 (December 2004 – January 2005): 197-216.

81. Cited in Sallie Westwood, "Re-Branding Britain: Sociology, Futures and Futurology," *Sociology* 34, no. 1 (February 2000): 185-202.

82. See Schatz, "The Politics of Multiple Identities."

83. Surucu, "Modernity, Nationalism, Resistance," 391.

84. Vladimir Socor, "A Model for Central Asia," *Wall Street Journal*, 2-4 December 2005, 13.

85. Pål Kolstø, "Anticipating Demographic Superiority: Kazakh Thinking on Integration and Nation Building," *Europe-Asia Studies* 50, no. 1 (January 1998): 51-70.

86. Jill E. Hickson, "Using Law to Create National Identity: The Course to Democracy in Tajikistan," *Texas International Law Journal* 38, no. 2 (Spring 2003): 346-379.

87. Vincent Graff, "It's a Free Country, But This Ali G Guy Has Got It All Wrong," *The Evening Standard* (London), 3 April 2000, 36.

88. John Harris, "When Ali G Went to Kazakhstan (Or How a Cult Comedian Fell Out with an Entire Country," *The Independent*, Features Sec., 26 April 2000, 1.

89. In one skit, Borat extols the national festival of *shurik*: "We take dogs, shoot them in a field, and have a party;" Oliver Poole, "Ban Borat, Say Offended Kazakhs," *Telegraph*, 23 April 2000.

90. For more on Cold War media framing, see Silvo Lenart and Harry R. Targ, "Framing the Enemy," *Peace & Change* 17, no. 3 (July 1992): 341-62.

91. Harris, "When Ali G Went to Kazakhstan," 1.

92. Harris, "When Ali G Went to Kazakhstan."

93. Victor Lewis-Smith, "A Kazakhstanding Ovation," *Mirror*, 29 April 2000, 6.

94. Lewis-Smith "A Kazakhstanding Ovation."

95. Harris, "When Ali G Went to Kazakhstan."

96. Kelaart, Lucy. "Inside Story: 'Is It Cos I Is Kazakh?'" *Guardian*, 11 April 2003, 7

97. Sarah Baxter, "We Are Not Liking This Ali G Joke, Says Kazakhstan," *Sunday Times*, 19 September 2004, 14.

98. Today, the site is a simple placeholder for Twentieth Century Fox.

99. I use this term as a convenient shorthand for the imaginary country that Baron Cohen has created through a decade of sustained myth-making via his performance art. According to historian Paula A. Michaels, "this fictitious place has become more potent in the western collective imagination than the real Kazakhstan, in large part because of the lack of any impression about this former Soviet republic in the popular consciousness;" Paula A. Michaels, "If the Subaltern Speaks in the Woods and Nobody's Listening, Does He Make a Sound?" *Slavic Review* 66, no. 1 (Spring 2008): 81-83.

100. Vassilenko considers himself a representative Kazakhstani. While he is of Ukrainian origin, he speaks fluent Kazakh and links his own identity with the Central Asian republic where he was born.

101. Baxter, "We Are Not Liking This Ali G Joke."

102. A scan of relevant fan-based web logs pointed the finger at Uzbekistan as the most likely culprit.

103. "Hear IS wat Thay Say," Official Borat Web site, http://www.borat.tv (2 February 2006).

104. "I Innocent!@," Official Borat Web site, http://www.borat.tv (2 February 2006). The Tuleyakiv reforms are again a figment of Baron Cohen's imagination; Kazakhstan decriminalized homosexuality in 1997 and, according to the Interpol web site, the country's age of consent for sexual activity is 18.

105. Sarah Hall, "Kazakhstan Strips Borat of Site," *Yahoo! News*, 13 December 2005, http://news.yahoo.com/s/eo/20051213/en_celeb_eo/17962 (10 January 2006).

106. "Ali G versus. Kazakhstan: Reporters without Borders Enters the Fray," *Associated Press*, 15 December 2005.

107. Doreen Carvajal, "Kazakh Officials Don't See Spoof's Humor," *International Herald Tribune*, 15 December 2005, http://www.iht.com/articles/2005/12/14/business/borat.php (2 January 2006).

108. Carvajal, "Kazakh Officials."

109. "War of words: Kazakhstan vs. Sacha Baron Cohen," *Good Morning America*, ABC News transcripts from 16 November 2005.

110. "War of words," *Good Morning America*.

111. See Harris, "When Ali G Went to," 1. In ethnographic interviews with Kazakhstani Russians, they invariably identified ethnic Kazakhs as being extremely welcoming and generous—cultural traits which were slowly rubbing off on the country's ethnic Russians after centuries of co-habitation. Scottish film star Ewan McGregor further evinced this point in *Long Way Round* (2004). The documentary recorded his and Charley Boorman's 20,000-mile motorcycle trip across Eurasia and North America. McGregor half-heartedly crabbed about the overzealous hospitality of the Kazakh people which at times slowed the pair's trek across the country.

112. Socor, "A Model for Central Asia," 13.

113. Katharine Barney, No title, *Evening Standard*, 2 December 2005, 3.

114. John R. Bradley, "Outrageous Comic Has Last Laugh," *The Straits Times*, 16 January 2006.

115. Mary Wiltenburg, "Backstory: The Most Unwanted Man in Kazakhstan," *Christian Science Monitor*, Features, 30 November 2005, 20.

116. See http://www.boratonline.co.uk/.

117. Geoffrey Gray, "Kazakh Elites Divided over Borat," *New York Magazine*, 28 August 2006, http://nymag.com/news/intelligencer/19391/index.html (15 September 2006).

118. "British Ambassador Comments on the British Comedian," *The Times of Central Asia*, 3 February 2006.

119. "Karsuli," like "chram," seems to be a purely Boratian construction (unlike his mangled Polish interjections or Hebrew borrowings).

120. While the ridiculousness of this schema is obvious, it does at least reflect some level of familiarity with Kazakh lifeways. In traditional nomadic Kazakh culture, the horse and hunting dog are highly valued—witness the old proverb, "There are three things which the real man should possess: a fast horse, a Tazy hound, and a Golden Eagle."

Chapter 5
Learning to Love Boratistan: Kazakhstan Buys into Brand Borat

Imagine a country where "women not only travel inside buses but also drive their own cars," where they make wine from, of all things, grapes, and where "Jews can freely attend synagogues."[1] In most countries, an official who praised his homeland's national customs in such bizarre terms would soon be looking for a new job. But Kazakhstan's Deputy Foreign Minister Rakhat Aliyev was not torpedoing his career as these words left his mouth, he was merely reflecting the latest turn in his government's vacillating relationship with the Cambridge-educated comedian Sacha Baron Cohen. When Aliyev made these statements a few weeks before the film's premiere, the critical acclaim and looming commercial success of the motion picture *Borat: Cultural Learnings of America for Make Benefit Glorious Nation of Kazakhstan* (2006) had effectively forced Kazakhstan's diplomatic staff to either get in on the joke or risk untold damage to the country's global brand in Europe and America.

As a satirist, Sacha Baron Cohen can be forgiven for attacking the aloof and disconnected political establishment in the United States and Great Britain; however, his utilization of Kazakhstan and its people to expand his own fame is, on many levels, indefensible. Despite the offensiveness of the parody, Kazakhstan has, after some false starts, entered into a querulous but symbiotic relationship with Borat's creator in order to raise the country's international profile and expand its brand recognition in the West. In the previous chapter, I detailed the dynamic official and "semi-official" positions on Baron Cohen's satire, which culminated in a tentative embrace of the parody immediately after the international premiere of *Borat*. This chapter explores the Kazakhstani government's use of the Borat controversy as a tool for nation branding. Through the use of the analytical tool of "nation branding," I discuss the realpolitik required of political elites[2] in dealing with mass-mediated threats to national image in the era of ubiquitous, deterritorialized media products (e.g., *MTV, Da Ali G Show,* etc.) and platforms (YouTube, MySpace, etc.).

Postmodern Foreign Policy, Brand Management, and the "National Image"

National image, that is, a country's reputation, has long been recognized for its effect on relations between countries and as a vital tool for any state to achieve its foreign policy goals. In international politics, the practices of policymakers are girded by their own national self-image (*Selbstbild*) and how other nations or cultures perceive their country (*Fremdbild*).[3] Harvard professor and former presidential advisor Joseph S. Nye suggests that a positive national image provides the ability to entice and attract other countries to it; such attraction often leads to acquiescence or imitation.[4] The relationship of national images, country reputation, and decision-makers' beliefs associated with both are major components in both alliance-building and international conflict.[5] A country's image stems from its "geography, history, proclamations, art and music, famous citizens and other features" and is strongly influenced by "the total of all descriptive, inferential and informational beliefs one has about a particular country."[6] World opinion, or the "more or less consensual perception" of a state's reputation, is integral to that country's negotiation of its national identity.[7] While older countries enjoy well-established national images at home and abroad, the past century has seen the emergence of roughly 100 new nations which face a double challenge: firstly, they are charged with crystallizing a coherent national image in the domestic realm, and, secondly, with transmitting a viable and positive national image to the world community.

The current global information age greatly heightens the importance of such images. The spread of information and communication technologies (ICTs), the purported victory of the neo-liberal system, and the deepening of complex economic interdependence have made governments ever more attentive to their national images. Borrowing from the field of business management, international relations scholars have begun to explore the management of national image through strategic policy initiatives, targeted public diplomacy, and discrete programs intended to alter global perception on the elite and mass levels. This new field of inquiry investigates nation or state branding, a phenomenon that is distinct from national image due to the active rather than passive nature of policy elites in shaping, changing, and maintaining their country's image. In short, nation branding is the practice of brand management applied to a country's national image.

In nearly every corner of the globe, polities are now actively engaged in the building, maintenance, and protection of their national brands. As some historians have pointed out, there is nothing new about nation branding except the explicit reference to country image building activities as such. In his essay "Branding the Nation—The Historical Context," Wally Olins argues that Napoleonic France, Bismarck's Germany, and Atatürk's Turkey all re-branded themselves for the age in which they existed. The term "nation branding" is, however, controversial. "Image and national identity are fine, but 'brand' sticks in the gullet."[8] While certain contemporary countries are reticent to embrace the full-blown corporatist approach to managing their national image (France prior to the election of President Nicolas Sarkozy, in particular), other nations have whole-heartedly endorsed the notion.

Spain and Ireland, in particular, successfully remade their images in the late 1980s and early 1990s by utilizing strategies which had previously allowed cities like New York, Sydney, and Shanghai to rebrand themselves. However, the paragon of nation branding remains "Cool Britannia."

In the late 1990s, Prime Minister Tony Blair's New Labourites began a large-scale effort to "re-brand" Britain as young, hip, modern, and most importantly "cool." A task force drawn from trade, tourism, and the culture industry launched "at high pitch with high gloss, a campaign aimed at convincing the world that Britain is about a lot more than tradition—and convincing Britons that [they] are the best in the world, at least in some things."[9] While Britain was branded as cool, Britons were taught to think of themselves as "young, vibrant, innovative, entrepreneurial, decent, open, tolerant, flexible, straight, radical, courteous, stylish, painstaking people."[10] Surprisingly, it worked. Britain went from being seen as old-fashioned, stodgy, and inefficient into a lean, mean European machine (with an Anglo-Saxon work ethic). In addition to the focus on values, the campaign also dashed the "stereotype of a stale, pale, male kingdom" by stressing the country's ethnic, regional, and religious diversity.[11] Following in the wake of Blair's successful re-branding of Britain, countries as diverse as Qatar, Latvia, and New Zealand have embraced nation branding as strategy for attracting foreign direct investment, promoting tourism, and expanding exports.[12]

Nation branding includes not only the activities of a given state's government actors, but also its celebrities, multinational corporations, and non-governmental organizations. Positive associations with various products are also vital to national brands.[13] In the current era of global commerce, individual corporate brands such as *Coca-Cola* (USA), *Sony* (Japan), and *Nokia* (Finland) have a significant role to play, as do Bollywood (India), Al-Jazeera (Qatar), basketball player Yao Ming (China), and other actors. Peter van Ham argues that the importance of creating a "brand state" through effective image projection and maintenance of a dependable reputation is now the paramount concern of the postmodern political system.[14] J. E. Peterson states, "Branding has emerged as a state asset to rival geopolitics and traditional considerations of power. Assertive branding is necessary for states as well as companies to stand out in the crowd, since they often offer similar products: territory, infrastructure, educated people, and, [in certain cases], almost identical systems of governance."[15]

Simon Anholt, who coined the term "nation branding" a decade ago, suggests that brands are gradually becoming "the dominant channel of communication for national identity."[16]

> Globalization means that countries compete with each other for the attention, respect and trust of investors, tourists, consumers, donors, immigrants, the media, and the governments of other nations: so a powerful and positive nation brand provides a crucial competitive advantage. It is essential for countries to understand how they are seen by publics around the world; how their achievements and failures, their assets and their liabilities, their people and their products are reflected in their brand image.[17]

State branding is particularly important for reinforcing positive images and blunting or negating unflattering ones.[18] Effective branding depends on the content, resonance, and reception of a country's image abroad. Like any product, a country's image is "multifaceted and may carry large amounts of both factual and affective information."[19] That brand (or image) plays a pivotal role in the decision-making process for those nations, firms, or individuals interested in doing business in said country.[20] However, unlike brands in the corporate world where imitation is the norm, nation brands are unique properties; in other words, no two nations are exactly alike.[21] Furthermore, national brands must reflect reality and avoid contradictory messages; failure to do so leaves the state open to charges of cynicism or hypocrisy and may result in severe damage to its reputation.[22] Finally, states must increasingly deal with alternative narrators to their national identity and state brand, a troubling reality that the Republic of Kazakhstan has confronted in its six-year feud with the comedian Baron Cohen.

Locating Kazakhstan: "A Stan Like No Other?"

Kazakhstan is part of what might be called the "Third Wave" of states which gained independence during the 20th century. In the wake of the Great War (1914-1918), the demise of the Ottoman, Habsburg, and Romanov empires launched a host of new nations onto the world stage including Iraq, Czechoslovakia, and Latvia. After World War II, decolonization nearly doubled the number of internationally-recognized states adding Ghana, Algeria, and Indonesia among others. Most recently, the dissolution of the federal states of the USSR and Yugoslavia in 1991 produced more than twenty new countries including Slovenia, Turkmenistan, and Belarus.[23] According to Vladimir Lebedenko of Russia's Ministry of Public Affairs, "most of these newly independent states were faced with the need for self-identification and assertion of their image in the international arena."[24] These countries debuted at a rather complicated juncture in history, one in which deterritorialized information and communications technologies have become nearly ubiquitous, economic interdependence and cultural interconnections are the norm, and the tools of public relations, advertising, and branding have become integral components of statecraft.[25] Given such changes, the community of nations has, in many ways, come to function as a marketplace.[26] This phenomenon acutely affects the newest countries of the world. As one of five new "Stans" created by the breakup of the USSR, Kazakhstan's situation is further complicated by brand confusion in the international marketplace as it is often confused with its less developed post-Soviet counterparts, as well as Afghanistan and Pakistan.[27]

Lacking a historically well-defined image beyond its borders, the Kazakhstani government has worked hard to build a unique, recognizable, and credible national brand. Whether or not the country's brand managers were happy with Jon Stewart's June 2007 reference to the southeastern European country of Albania as "a poor man's Kazakhstan" remains to be seen, but it is likely that Kazakhstan's press secretary in the US, Roman Vassilenko, and others prefer such comparisons to those with the nation's troubled fellow Stans to the south (Uzbekistan, Kyrgyzstan, Turkmenistan, and Tajikistan).[28] In particular, Kazakhstanis are uncomfortable being grouped together with Afghanistan, which possesses an entirely different history and socioeconomic character. According to Vassilenko, "It is frustrating when we are lumped together with a country where girls were prevented from going to school for a decade and where the *burqa* is worn. The confusion with countries like Pakistan is also annoying."[29]

Kazakhstan's quiddity is based on being a resource-rich, multi-cultural, and stable outpost in an otherwise troubled region of the globe. Uncomfortable with the "Central Asian" stereotype that combines Soviet and Islamic legacies of autocracy and authoritarianism, the Kazakhstani government has sought numerous venues to present a positive image to the world.[30] These include hosting the 2011 Asian Winter Games, close cooperation with the North Atlantic Treaty Organization, expansion of the Baikonur Cosmodrome, and a major tourism infrastructure overhaul.[31] As Vassilenko states: "We are not a typical Stan because of our ethnic diversity, our role as a bridge to Europe, and a different mentality from our southern neighbors . . . we don't fit the stereotype of a Central Asian country." [32] While Vassilenko is quick to advertise the positive, there has been bad press as well, including a "poor" rating on human rights by the US State Department, Western criticism of the country's elections, and the "Kazakhgate" scandal, in which an American businessman allegedly paid $78 million in bribes to unnamed Kazakhstani officials to secure contracts for Western oil companies. As a major recipient of foreign direct investment (FDI) from the US and UK, Kazakhstan is extremely sensitive to any negative associations with its new and rather fragile brand in the West.

It is therefore not surprising that Baron Cohen touched a raw nerve with his increasingly high profile parodies of Kazakhstan and its people as "benighted and backward."[33] In late 2006, the character rose to global stardom with an eponymous feature-length film. The movie unfairly portrays the Central Asian republic as a medieval backwater populated by rapists and anti-Semites (see Chapter 6), a far cry from the reality of 21st century Kazakhstan with its modern skylines, well-educated and tech-savvy populace, and myriad ethnic and religious groups living in relative harmony.[34] While *Borat* is an undeniably grotesque and spurious representation of Kazakhstan and its people, the film has unexpectedly provided the country with a precipitous increase in its global profile, though one that comes at a hefty price.

Imagining Boratistan: The Battle for Control
of Kazakhstan's National Image

The premiere of the *Borat* film signaled the high-water mark in the controversy between the government of Kazakhstan and Sacha Baron Cohen. As explored in the previous chapter, the feud dates back to 2000 when the Kazakh diplomat Talgat Kaliyev condemned Borat's portrayal of his country stating: "We can take a joke like anyone else. But this has gone too far—it's a form of racism. We want Borat banned."[35] At the time, this was widely-viewed as a laughable overreaction, but as Sacha Baron Cohen increased his usage of Kazakhstan as an artistic tool to advance his own fame, it became clear that the comedian was doing a great disservice to the nation, though, as I will argue, Kazakhstan will reap the benefits of *Borat* long after Sacha Baron Cohen has exited the stage.

Towards Détente: Astana Seeks Redress on the "Borat Problem"

When foreign ministry spokesperson Yerzhan Ashykbayev declared Baron Cohen to be a potential foreign agent and threatened the comedian with legal action, Kazakhstan crossed the boundary from managing the Borat problem to actively—albeit unwittingly—contributing to Sacha Baron Cohen's comedic project. Prior to the MTV appearance, the government's policy towards its unwanted "son" was entirely appropriate. Given the young country's acute sensitivity to its perception abroad, particularly in the English-speaking world, its policies of cool disregard peppered with the occasional denial of the veracity of Borat's outlandish claims followed standard diplomatic protocols. When an official representative of the Kazakhstani government issued a thinly-veiled threat to the British comedian, however, Kazakhstan entered into uncharted political territory. The country had begun to wage war on a mass-mediated, fictional persona for the right to determine the content of Kazakhstan's national brand.

With the MTV Europe controversy, it had become undeniable that Kazakhstan's national brand was being hijacked by a foreign actor who was making a mockery of its people and customs through his absolutely preposterous "Boratistan" parody. While countries and corporations tend to have a dominant role in determining the content of their own brands, there are certain cases where the creator or owner of a product—whether it be a country, a firm, or a pair of sneakers—loses control of the discourse surrounding its product. This happened to Kazakhstan in early years of the 2000s as it sought to make itself known to a world obsessed with consumer culture, international terrorism, and American power (not necessarily in that order). In the mass-mediated global marketplace of ideas, Baron Cohen, as a hip and savvy social interlocutor, proved that he commanded more influence among certain segments of the "West" than did the Kazakhstani elite. In the words of Dickie Wallace: "For Baron Cohen's primary target audience in the west, Borat's representation of Kazakhstan [had] replaced the real Kazakhstan. And, if we consider Americans' notoriously poor sense of world geography, we can almost assume that for most, there may not have been any such original Kazakhstan in American thinking in the first place."[36] Kazakhstan, unlike some of its Central Asian peers, was (and is) dedicated to preserving its brand name, recognizing that without a protected brand, there is no brand.[37] Protecting the image of country is much more difficult than engaging in brand management of other products (clothing, refrigerators, cars, etc.). As van Ham points out, states have no monopoly over the use of their names; as such, those countries wishing to become "brand states"—that is, instantly recognizable polities which evoke positive associations among key actors in international politics and economics—must manage their external perceptions in new and innovative ways.[38] In effect, Sacha Baron Cohen forced Kazakhstan to either abandon its attempts to become a brand state or take him on in the global arena. They chose the latter.

While *Da Ali G Show* had no direct impact on Kazakhstan since it never aired there, this did not mean that it was insignificant.[39] The program did prove to have some influence on views of Kazakh culture held by those outside the country. As such, the popularity, ubiquity, and grotesqueness of Borat struck fear in the hearts of Kazakhstan's national elites, whose attempts at "imagining a community" and wooing the West were being disrupted by a British prankster.[40] Kazakhstan, by its very name and geopolitical location, is constantly forced to contend with negative stereotypes of authoritarianism, corruption, and instability. According to Rachid Nougmanov, a member of Kazakhstan's political opposition forces operating from London, "Most people in the West don't know anything about Kazakhstan. They just think we're between China and Dracula somewhere."[41] As such, Baron Cohen's ethno-national pantomime proved to be an acute danger to Astana's efforts to market the country to the Western masses. Reaching the upper echelons was not as difficult. The country's uranium, oil, and natural gas reserves, however, tend to figure prominently in the minds of Western multinational corporations. The country's firm stance against radical Islamism appeals to foreign policy elites. But postmodern statecraft takes more than just marketing to business executives and policymakers. To effectively brand a state, it takes a top-to-bottom approach focusing on both image and reputation, and reaching out to the masses, as well as traditional elites.[42]

Protecting "Brand Kazakhstan" in the UK and USA—the two countries where *Da Ali G Show* aired in its original form (though much of the show later became accessible in cyberspace)—is an especially sensitive issue. Taken together, multinational corporations based in these two countries command the lion's share of foreign direct investment (FDI) into Kazakhstan, accounting for nearly 50 percent of the country's overall FDI of $8.4 billion in 2004.[43] A positive brand is absolutely necessary for states seeking foreign investment, new security alliances, and diplomatic prowess.

> Globalization and the media revolution have made each state more aware of itself, its image, its reputation, and its attitude—in short, its brand . . . state branding is gradually supplanting nationalism. The brand state's use of its history, geography, and ethnic motifs to construct its own distinct image is a benign campaign that lacks the deep-rooted and often antagonistic sense of national identity and uniqueness that can accompany nationalism.[44]

While I am not entirely convinced that "old school" nationalism has been left by the wayside, my own interactions with Kazakhstani immigrants and elites within the country suggest they are more concerned with external views of their country and its ability to adapt to the global system rather than with the promotion of their own ideology over competing nationalisms. Unfortunately, Borat short-circuited the "benign process" of branding and began generating unwanted and unwarranted stereotypes for Kazakhstan. As one author put it, "Instead of being a regional leader and a growing economic and geopolitical power, Kazakhstan emerges as a country lost somewhere in the steppe, by turns absurd and quaint, but always gauche."[45] Add to this the complications of globalization that insidiously undermine the "naturalization of national identities through place, history, and ethno-racial origins" and a real problem emerges.[46]

Paradoxically, the ensuing controversy promoted tourism to Kazakhstan, something economic elites in Almaty and Astana have long desired and spent countless millions on making a reality. Many young Westerners realized that Baron Cohen's Boratistan was purely a plot device for his strange brand of humor. As a result, they wished to learn more about the real Kazakhstan. Kazakhstan's embassy in the UK reported record numbers of visa applications for British tourists in the wake of the MTV awards

show, which ambassadorial staff readily attributed to Borat's burlesque.[47]
"More people are applying for visas to Kazakhstan than ever. . . . It seems
that many are intrigued by [Borat] and he's introduced them to the country."
The official added: "There will be no legal action against Mr. Cohen. Our
country is a democratic nation and we recognize the right for freedom of
speech. We understand that it is satire and it appears his target is not the
Kazakh people but foreigners stupid enough to believe all this rubbish about
our country."[48] This unintended outcome was not a trivial one. According to
Morgan, "Branding is perhaps the most powerful marketing weapon available to temporary destination marketers confronted by increasing product
parity, substitutability and competition."[49] While Borat may have intrigued
many Westerners by drawing their attention to Kazakhstan and then telling
them nothing factual about it, *Borat*'s deft exposure of American homophobia, racism, and anti-Semitism contributed to the branding of the United
States, or at least some of its regions, as an undesirable destination.

Despite the serendipitous increase in British tourism, Astana's denunciations of Borat grew in intensity. Governmental representatives spent both
time and effort in the first half of 2006 berating Sacha Baron Cohen and
trying to tame Kazakhstan's anarchic brand. In the late summer of 2006, a
rumor started to circulate in international circles that President Nazarbayev
was planning to ask his American counterpart, George W. Bush, to "do
something about Borat" during their October meeting at the White House.[50]
This rumor quickly emerged as a starting point for the media's discussion of
Kazakhstan's national image, much to the chagrin of those who managed
the country's brand. A case in point, Richard Goldstein argued that the government's "vehement" response to the comedian's antics saved the film
from fading into "date-movie oblivion" by endowing Baron Cohen with
"politically incorrect creds."[51] (In fact, neither the comedian nor the movie
was discussed at the presidential summit. According to government sources,
this was a strategic decision in order to deny the movie further promotion
and publicity.)[52] *Guardian* film critic Peter Bradshaw goes further: "The
taxpayers from the sovereign state of Kazakhstan have been lavishly subsi-
dizing the publicity for Baron Cohen's new movie with fury-filled full-page
government ads in the *New York Times* [and] a personal complaint from the
Kazakh president to Mr. George W. Bush."[53] While Bradshaw's description
"fury-filled" is wildly off-the-mark, the author's own discussions with Kazakhstan's political elite suggest that there was a good deal of ire directed at
the comedian and some of that translated into greater spending on public
diplomacy efforts. However, as explored later, Kazakhstan ultimately came
to welcome Baron Cohen's spoofery.

Baron Cohen seems to have done everything in his power to goad Astana into further condemnation, hoping that a perceived over-reaction on the
part of the Kazakhstani government would function as a valuable add-on to
his unorthodox marketing campaign. Baron Cohen was no longer employing
Kazakhstan because it was unknown. Ironically, he was now hoping to leverage the previously mysterious and even "unreal" country of Kazakhstan to
gain access to the various mechanisms of public diplomacy to market his
film.[54] The comedian's ability to deftly re-vector his game plan is not surprising, for when it comes to courting controversy to raise his own profile,
Baron Cohen is an experienced operator. Long before bringing his act to the
United States, he provoked public outcry in Britain with his gratuitous use

of foul language, parody of blacks, and insensitive comments about gays and the physically-handicapped, seemingly only to garner larger viewing audiences. By eschewing interviews out-of-character and maintaining strict secrecy about his private life, Baron Cohen has been able to shield himself from having to answer his critics. Despite the fact that his humor insulted the Kazakhstani government, Kazakh immigrants in the US and the UK, and the families of thousands of Kazakhstani adoptees in the West, Sacha Baron Cohen demonstrated no remorse as the movie's premiere approached.

Not all Kazakhstanis were displeased by Baron Cohen's interloping. Responding to his nation's new-found popularity, the Kazakh novelist Sapabek Asip-uly called on the Kazakh Club of Art Patrons to give Baron Cohen its annual award for popularizing Kazakhstan, stating: "[Borat] has managed to spark an immense interest of the whole world in Kazakhstan, something our authorities could not do during the years of independence." He further noted, "I truly hope my initiative will be supported for the benefit of the glorious nation of Kazakhstan."[55] Diasporic Kazakhstanis, generally quite proud of their country, did what they could to dispel the Boratian ramblings by giving interviews to the press and engaging in people-to-people diplomacy.[56] According to one, "Before *Borat* I had to tell people I was from Russia because they had no idea what or where Kazakhstan was. Now at least, they know the country and that it's different from Russia" (female Kazakhstani, age 23).

While most parents of children adopted from Kazakhstan loathe Borat, most of those with whom I spoke suggest it is now easier to talk to people about their children's birth country because, in the words of one mother, "Borat is memorable . . . he makes Kazakhstan stick in people's minds" (adoptive mother, age 49). A Kazakhstani living in the US stated, "Borat gave me a chance to tell people about my country, the people, and other things. It wasn't just some far away place anymore. Now it was a real country and they ask lots of questions about it" (female Kazakhstani, age 42). Another stated, "I wouldn't say that it was the best venue to start educating Americans about Kazakhstan, but, in the absence of any[thing else], it's a start" (male Kazakhstani, age 28). In a *Washington Post* editorial entitled "My 'Glorious Nation of Kazakhstan,'" Gauhar Abdygaliyeva, a Kazakh student studying in America echoed some of these findings: "The movie has already created unprecedented interest in Kazakhstan. Not only has Borat promoted our name and flag, he has also indirectly fueled a great wave of patriotism among my fellow citizens."[57]

Gradually, a subtle shift towards Borat began among the Kazakhstani political elite. Dariga Nazarbayeva, the president's daughter and then heir-apparent, grumbled in April 2006 that the Borat website "damaged our image much less than its closure, which was covered by all global news agencies." The former head of the state-run news organ *Khabar* went on to state, "We should not be afraid of humor and we shouldn't try to control everything."[58] This modest reorientation signaled by Dariga Nazarbayev's criticism soon gave way to a complete revision of Kazakhstan's position on Borat as it became clear that Baron Cohen's "moviefilm" was going to achieve both critical and commercial success.[59]

An advance screening at the Toronto Film Festival produced a significant buzz for the motion picture, and enabled Borat, i.e., Baron Cohen, to dominate the American talk show circuit in the crucial weeks before the movie's premiere. At the Toronto premiere of "his" movie in September 2006, Borat responded to the question of whether Kazakhstan is oppressive with "Yes—Thank you very much." It is possible to read this response two ways. The first is to take it as a Boratian quip. The alternative reading suggests that Sacha Baron Cohen's own "voice" is bleeding through, and he is expressing his gratitude to the Kazakhstani government for creating serendipitous buzz for his new movie. While *Ali G Indahouse* went straight to video in the US market, *Borat* was already shaping up as one of the most anticipated movies of the fall season.

Borat also benefited from an innovative Web-based marketing strategy backed by the film's production company, Twentieth Century Fox, which is owned by Rupert Murdoch's News Corp. The social networking site MySpace, currently the world's fourth most popular English-language website, used *Borat* to launch its new "Black Carpet" service which allows selected MySpace members to pre-screen movies. According to *AdWeek*, "The goal of Black Carpet is to encourage MySpace users to build buzz for a movie before its release. . . . Nearly every movie released now has a MySpace page, where fans can add it as a "friend." Black Carpet will promote the featured film's profiles. Borat's MySpace page already has 111,000 friends."[60] However, *Borat*'s greatest asset was Baron Cohen's tireless guerrilla marketing, which included dozens of in-character appearances on various mainstream American talk shows and news programs before the film's release.

A memorable example of Baron Cohen's unorthodox self-promotion occurred on 29 September 2006, when Borat called a press conference outside the Kazakhstani embassy in Washington, DC to coincide with President Nazarbayev's visit to the White House. Flanked by stony-faced, Stalinesque actors, Borat made several spurious claims about "his" country before threatening to bombard the "evil nitwits" of Uzbekistan with his catapults in response to their vicious "propaganda campaign" against his movie. While this act of marketing was ingenious, it was also irresponsible. Kazakh-Uzbek relations are fairly sensitive, and have been further complicated by Uzbekistan's estrangement from the international community since the 2005 Andijan massacre.[61] While a few savvy Americans might have chuckled at Baron Cohen's threats to Kazakhstan's southern neighbor, the risk vastly outweighed the reward.

In his mention of "propaganda," Borat made reference to Kazakhstan's ongoing multimillion-dollar "Heart of Eurasia" advertising campaign. Some members of the Western press cynically characterized the campaign as a response to the Boratistan parody, but the new program was simply an expansion of growing public diplomacy effort in the US, the UK, Russia, and China.[62] Since 2001, Kazakhstan has regularly placed ads in the *Washington Post*, but beginning in 2006 an attempt was made to branch out to a larger pool of opinion leaders in the United States. This shift was reflective of a deepening relationship between the US and Kazakhstan and timed to coincide with American Vice-President Cheney's springtime visit to Kazakhstan and President Nazarbayev's autumnal trip to the United States.

The new campaign included spots on local DC television stations and informational inserts and ads in *New York Times, Foreign Affairs, Newsweek, Fortune,* and the *International Herald Tribune*. The messaging focused on the following themes: 1) tolerance and efforts to spread such policies across the region; 2) energy production and stability; 3) Kazakhstan as a friend and partner to the US in the "war on terror;" and 4) Kazakhstan as a modern country. While Borat's anti-diplomacy may have had some impact on the tone of the advertisements, the bilious reporter does not deserve the lion's share of credit for the campaign itself. However, Vassilenko confirmed that forthcoming programs will take the "Borat effect" into account explaining, "We plan to reorient our branding campaign to a younger audience. We will be focusing less on heavy political issues and more on culture and tourism."[63] This is an especially interesting finding. With its Tengiz oil field, a propitious location between East Asia and Europe, and solid relationships with Russia and China, Kazakhstan can easily afford to ignore public—that is, non-elite—opinion in the West. That it has chosen not to underscores the country's multifaceted, long-term plan for achieving internationally recognized greatness in the 21st century.[64]

Kazakhstan, while still condemning Borat's representation of Kazakhs as ludicrous, started to get in on the joke as the movie's premiere approached. In October, Kazakhstan's deputy foreign minister, Rakhat Aliyev, invited Baron Cohen to visit his country. Not surprisingly, the comedian demurred. He would have either had to visit as Sacha Baron Cohen, with all the fanfare and press scrutiny that such a departure from his modus operandi would entail, or as Borat, in which case he would have faced the entirely appropriate indignation of a wronged nation. In another deft move, Kazakhstan enlisted one its most popular comedians, Jantemir Baimukhamedov, to attend the London premiere of *Borat*, where he handed out free horsemeat sausages and dispelled myths about his homeland.[65] Most notably, Kazakhstan's ambassador to the United Kingdom Erlan Idrissov, who had condemned Baron Cohen's characterizations of his country as "racist and slanderous" in early October 2006, penned an editorial after the film's premiere thanking Baron Cohen for drumming up the "kind of media attention of which previously I could only dream."[66] Despite the massive capital investment in what has been officially termed "educational" advertising about Kazakhstan and its people, Idrissov admitted, "The reality is that the only thing many millions of people in the West know about Kazakhstan—or think they know—comes from Borat." [67] In the words of Idrissov, Borat had "put Kazakhstan on the map."[68]

This is no mean feat. Despite the fact that Kazakhstan is the ninth largest country in the world and will soon rank as its fifth-largest oil exporter, before *Borat* few Americans could distinguish it from "Kreplachistan," i.e., the fictional country which is repeatedly referenced in the *Austin Powers* films. Unfortunately this recognition has come at a hefty price.[69] The *Economist* framed Kazakhstan's dilemma succinctly:

> For 15 years you have tried to make the world aware of your newly born country. It is huge—the size of Western Europe—rich in natural resources, modernizing fast. But progress is frustratingly slow. Then a pestilential foreign comedian makes you (in)famous overnight, for grotesque but fictional squalor, cruelty and vulgarity. Should you be pleased, cross or both?[70]

The answer to this rhetorical question lies in a country's wherewithal to change perceptions once its brand has exploded on the marketplace. Kazakhstan possesses both the desire and capacity to re-brand itself. More importantly, the country has much to gain from such an undertaking. That being said, Kazakhstan is in need of a massive post-*Borat* brand management effort. But as Jeremy Kahn points out, re-branding countries is not as simple as slapping a new label on an old product and then spending millions on TV campaigns. It needs to be backed up with "real work—reforming legal systems, building new roads, [and] reducing poverty—[which] can take decades."[71] However, Kazakhstan has done all that and more since the collapse of the USSR fifteen years ago. Successful reforms include an economy which has grown by 10% or more the past five years, a reduction in the percentage of the population living below the poverty line from 40% to 16% since 2001, and a five-fold increase in average income over the past decade. Furthermore, Kazakhstan has recently expanded its diplomatic presence and helped found the important regional security alliance, the Shanghai Cooperation Organization.

Learning to Love Boratistan: Re-branding Kazakhstan in Sacha Baron Cohen's Wake

Defining and defending Kazakshilik ('Kazakhness'), or more accurately Kazakstanshilik, i.e., what it means to be from Kazakhstan, have gone hand-in-hand since independence. In a perfect world, Kazakhstan's national brand would be the result of the work of the state in the realms of politics, economics, science, sport, and culture. In the postmodern, interconnected world of MTV, iPods, and YouTube, Kazakhstan has to deal with the likes of Borat as well, an alternate and unwelcome narrator of Kazakhness. As Philip Kotler and David Gertner point out, "The entertainment industry and the media play a particularly important role in shaping people's perceptions of place, especially those viewed negatively."[72] Unlike their counterparts in Turkmenistan and Uzbekistan who appear to care little about global opinion, Kazakhstani elites crave international respect and to be welcomed into the club of First World nations. However, as Martinović points out, national brand management is "not a simple operation, as no country can determine its identity by itself."[73] Other actors, both genuine and spurious, have the ability to affect global views of the nation.

As globalization becomes more deeply embedded, the proliferation of voices grows more cacophonous and the state's domination over its messaging becomes more difficult. "With worldwide proliferation of media technologies and facile and affordable information access, the credibility and efficacy of the national government, as the primary communicator, are now often suspect."[74] The issue is further problematized when governments are forced to confront evocative, mass-mediated narratives about their countries whether through films such as *Blood Diamond* (Sierra Leone), novels such as *The Kite Runner* (Afghanistan), or television programs like the National Geographic Channel's *Worlds Apart* (Kenya).[75] According to Edward Schatz, "transnational images are difficult to manage. Their sources are varied, they travel easily across physical space, completely preventing their distribution is impossible, they emerge quickly and sporadically, and they are mediated and transformed by many layers of cultural difference."[76]

Nevertheless, Kazakhstan, like other modern nations, is committed to managing its brand. In 2008, the government plans to establish a Committee on International Information within the Ministry of Foreign Affairs to coordinate branding activities across various agencies of the government that deal with the public.[77] There are two audiences for Kazakhstan's brand: opinion-makers and everyone else. Vassilenko states:

> We need to be clear that there are distinctions between the multinational corporations, academics, and political elites in the [USA] who are savvy about the country and the general public who are not aware of Kazakhstan's existence. When the latter saw the Borat movie, they did not realize it was a real country. Today, there is a trend toward greater name recognition. Tens of millions don't know about Kazakhstan and don't care to know about it. We are not particularly concerned about reaching these people. We are most concerned with opinion leader. . . . However, [Borat] put Kazakhstan on the map for people who did not know us before. As I have said before, this was a blessing in "heavy disguise." There is the matter of how we were put on the map and how we should use this opportunity. It is going to take a lot of work.

When initially confronted with the Boratian nightmare, Kazakhstan tried to manage and then quash the threat. However, as the Boratistan parody grew in both scale and scope, Astana wisely responded by engaging Borat's antics in a panoply of ways in an effort to raise its country profile and expand the reach of its national image. When asked if he had any regrets about the way he or his government handled the battle over Borat, Vassilenko responded tellingly:

> No regrets. Perhaps the only one is that we have not done more to capitalize on the opportunity. [Baron Cohen] helped us do our job. The original condemnation [of Borat] prompted more questions from the media which in turn led to further opportunities to discuss Kazakhstan. If we had laughed it off or ignored it, we wouldn't be anywhere near where we are today in terms of recognition and public visibility. Many countries ignore negative portrayals. You can afford to do this only if you have the advantage of a national brand which is already established. Our brand is in its infancy. It was important to protest and use every wave of interest created by the protests to maximize our opportunities.[78]

According to Anholt, "Having a brand means living in the limelight, with all the benefits and obligations this confers. . . . It is within the power and nature of brands to bring transparency, honesty and fairness to all transactions."[79] Under international media scrutiny, there came a realization that a new realpolitik was required for dealing with external threats to the national identity. In the words of Schatz, "Kazakhstan, for all its energy wealth and emergent ability to project power regionally, could not contend with Hollywood's resources and marketing expertise, as well as the commercial muscle of the world's most powerful consumer driven society."[80] Growing consciousness of the vagaries of the "global supermarket" of nation brands bleeds through in Ambassador Idrissov's ruminations on why Baron Cohen picked his country as a comedic vehicle:[81]

We are an easy target. Borat could have been made the citizen of a country
with a truly awful record on human rights—say Afghanistan in the days of
the Taliban. But that would have been risky for Baron Cohen. Many
Kazakhs who have seen Borat on television have been offended and
incredulous. But the critics of my country, including Baron Cohen, are
more likely to receive an invitation to address their concerns at an
expenses-paid conference in Kazakhstan than they are to receive a fatwa.
Nor does Kazakhstan have the advantages of a well-connected diaspora to
defend its interests in the same way as Israelis, Palestinians or Armenians.
Again, Baron Cohen could have caricatured a powerful developing
country—like Turkey, Brazil or India—but there would have been sharp
reactions, perhaps even at a political level.[82]

Although Baron Cohen is often applauded for his comedic bravery, it seems
he may have chosen his target for reasons of safety. His previous loci for the
Borat character were Moldova and Albania.[83] Had he preserved either of
these or chosen another "Stan" as his cover, he might have faced legal or
political hurdles and may have even put himself in harm's way. Kazakhstan,
as a country worried about world opinion, treated him quite well much to its
own credit. The managers of Brand Kazakhstan essentially took lemons and
decided, after painful consideration, to make lemonade.

This change in policy became readily apparent in autumn 2006 when
official publications including *Kazakhstan's Echo,* a government-issued
periodical, and the official newsletter of the Embassy of Kazakhstan to the
USA and Canada began to market the country via the mass-market vehicle
of *Borat.* In late October 2006, *Kazakhstan News Bulletin's* lead story was
"Our Take on Borat" which highlighted key positive attributes of Kazakhstan, including its voluntary decommissioning of the world's forth largest nuclear arsenal, religious harmony, and US foreign direct investment.[84]
The 2 November 2006 issue which came out a day before the film's US
premiere included the header: "Today, we offer our readers three stories on
what the people in and around Kazakhstan do to make Kazakhstan better
known in America and bring our peoples closer. These stories are also telling about how different people in Kazakhstan and in the United States react
to the upcoming movie 'Borat.'"[85] The issue's lead story heralded the
launch of two Borat-themed vacation itineraries by Sayat Tours entitled
"Kazakhstan vs. Boratistan" and "Jagzhemash!!! See the Real Kazakhstan."[86] The article included a quote from Marianna Tolekenova,
Sayat's Executive Director, stating: "With the release of Borat: Cultural
Learnings of America for Make Benefit Glorious Nation of Kazakhstan, we
are hoping many Americans will want to engage in 'cultural learnings' of
that unknown 'glorious nation' for their own 'make benefit.' That is why we
are launching these new tours and hoping the Americans will come visit us."
Kazakhstan's Ministry of Tourism has since begun sponsoring press junkets
for tourism reporters from select countries to generate increased press coverage in the West, particularly Western Europe.

Just after the film's debut, the embassy helped introduce the inaugural
issue of the new Central Asian-themed magazine *Steppe.* Piggybacking on
the presumed success of Baron Cohen's movie, the first sentence in the ad-
vertisement reads: "Central Asia—one of the least known and understood
regions of the world—is the perfect home for this autumn's hottest comedian: BORAT SAGDIEV. Perfect, because few people know much about

Kazakhstan, or any of the 'stans that make up the region, which has allowed Borat to use his interviewees' ignorance to brilliant comic effect."[87] Throughout the month of November, *Echo* and the *News Bulletin* continued to use *Borat*'s popularity as a springboard for getting out the "good word" on Kazakhstan. This included providing a reprint of a *Washington Post* article on Central Asian (particularly Kazakh) high fashion entitled "Forget 'Borat': Fashion Looks from the 'Stans," and a synopsis of the *Rolling Stone* interview in which Baron Cohen begged forgiveness of Kazakhs for his portrayal, stating the joke was on those who actually believe there is a country where "homosexuals wear blue hats."[88]

The most important development in the "Battle over Borat" was chronicled in the 22 November 2006 issue of the *News Bulletin*. The lead story recounted President Nazarbayev's about-face on Borat in which he declared that there is no such thing as bad publicity. "This film was created by a comedian so let's laugh at it, that's my attitude."[89] According to ethnographer Steven S. Lee, Nazarbayev had good reason to reevaluate his opinion of Baron Cohen's antics since the media circus had obviated the need to conduct damage control on other sensitive issues. "As a result, when Kazakhstani president Nursultan Nazarbaev visited the White House just prior to *Borat*'s release, almost no coverage was devoted to his government's alleged human rights violations, nor to the long-delayed New York trial of James Giffen, a businessman accused of funneling millions of dollars from U.S. oil companies to the Nazarbaev family."[90] At the press conference, Nazarbayev jokingly added, "Maybe the journalist himself Borat Sagdiyev is here representing Kazakhstan? I would very much like to speak to him if he is." The turnabout, which occurred during a joint press conference with British Prime Minister Tony Blair, represented the symbolic end of a six-year struggle that had produced significant financial, political, and cultural changes for Kazakhstan. In a curious juxtaposition of Borat-style branding and state-crafted messaging, Britain's *Spectator* magazine published a 23 November 2006 article penned by Kazakhstan's president with the following header: "In this exclusive article, Nursultan Nazarbayev presents a different picture of his homeland to the caricature of Sacha Baron Cohen's film. It is a thriving, optimistic nation. We like!"[91] The use of the Borat catchphrase 'we like' to introduce an important public statement by the leader of the world's ninth largest country speaks volumes about how deeply embedded Baron Cohen's branding had become.

"Glorious Kazakhstan": Battered, but Branded for the 21st Century

While still chafing at Borat's spurious characterizations, the Kazakhstani elite ultimately made the best of what began as a humiliating experience brought on by the gross misrepresentations of the Boratistan parody. Despite this willingness to negotiate what Kazakshilik means in the West, the decision to keep Borat out of the nation's theatres showed that the government remains intensely concerned about protecting Kazakhstanis' fragile national identity at home. Yet, the country's political elite seems to have settled into a querulous yet symbiotic relationship with Baron Cohen beyond its borders. This paradoxical turn of events stems from the way in which much of the West has been affected by the Borat parody. As van

Ham sees it, "Branding goes beyond PR and marketing. It tries to transform products and services as well as places into something more by giving them an emotional dimension with which people can identify. Branding touches those parts of the human psyche which rational arguments just cannot reach."[92] *Borat* has touched people, though not in the way that Kazakhstani elites could have ever imagined or would have necessarily wanted. Regardless, a connection has been made. Anholt argues that this is a watershed event for the Kazakhstanis. "At least they have a reputation now. It may be a bad one, but it's much easier to turn a negative into a positive than nothing into something."[93] It is also important to note that Borat's impact on the Kazakhstan's brand is likely to be ephemeral considering the average lifespan of a country versus that of a comedian.

As a new, potentially wealthy country with a relatively small population, Kazakhstan has some built-in advantages when it comes to taming its currently out-of-control brand. "Young nations are in a unique position to brand themselves because they are at an early stage of development and . . . any negative perceptions or associations . . . have not yet had time to embed themselves. Smaller, younger countries may have smaller populations, and are leaner, meaner and easier to manage. They have citizens who feel a greater loyalty and drive to serve their country and potentially to realize its brand."[94] Kazakhstanis, who see themselves as tolerant, hospitable, and generous people, demonstrated these tendencies throughout the Borat debacle and thus helped market their country by showcasing these values. Expatriates in the west rallied around the flag, not because of war or even sports, but out of pride in their nation when it was besmirched by a British mountebank. The parents of Kazakhstanis adopted into the United States have also emerged as vociferous defenders of the country's national image, using every opportunity to re-brand Kazakhstan in positive ways.[95] Additionally, Borat has endowed "Brand Kazakhstan" with an elusive trait that cannot be bought at any price: *the "cool" factor.* Kazakhstani symbols now adorn countless Borat T-shirts, buttons, magnets, and other paraphernalia which can be purchased in novelty shops and over the Internet. Just like the British and Swiss flags, the Kazakhstani flag is now fashionable. Although the residual "funhouse" version of Kazakhstan somewhat taints this public relations coup, Astana has demonstrated both the will and the capacity to capitalize on its incipient "Glorious Kazakhstan" brand, though much hard work still lies ahead to turn this into a genuine victory in nation branding.

The country's domestic political situation remains the greatest impediment to realizing this goal. Coincidentally, Rakhat Aliyev, whose quote opened this chapter, personifies Kazakhstan's image problems in this arena. Aliyev, who was married to Dariga Nazarbayeva until June 2007, ultimately did torpedo his career with Borat playing a small part in his downfall. The president's (now former) son-in-law made his own presidential ambitions overly clear in 2007, which may have led to an international arrest warrant being issued for his alleged role in a banking scandal and kidnap case. Attempting to avoid extradition from Austria to his home country, Aliyev publicly criticized Nazarbayev's personal rule by paraphrasing Borat. He suggested that both he and Borat would only be free to run for the office of president when the next elections are held in 2045.[96] This very public spat within the Nazarbayev clan has once again underscored the Byzantine nature of power and political culture in Kazakhstan, a country where power rests solely within the presidential palace. Returning to the protagonist of this narrative, in all his various representations of Kazakhstan and Kazakh national identity, Sacha Baron Cohen (Borat) has gotten it dead wrong—with one important exception. At a patriot rally in the United States, Borat was asked the following question by an American woman: "Are you totally free in your country?" After an uncharacteristic moment of introspection, Borat replied, "Not so much."

Notes

1. See "Kazakh Official to Borat: Come Visit," *Associated Press,* 16 October 2006.

2. Boulding distinguishes between *elites,* i.e., "the small group of people who make the actual decisions which lead to war or peace, the making or breaking of treaties, the invasions or withdrawals, alliances, and enmities which make up the major events of international relations," and the *masses,* i.e., "ordinary people who are deeply effected by these decisions but who take little or no direct part in making them;" see Kenneth E. Boulding, "National Images and International Systems," *The Journal of Conflict Resolution* 3, no. 2 (June 1959): 120-131.

3. See Frank Louis Rusciano, "The Construction of National Identity—A 23-Nation Study," *Political Research Quarterly* 56, no. 3 (September 2003): 361-366.

4. Joseph S. Nye, Jr., *Soft Power: The Means to Success in World Politics* (New York: Public Affairs, 2004), 11-15.

5. See Robert Keohane, *After Hegemony: Cooperation and Discord in the World Political Economy* (Princeton: Princeton University Press, 1984), 116 and Ole R. Holsti, "The Belief System and National images: A Case Study," *The Journal of Conflict Resolution* 5, no. 3 (September 1962): 244-252.

6. Philip Kotler and David Gertner, "Country as Brand, Product, and Beyond: A Place Marketing and Brand Management Perspective," *Brand Management* 9, nos. 4-5 (April 2002): 249-261; cited in Ingeborg Astrid Kleppe, "Country Images in Marketing Strategies: Conceptual Issues and an Empirical Asian Illustration," *Brand Management* 10, no. 1 (September 2002): 61–74.

7. Rusciano, "The Construction of National Identity," 361.

8. Wally Olins, "Branding the Nation—The Historical Context," *Brand Management* 9, nos. 4-5 (April 2002): 241-248.

9. John Lloyd, "Cool Britannia Warms Up," *New Statesman* 127, no. 4376 (12 March 1998): 10-11.

10. While "Cool Britannia" may have attempted to brand the nation as "straight," the successful BBC comedy series *Little Britain* (2003-2005) has done much to erase such marketing by implying that nearly everyone in the country (perhaps even the Blairesque Prime Minister himself) is gay. Interestingly, one of the show's two writers, Matt Lucas, attended Sacha Baron Cohen's alma mater, Haberdashers' Aske's Boys School. Further deepening the Baron Cohen connection, HBO has also licensed Lucas and his co-writer David Walliams to create an American version of *Little Britain,* using what has become known as "Da Ali G Show" model for converting British comedies into American fare; Lloyd, "Cool Britannia," 10.

11. Daniel H. Pink, "The Brand Called UK," *Fast Company* 22 (January 1999): 172.

12. J. E. Peterson, "Qatar and the World: Branding for a Micro-State," *Middle East Journal* 60, no. 4 (Autumn 2006): 732-48; See Dace Dzenovska, "Remaking the Nation of Latvia: Anthropological Perspectives on Nation Branding," *Place Branding* 1, no. 2 (March 2005): 173–186; Nigel Morgan, Annette Pritchard, and Rachel Piggott, "New Zealand, 100% Pure. The Creation of Power Niche Destination Brand," *Brand Management* 9, nos. 4-5 (April 2002): 335-354.

13. The inverse is also true; according to the architect of the "Cool Britannia" strategy, Geoff Mulgan, "When a nation builds an attractive brand, it creates a patina—an "identity premium"—that attaches to businesses operating out of that country;" see Pink, "The Brand Called UK," 172.

14. Peter van Ham, "The Rise of the Brand State: The Postmodern Politics of Image and Reputation," *Foreign Affairs* 80, no. 5 (September-October 2001): 2-7.

15. Peterson, "Qatar and the World," 746.

16. Simon Anholt, "Forward," *Brand Management* 9, nos. 4-5 (April 2002): 229-239; see, also, Simon Anholt, *Competitive Identity: The New Brand Management for Nations, Cities and Regions* (New York: Palgrave Macmillan, 2007).

17. Anholt, "Anholt-GMI Nation Brands Index."

18. Jorge de Vicente, *State Branding in the 21st Century*, Master of Arts in Law and Diplomacy Thesis, The Fletcher School of Diplomacy at Tufts University (May 2004), 1.

19. Nicolas Papadopoulos and Louise Heslop, "Country Equity and Country Branding: Problems and Prospects," *Brand Management* 9, nos. 4-5 (April 2002): 294-314.

20. de Vincente, *State Branding*, 4.

21. Stefan Paul Jaworski and Don Fosher, "National Brand Identity & Its Effect on Corporate Brands: The Nation Brand Effect," *Multinational Business Review* 11, no. 2 (Fall 2003): 99-113.

22. William Grimes, "Japan as the 'Indispensable Nation' in Asia: A Financial Brand for the 21st Century," *Asia-Pacific Review* 12, no. 1 (May 2005): 40-54.

23. In 1991, the Soviet Union's fifteen socialist republics (Russia, Ukraine, Belarus, Moldova, Estonia, Latvia, Lithuania, Georgia, Armenia, Azerbaijan, Kazakhstan, Uzbekistan, Turkmenistan, Kyrgyzstan, and Tajikistan) gained independence. Since that time, certain break-away regions—such as Transnistria (in eastern Moldova), Abkhazia (a region of Georgia), and Chechnya (an ethnic republic of the Russian Federation)—have claimed sovereignty. However, they have all, thus far, failed to secure international recognition as independent states. Each of the Socialist Federal Republic of Yugoslavia's six constituent republics ultimately gained independence, though only Croatia and Slovenia functioned as independent states by the end of 1991. Czechoslovakia's dissolution in 1993 added two more countries to the grouping.

24. Vladimir Lebedenko, "Russia's National Identity and Image-Building," *International Affairs: A Russian Journal of World Politics, Diplomacy & International Relations* 50, no. 4 (September-October 2004): 71-77.

25. See Lebedenko, "Russia's National Identity."

26. Quoted in Clay Risen, "Branding Nations," *New York Times Magazine* 155, no. 53425 (11 December 2005): 61.

27. My usage of this rather informal term to describe the former Soviet states of Central Asia is a reflection of Kazakhstan's own branding strategy. The term is regularly used by diplomatic personnel in formal settings, including public statements, press interviews, etc.

28. Interestingly, Albania has itself been the victim of remarkably similar attacks on its nation brand. For instance, J. K. Rowling has repeatedly depicted Albania as a den of iniquity in her fabulously successful *Harry Potter* series. Gëzim Alpion writes, "I do not know why, of all countries, Rowling has chosen Albania as the place that harbours evil creatures. If she has done this for a laugh, then this is a cheap and irresponsible laugh at the expense of a European country that has become small, 'insignificant' and 'voiceless' largely as a result of political witchcraft and wizardry practiced beyond its artificially drawn and imposed borders. I am inclined to believe that Rowling's choice of Albania is an indication of the intellectual arrogance and ignorance often displayed by Western authors when writing about, to borrow Edward W. Said's phrase, 'lesser peoples.' By choosing Albania as the right habitat for

the evil to reside in, Rowling reveals how little she knows about the world beyond the British shores, and in particular about a tiny spot like Albania;" Gëzim Alpion, "Images of Albania and Albanians in English Literature from Edith Durham's *High Albania* to J. K. Rowling's *Harry Potter*," *BESA Journal* 6, no. 2 (Spring 2002): 30-34; see Jon Stewart, "Albaniacs," *The Daily Show with Jon Stewart* (4 June 2007).

29. Roman Vassilenko. Interview by author, Embassy of the Republic of Kazakhstan, Washington, DC (13 April 2007).

30. See, for instance, Yaacov Ro'i, "Introduction," in Y. Ro'i, ed., *Democracy and Pluralism in Muslim Eurasia* (London: Frank Cass, 2004). Stephen Kotkin described the region as a "dreadful checkerboard of parasitic states and statelets, government-led extortion rackets and gangs in power, mass refugee camps, and shadow economies;" see Stephen Kotkin, "Trashcanistan," *New Republic* 226, no. 14 (15 April 2002): 26-38.

31. Baikonur Cosmodrome is the oldest and largest operational space facility in the world. It was the site of the launch of *Sputnik* in 1957 and Yuri Gagarin's first manned-spaceflight aboard *Vostok 1* in 1961. While the site remains Russia's primary location for launching space missions, it also serves the growing needs of international corporations which are dependent on satellite technologies.

32. In a 2005 interview with *National Public Radio*, Kazakhstan's press secretary in the US stated, "Every Stan is very different and Kazakhstan right now is a Stan like no other;" see Madeleine Brand, "Kazakhstan Not Laughing at TV's 'Ali G,'" *NPR's Day to Day*, 17 November 2005.

33. "By the Horns," *New Republic,* 235, no. 16 (16 October 2006): 7.

34. While the country does have much to brag about, there is a growing gap between rich and poor, the countryside remains underdeveloped, and ethnically-charged clashes are not unknown (usually this involves disputes between Uzbeks and Kazakhs, but recently there have been problems with the country's Chechens as well). However, it should be said that Kazakhstan shares these problems with even the most "developed" of the former Soviet republics, such as Estonia and Latvia.

35. John Harris, "When Ali G Went to Kazakhstan," *Independent*, Features Sec. (26 April 2000), 1.

36. Dickie Wallace, "Hyperrealizing 'Borat' with the Map of the European 'Other,'" *Slavic Review* 66, no. 1 (Spring 2008): 35-49.

37. See Robert E. Moore, "From Genericide to Viral Marketing: On 'Brand,'" *Language and Communication* 23, nos. 3-4 (July-October 2003): 331-357.

38. See van Ham, "The Rise of the Brand State."

39. While some in Kazakhstan may have been able to view the program via bootlegged DVDs and some satellite television services, I did not encounter a single Kazakhstani who was familiar with the program until the months after the MTV Europe imbroglio in 2005. My discussions with Kazakhstani-Americans elicited similar findings, i.e., their friends and relations did not know of Borat until 2006.

40. I borrow here from Benedict Anderson's *Imagined Communities*.

41. Mary Wiltenburg, "Backstory: The Most Unwanted Man in Kazakhstan," *Christian Science Monitor*, 30 November 2005.

42. van Ham, "The Rise of the Brand State," 3-5.

43. The US was the largest contributor of FDI in 2004 with $3.1 billion and British investment totaled $924 million; "News & Trends: Central Asia," *Alexander's Gas & Oil Connection*, 10, no. 9 (10 May 2005), http://www.gasandoil.com/goc/news/ntc51936.htm (12 December 2005). In 2006, the US accounted for 27 percent of Kazakhstan's total FDI of $6 billion.

44. van Ham, "The Rise of the Brand State," 3.

45. "Kazakhstan: Ali G and the Emperor's New Clothes," *Transitions Online*, 28 November 2005, http://www.tol.cz/.

46. Sallie Westwood, "Re-Branding Britain: Sociology, Futures and Futurology," *Sociology* 34, no. 1 (February 2000): 185-202.

47. The foreign currency firm Travelex was recently forced to increase its reservoir of the tenge, Kazakhstan's currency, to accommodate the increased demand by British travelers; see Laura Bly, "Finding the Real Kazakhstan," *USA Today*, 16 November 2006.

48. Andy Lea, "Come Home Borat, All is Forgiven," *Daily Star*, 20 November 2005.

49. Nigel Morgan, Annette Pritchard, and Rachel Piggott, "New Zealand, 100% Pure: The Creation of Power Niche Destination Brand," *Brand Management* 9, nos. 4-5 (April 2002): 335-354.

50. *New Republic*, "By the Horns."

51. Richard Goldstein, "The Tao of Borat," *Nation* 283, no. 17 (20 November 2006): 8.

52. Vassilenko, personal interview.

53. Peter Bradshaw, "Bear-Baiting in Bushville," *Guardian*, 27 October 2006, 7.

54. In my interviews with Kazakhstani in the diaspora and parents of children adopted from Kazakhstan, respondents regularly told me that they often found that "average" Americans thought Sacha Baron Cohen had made up the country for his comedy act and were surprised to learn of its existence.

55. "Kazakhs Warm to Borat's Humor," *CBC* website, 24 November 2006, http://www.cbc.ca/arts/film/story/2006/11/24/borat-kazakh.html (31 December 2006).

56. As an ethnographer, I actively sought out such "people-to-people" diplomats. I conducted open-ended, qualitative interviews with a dozen Kazakhstanis living in the United States ranging in age from 18 to 45. Using a similar methodology, I interviewed some 20 Americans who had adopted Kazakhstani children since 2000; these respondents were between the age of 35 and 55. These data were collected between November 2002 and May 2007; for more on the concept of people-to-people diplomacy, see Ralph N. Clough, *Reaching across the Taiwan Straight: People-to-People Diplomacy* (Boulder, CO: Westview Press, 1993).

57. Gauhar Abdygaliyeva, "My 'Glorious Nation of Kazakhstan,'" *Washington Post*, 7 November 2006. In the film, the country's name is mentioned 41 times and its pale blue flag adorned with the Golden Eagle appears frequently.

58. "Daughter of Kazakhstan's President Defends Borat," *CBC* website, 21 April 2006, http://www.cbc.ca/story/arts/national/2006/04/21/borat-kazakhstan-defence.html?ref=rss (16 September 2006).

59. Baron Cohen ultimately won the prestigious Golden Globe for Best Actor in the US. Kazakhstan's leading weekly *Karavan* sent its movie reviewer to a Vienna screening of the film who declared it the "best film of the year;" see "Borat 'Best Film' of Year: Kazakh Reviewer," *CBC* website, 19 November 2006, http://www.cbc.ca/arts/film/story/2006/11/19/borat-kazakhstan-review.html (31 January 2006).

60. Brian Morrissey, "MySpace Rolls Out 'Black Carpet' for Movies, *AdWeek*, 15 September 2006, http://www.adweek.com/aw/iq_interactive/article_display.jsp?vnu_content_id=1003122827 (17 September 2006).

61. The massacre occurred when Uzbek security forces fired on a group of protestors in the eastern city of Andijan on 13 May 2005. Government figures state that 187 people were killed, but other sources suggest the number of dead to be in the hundreds. Tashkent refused to allow an international investigation into the event, prompting international condemnation. In response, the Karimov government ordered the closing of the US airbase at Karshi-Khanabad and reoriented its foreign policy towards Russia and China. Kazakhstan's excellent relations with the United States, territorial disputes with Uzbekistan, cross-border trade problems, and the country's disaffected Uzbek minority all contribute to a less than perfect bilateral relationship between Astana and Tashkent.

62. See, for instance, John R. Bradley, "Comic Has Last Laugh," *Straits Times*, 16 January 2006.

63. Vassilenko, personal interview.

64. On this topic, the date 2030 is found in numerous, high-profile locations in Kazakhstan; in fact, it is visible at night from almost everywhere in the country's largest city, Almaty. This date is when President Nazarbayev expects the country to successfully achieve "First World" status. It is also an integral part of Kazakhstan's internal branding effort to become the "Snow Leopard of Asia," i.e., an economic trailblazer following the Asian Tiger model of South Korea, Hong Kong, etc. See Nursultan Nazarbayev, "Message of the President of the Country to the People of Kazakhstan" Embassy of the Republic of Kazakhstan to the United Kingdom of Great Britain and Northern Ireland website, http://www.kazakhstanembassy.org.uk/ (25 April 2007).

65. Tim Cornwell, "Wish You Were Here, Mr Borat," *Scotsman*, 20 October 2006, http://news.scotsman.com/uk.cfm?id=1552572006 (21 October 2006).

66. See Erlan Idrissov, "Sacha Baron Cohen Exploits the West's Ignorance of Kazakhstan," *Guardian*, 4 October 2006 and Erlan Idrissov, "We Survived Stalin and We Can Certainly Overcome Borat's Slurs," *Times*, 4 November 2006.

67. Idrissov, "We Survived."

68. Idrissov, "We Survived."

69. As the parent of a child born in Kazakhstan, I have seen the predominant American response to the initial mention of Kazakhstan transformed from "Kazakhstan . . . where is that?" to "Kazakhstan . . . oh, where Borat is from."

70. "National Branding: A New Sort of Beauty Contest," *Economist* 381, No. 8503 (11 November 2006): 69.

71. Jeremy Kahn, "A Brand-New Approach," *Foreign Policy* 157 (November-December 2006): 90-92.

72. Kotler and Gertner, "Country as Brand," 251.

73. Stjepo Martinović, "Branding Hrvatska—A Mixed Blessing that Might Work," *Brand Management* 9, nos. 4-5 (April 2002): 315-322.

74. Jian Wang, "Localising Public Diplomacy: The Role of Sub-national Actors in Nation Branding," *Place Branding* 2, no. 1 (January 2006): 32–42.

75. See Ishita Sinha Roy, "*Worlds Apart*: Nation-branding on the National Geographic Channel," *Media, Culture & Society* 29, no. 4 (July 2007): 569-592 for more on American "edutainment" programs and nation branding.

76. Edward Schatz, "Transnational Image Making and Soft Authoritarian Kazakhstan," *Slavic Review* 66, no. 1 (Spring 2008): 50-62.

77. Vassilenko, personal interview.

78. Vassilenko, personal interview. When I asked him if he wished Sacha Baron Cohen had never come up with the character of Borat, he quickly responded in the negative. He smiled and after a long pause told me, "I am planning to write a book on my experiences with Borat."

79. Simon Anholt, "Nation Branding: A Continuing Theme," *Brand Management* 10, no. 1 (September 2002): 59-60.

80. Schatz, "Transnational Image Making and Soft Authoritarian Kazakhstan," 61.

81. Anholt states, "It does sometimes seem as if globalization is turning the world into a giant supermarket where nations are nothing more than products on a shelf, frantically trying to attract the attention of each passing customer;" see Anholt, "Forward," 234.

82. Idrissov, "Sacha Baron Cohen."

83. See Neil Strauss, "The Man behind the Moustache," *Rolling Stone* 1014 (11 November 2006): 58-70.

84. Embassy of Kazakhstan to the USA and Canada (EKUC), "Our Take on Borat," *Kazakhstan News Bulletin* (KNB) 6, no. 38 (27 October 2006).

85. EKUC, "Our Take."

86. EKUC, "Take that, Borat: Sayat Announces Tours to 'Glorious Nation of Kazakhstan,'" *KNB* 6, no. 39 (2 November 2006).

87. "Steppe Magazine Press Release Nov 2006," EKUC. Email received 6 November 2006.

88. EKUC, "Forget 'Borat': Fashion Looks from the 'Stans," *KNB* 6, no. 40 (17 November 2006); EKUC, "'Borat' Actor Says He Means No Offense to Kazakhstan" *KNB* 6, no. 41 (17 November 2006).

89. EKUC, "Kazakh President Laughs of 'Borat' Controversy," *KNB* 6, no. 42 (22 November 2006).

90. Steven S. Lee, "*Borat*, Multiculturalism, *Mnogonatsional'nost'*," *Slavic Review* 66, no. 1 (Spring 2008): 19-34.

91. Nursultan Nazarbayev, "Who Needs Borat?" *The Spectator* (UK), 25 November 2006.

92. Peter van Ham, "Branding European Power," *Place Branding* 1, no. 2 (March 2005): 122-126.

93. Oliver Burkeman, "Problem with Your Country's Image?" *Guardian*, 11 November 2006.

94. Fiona Gilmore, "Spain—A Success Story of Country Branding," *Brand Management* 9, nos. 4-5 (April 2002): 281-93.

95. Prior to *Borat*, these families had developed their skills by disabusing the uninitiated of the notion that Kazakhstan was a hotbed of Islamic terrorism, the prevailing corrigendum before Sacha Baron Cohen's rise to global stardom.

96. See Anne Penketh, "After Nazarbayev: The Dictator, His Daughter, and a Dynasty at War," *Independent*, 30 May 2007.

Chapter 6
Under Fire and Loving It: The Cultural Impact, Criticisms, and Controversies of *Borat*

While the early fall of 2006 saw the Kazakhstanis burying the hatchet with Borat, Sacha Baron Cohen saw the rise of a host of new critics. The film premiered to sold-out audiences and critical acclaim, breaking box office records for a "mockumentary."[1] Almost overnight, Borat became a lightning rod for debates over sex, politics, and religion. Reviewers from all points on the political spectrum commented on his centrality to various phenomena from the "war on terror" to bedroom politics. Sacha Baron Cohen—no stranger to controversy—also became a magnet for lawsuits with nearly a dozen of the film's supporting "actors" suing the comedian and his production company for their portrayal in *Borat*. Baron Cohen could not have been happier, as each new controversy helped build his brand as a guerilla comedian whose reach had now become truly global.

Welcome to Absurdistan: Borat's Transamerican Romp

Borat: Cultural Learnings of America for Make Benefit Glorious Nation of Kazakhstan opens with a tongue-in-cheek tour of our protagonist's purported home village of "Kuzçek" which, according to Borat, lies "three mile north of fence to Jewtown" in Kazakhstan. In fact, the village scene was filmed in the Romanian town of Glod, which translates as 'mud.'[2] Borat proudly struts around the trash-strewn hamlet introducing his motley neighbors who range from rapists to amputees. As Borat speaks about his own achievements as a respected Kazakhstani journalist, the viewer is treated to a brief montage of old Borat clips from the *Ali G Show* and other performances. This is followed by the now infamous "The Running of the Jew 2004" segment. The parody of Pamplona's running of the bulls includes a gaggle of men dressed in white with green sashes being pursued by two ten-foot effigies, which grotesquely ape the medieval caricatures of the horned Jew and fanged Jewess. The latter stops in mid-pursuit of the villagers to lay an egg that the local children then punch and destroy before it can "hatch." Borat, looking a bit like a Middle Eastern Howard Cosell, reports the spectacle as if it were a weekend football match.

Borat's tour of Eastern European backwardness serves to explain why his government has commissioned him to travel to the "greatest country in the world—U.S. and A" to "learn a lessons" to benefit the "glorious nation of Kazakhstan." After a ceremonial (and Sovietesque) photo-op with members of the fictitious Kazakhstan Ministry of Information, Borat and his sidekick Azamat Bagatov (played by the obese, Armenian-American character actor Ken Davitian) strike out for America.[3] After a tortuous flight from Kazakhstan to New York, Borat begins filming his documentary. Early encounters with Americans produce frightening moments of culture clash as Borat tries to hug and kiss perfect strangers on the streets of Manhattan and lets his pet chicken loose as he rides the subway.

Later while relaxing in his hotel room, Borat views an episode of the now defunct series *Baywatch* and instantly falls in love with the buxom character, CJ (played by actress Pamela Anderson). His mission to understand America steadily becomes consumed by a desire to meet and marry the *Baywatch* beauty. Upon learning her real name and probable location from the "Veteran Feminists of America," Borat convinces Azamat to join him in a cross-country trek to California. Hoping to avoid any repetition of the "Jews' attack of 9/11" they opt to drive rather than fly to the West Coast.

From this point forward, *Borat* adheres to the 1940s "road movie" style made famous by the comedic duo of Bob Hope and Bing Crosby.[4] Cinematically, this genre provides almost limitless possibilities for exploration of the themes discussed earlier in this text, including fear of the other, respect for diversity, etc. According to film historian David Laderman, "The driving force propelling most road movies . . . is an embrace of the journey as a means of cultural critique. Road movies generally aim beyond the borders of cultural familiarity, seeking the unfamiliar for revelation, or at least for the thrill of the unknown."[5] Given Baron Cohen's penchant for exposing the bigotry simmering beneath society's thin veneer of acceptance of diversity, it is not surprising that he and his director chose such a genre for *Borat.* The internal dynamic between Borat and Azamat is also worth highlighting. Cultural studies professor Nancy Condee asserts that Borat and Azamat are the "distant progeny of Laurel and Hardy, Abbott and Costello, Amos 'n' Andy, Two Black Crows [and] Mutt and Jeff."[6] There are shades of *Don Quixote* (1605) as well, especially given the pairing of the squat, portly, and world-weary Azamat (Sancho Panza) with the tall, lanky dreamer Borat (Quixote). The later scenes involving Pamela Anderson also mirror Miguel de Cervantes' 17th century spoof of chivalric romance.

Borat and Azamat steadily venture deeper into "Red-State" America, replete with pawn shops and pickup trucks. In Jackson, Mississippi, Borat makes a mockery of a local news and talk show by childishly standing when he should sit during an interview, obsessing about his need to go to the bathroom on live TV, and screaming into his mic.[7] Borat's pranks then turn potentially dangerous as he takes his pantomime into that swirling vortex of patriotism, machismo, and animal cruelty known as the American rodeo. Borat's starring role in the 38th annual Kroger/Valleydale championship rodeo at the James E. Taliaferro Sports & Entertainment Complex in Salem, Virginia made local headlines at the time, and served as the focal point for nearly every review of the film when it premiered. The scene begins with the rodeo's general manager Bobby Rowe lecturing Borat, who is clad in an American flag shirt, a bolo tie, and cowboy hat, about the "images" beamed back to America from Iraq. He wrathfully grumbles, "The terrorists . . . the Muslims, they look like you. Black hair, black mustache. Shave that dadgummed moustache off so you're not so conspicuous. So you look maybe like an *Aiy-talian* or something. . . . I see a lot and I think there's a dadgummed Muslim. I wonder what kind bomb he's got strapped to him." The conversation then turns to homosexuality and Rowe malevolently affirms his support for taking gays out and hanging them.[8]

Borat's ostensible reason for being at the rodeo is to perform the national anthem. However, before he commences singing he warms up the crowd by enthusiastically declaring on behalf of Kazakhstan, "We support your war of terror." A round of applause then emanates from the audience. Borat, playing on the crowd's swelling patriotism, continues: "May U.S. and A. kill every single terrorist. May George Bush drink the blood of every single man, woman, and child of Iraq. May you destroy their country so that for the next thousand years not even a single lizard will survive in their desert." He then delivers a faux Kazakhstani anthem to the tune of "The Star-Spangled Banner" declaring all other countries to be run by "little girls" and lauding his country's potassium output. The crowd quickly turns against him. In a scene which could not have been more apropos given Sacha Baron Cohen's implied condemnation of America's current actions and tarnished image in the world, the boos startle a horse which bucks its rider, a cowgirl bearing an over-sized American flag, sending her and "Old Glory" into the mud. According to news reports, the production crew fled the civic center immediately, fearing for Baron Cohen's safety.[9]

Later, Borat takes on the patrician mores of the Deep South, providing some of the most uncomfortable moments for the viewing audience. Borat goes to a dinner party at the Magnolia Mansion Dining Society, attended by genteel Southerners in their sunset years. It must have been this scene that prompted Anthony Lane to write of Sacha Baron Cohen: "He is a squirmist: a master of SECS, or Socio-Ethnophobic Comic simulations, in which he adopts fictional personae and then marches briskly into the real world with a mission to embarrass its inhabitants."[10] The soirée begins well enough, with Borat engaging in some of the niceties he had learned earlier from an etiquette coach. However, the evening quickly degenerates. After Borat excuses himself from the table, his hostess remarks, "I think that the cultural differences are vast. I think he is a delightful man. It wouldn't take very much time for him to become Americanized." Cut to Borat returning with a plastic bag full of his own feces.

This scene is carnivalesque in its transposition of the fecal with formal. As discussed earlier, the medieval tradition of undermining authority by confronting artifice with grotesque realism is very much a part of Baron Cohen's humor. Borat strikes below the belt and attempts to drag his subjects down with him. The scene also plays on the hallowed British tradition of the "comedy of manners," which underpinned such gems as Oscar Wilde's *The Importance of Being Earnest* (1895), *Fawlty Towers* (1975-79), and *The Office* (2001-2003). Reflective of the English obsession with class and social standing, comedic tension is supplied through cultural violations by those who are unaware of the norms of "polite society." As Borat begins to breach seemingly obvious societal norms associated with personal hygiene, his hostess keeps her cool and accompanies him to the toilet where she patiently instructs him on the finer points of bathroom etiquette, including who wipes whom.

Shortly thereafter, *Borat* briefly falls victim to Paul Gilroy's previously-discussed "Beavis and Butthead syndrome" by becoming overly self-aware and a parody of itself. This is a result of the introduction of Leunell Campbell, a comedian and one of the few genuine actors in the film besides Baron Cohen and Davitian. Leunell's character arrives at the party after Borat surreptitiously called on her "services" after seeing an ad in a local paper. Refusing to break bread with an obvious prostitute (and a black one at that), the sheriff is called and Borat and Luenell flee the mansion.[11] The scenes which follow between Baron Cohen and Luenell are clearly scripted and create artistic dissonance with the rest of film.

Back on the road, Borat stops at an antique store in Vicksburg, Mississippi (though the audience is informed its location is Texas). The store is packed with the symbols of the Confederacy which, according to the owner Larry Walker, is a way of "honoring our heritage." Paradoxically, Borat's intention is to buy a gift for Pamela Anderson to allow him entry into her "vazheen." Dozens of pratfalls later, Adolph Rose Antiques is in shambles with hundreds of dollars of damage incurred by the Kazakhstani pretender. The owner later commented, "You have to laugh at it now. But at the time, we were just glad to get rid of him."[12] This scene represents one of the more politicized moments in the film. As Baron Cohen trashes dozens of pieces of Confederate "heritage," he seems to be engaging in a staged catharsis. His symbolic attacks on the iconography of American slavery, the country's bloody Civil War, and the idealized "old South" are thinly disguised and, more importantly, are intended for worldwide consumption. For a moment, the film lingers on the threshold of degenerating into a cathartic vigilante-melodrama akin to *Falling Down* (1993) or *Sling Blade* (1996), but safely returns to its satirical foundation after Borat exits the antique shop.

Later at the hotel, Borat exits the bathroom only to find his compatriot masturbating to his prized possession, a *Baywatch* fanzine in which Pamela figures prominently. Borat flies into a rage, attacking Azamat for making "hand-party over Pamela." Thus begins an extended scene of flesh, flab, and body hair the likes of which the mainstream viewing public has never seen before. Unlike the innocuous Protestant male nudity that characterized earlier British comedies such as *Monty Python's Flying Circus,* the nakedness of *Borat* is primordial, dangerous, and ethnic. Baron Cohen's manhood is obscured by an overly-generous black bar (suggesting his penis is at least twelve inches long), while Davitian's privates are safely obscured beneath layers of his own fat. After a bit of Pro Wrestling-style sparring, the two become locked in a horrific and hairy *soixante-neuf*, with Davitian screaming in Armenian, "Eat my asshole."[13] After extricating himself from the compromising position, Azamat runs out of the hotel room with Borat in hot pursuit. The two quiescently cease their melee while riding the elevator down to the lobby as strangely unflustered hotel guests attempt to avoid eye contact with the naked foreigners. The chase resumes and soon interrupts a mortgage brokers' convention. Security guards brusquely separate the two after their grotesque nude wrestling match spills onto the main stage.[14]

Sacha Baron Cohen also recalled the unforgettable scene when he accepted the Golden Globe award for Best Actor in a Comedy or Musical in 2007.[15] After describing how filming the movie allowed him to see America

in all its beauty, as well its dark underbelly, he sardonically noted that he got
to see "a side of America that rarely sees the light of day" referring to Ken
Davitian's derrière. He added, addressing his co-star in the audience, "I
stared down and saw your two wrinkled golden globes on my chin. I thought
to myself, 'I'd better win a bloody award for this.'" The morning after the
pornographic tussle, Borat finds himself abandoned by his handler Azamat,
who has absconded with their bear, the remainder of their funds, and Borat's
passport, leaving our hero with only a return ticket to Kazakhstan, his pet
chicken, the ice cream truck, and the *Baywatch* magazine. Penniless, he runs
out of gas in the American Southwest and begins walking westward. He
successfully "hike-a-hitchings with a group young scholars" also heading
across the country in a recreational vehicle. The three inebriated Chi Psi
fraternity brothers from the University of South Carolina (USC) salute him
with "Welcome to fucking America, baby," before launching into alternat-
ing tirades against women and minorities. Borat asks, "Do you have slaves
here?" to which one of the "scholars" replies repeatedly, "we wish." The
scurrilous exchanges subside only when they decide to watch the sex-tape
Pam & Tommy Lee: Stolen Honeymoon (1998) and Borat learns that the
object of his desire is somewhat less than pure. They bid the crestfallen
journalist farewell, affirming "Boris . . . we'll remember you always. You're
an American now." This scene, in which the main protagonist falls in with
the wrong crowd after quarreling with his traveling partner, is a common
element of the buddy film/road show genre.

Borat's misadventures also bear an uncanny resemblance to certain
elements of Carlo Collodi's *Le avventure di Pinocchio* (1883). After being
separated from their symbolic fathers (Azamat and Geppetto, respectively),
both heroes fall off the straight and narrow path. The allusion to Jonah and
the belly of the whale myth is also evident in both texts, suggesting a transition from the real world into a sort of purgatory. While Pinocchio's parallel
with Jonah is explicit (both character's enter a whale's belly), Borat is swallowed up within the claustrophobic confines of a dingy RV. In both cases,
the characters escape their purgatories and continue their journeys. The belly of the whale metaphor, which the late mythology expert Joseph Campbell
equates with a symbolic death, is a common element of mythology, literature, and film from the legend of Finn MacCool to *The Lord of the Rings* to
Star Wars.[16]

After escaping the RV, Borat hits rock bottom and ceremonially burns
all his possessions and frees his chicken. This symbolic death sets the stage
for the obligatory rebirth scene. After spending the night outside a megachurch, he begins his resurrection via American Pentecostalism.[17] The scene
was filmed at the United Pentecostal Church (UPC) camp in Mississippi,
and features genuine attempts on the part of the church-goers to "pray Borat
through to the Holy Spirit," i.e., cause him to speak in tongues.[18] Instances
of glossolalia pepper the entire scene, which also includes unscripted ca-
meos by Congressman Charles "Chip" Pickering (R-MS) and Chief Justice
James W. Smith, Jr. of the State Supreme Court of Mississippi. The service
soon turns to the "olde tyme" religion of the American Charismatic movement. A congregant leads Borat to the altar where he is introduced to the
church by UPC evangelist Greg Godwin as 'Bolak.' Borat gives testimony[19]
and then asks, "Can Jesus heal the pain that is in my heart?" After this is
confirmed, he begins speaking in tongues (a phenomenon with which the

ethnic transvestite Baron Cohen is all too familiar) at the forceful command of the preacher. He then takes a bus to Los Angeles with "some friends of Mr. Jesus," i.e., missionaries. After his symbolic death and rebirth, Borat has now crossed the last threshold of his journey; he is ready to marry Pamela.

Upon arriving on the West Coast, Borat immediately reunites with Azamat in front of Grauman's Chinese Theatre on Hollywood Boulevard— again, a necessary component of the "road film" formula. To add a few laughs, Azamat has taken to dressing as Oliver Hardy and is mistaken by Borat for Hitler. They reconcile and head to Pamela Anderson's book-signing at a Virgin Megastore in Orange County. Their reunion reinforces Borat's metamorphosis and provides further proof that he is now ready to ask for the *Baywatch* star's hand in marriage. Promising to show America a Kazakh-style wedding, Borat enters the store bearing a blanket that eerily resembles the Kazakh dream quilt, a traditional yurt wall hanging. Upon meeting the blond bombshell, Borat recites his family lineage (again a nod to traditional Kazakh culture). After showing her the quilt, he proposes marriage. Anderson naturally declines to which Borat replies, "No agreement necessary." We then see the quilt is actually a bag which Borat puts over the head of the *Baywatch* star to the dismay of the crowd.[20] The bride-kidnapping, a genuine Kazakh tradition, fails and Borat is tackled and hand-cuffed by security guards.[21] Despite the fact that Pamela Anderson is in on the gag, the scene does not seem stilted like those featuring Luenell. Given the quality of Anderson's past performances in such theatrical clunkers as *Raw Justice* (1994) and *No Rules* (2005), her role in *Borat* is more than just convincing, it is probably the best acting she has ever done.

A maudlin, if not schmaltzy, exode follows with Borat realizing that Luenell is the true love of his life. This occurs only after his unrequited love for the "dream girl," once exposed, ends in disaster. In what is perhaps the most unoriginal element of the entire film, he seeks her out and they return to "Kazakhstan" together. In the epilogue supposedly filmed eight months later, we find Borat back in Kuzçek looking hale and hearty and no longer sporting his gray suit. He details the improvements his "cultural learnings" have brought to his country. "We no longer have a running of the Jew. It's cruel. We Christians now." Cut to a scene of bloodthirsty babushkas poking a crucified Jew with their wooden pitchforks. We then learn that Luenell is a hit, selling her breast milk to the villagers who line up in droves for a taste of her foreign lactations. The film credits run over a scintillating visual bricolage of Soviet television commercials and musical accompaniment. The latter comes in the form of Erran Baron Cohen's "O, Kazakhstan," in which the Central Asian nation is declared the greatest country in the world, its leading potassium exporter, and a leader in industry due to its invention of toffee and the trouser belt. Kazakhstan's neighbors are then roundly denounced for their backwardness, before an invitation is issued in the final lines to visit the country in order to grasp the "mighty" penis of its leader. True to form, Baron Cohen's "moviefilm" ends where it begins—below the waist. Feces, genitalia, and profanations combine in a swirling nexus that might be dismissed as simply another iteration of the teen-oriented stunt film.

However, on a deeper level, *Borat* represents the classic quest myth. The film adheres religiously to the three phases of Joseph Campbell's transformation of the hero: departure, initiation, and return.[22] In the first phase, Borat experiences the *call to adventure*. He accepts the call and departs from his place of origin for a strange new world, thus *crossing the threshold*. As a result, he is forced to abandon those things which are familiar to him (hearth, family, etc.), but like all great heroes, he does not travel alone. In the second stage, Borat is tested on the *road of trials*. He faces challenges, is abandoned by his companion, loses most of his possessions, and ultimately experiences a symbolic death and rebirth. By being "saved" at the megachurch, Borat has experienced an *expansion of consciousness* or *apotheosis*; with this, his initiation as the hero is complete. He is now free to seek his boon. Despite his failure to *capture the boon* (i.e., Pamela Anderson), he finds love and happiness with Luenell. His marriage to her comes to represent the *ultimate boon*. Borat then makes a triumphant *return to the ordinary world* of his make-believe Kazakhstan. Once there, he demonstrates how the trials and tribulations of his quest have granted him self-knowledge. As *master of the two worlds* (i.e., culturally fluent in both the mores of "glorious Kazakhstan" and the "greatest nation on Earth, the "U. S. and A."), he has now opened the door to a new and enlightened future for both himself and his countrymen. The epilogue shows scenes of Borat's transfer of knowledge to the purported Kazakhs, what Campbell calls the *application of the boon*. By successfully passing through these stages, Borat joins the ranks of Ulysses, Buddha, Frodo Baggins, Luke Skywalker, and countless other questing heroes of myth.

Assessing the Critical Reception of Baron Cohen's "Cultural Learnings" through the Prism of Politics

Borat opened to rave reviews and sold-out audiences in North America and Europe in November 2006. Topping the box office, Borat took in £6.2 million in the UK and over $26 million in America during its first weekend in distribution, ultimately generating a worldwide box office gross in excess of $250 million.[23] *Borat* ranked as the sixteenth highest grossing film of 2007. This statistic is especially compelling given that the movie only played in about half of the theatres that showed the year's highest grossing film, *Pirates of the Caribbean: Dead Man's Chest*, and only cost $18 million to make. When Borat was released on DVD, it also topped the charts both in terms of sales and rentals during the week of 11 March 2007, generating more than $60 million in sales alone.

The film ultimately made the 2007 "Top" 10 lists of the American Film Institute, AOL Moviefone, *Rolling Stone*, Joel Siegel (ABC), *Time*, CNN, and various other organizations. In addition to critical accolades, the motion picture was also nominated for more than two dozen awards, including an Oscar nomination for "Best Writing, Adapted Screenplay." As mentioned earlier, Sacha Baron Cohen was awarded the prestigious "Best Actor in Comedy or Musical" by the Hollywood Foreign Press Association. He also won "Best Comedic Performance" by the youth-oriented MTV Movie Awards, as well as awards from the San Francisco Film Critics Circle, British Comedy Awards, *Evening Standard* British Film Awards, Online Film Critics Society Awards, Chicago Film Critics Association Awards, and Toronto Film Critics Association Awards.

With only a handful of exceptions, the reviews of the film invariably described the movie as funny—even dangerously so. The *Wall Street Journal*, which bookishly declared the film an instance of *Candide Camera*, joked that "*Borat* may be dangerous to your abdominal health; there must be a limit to how many convulsions a belly can take without trauma," which CNN's review echoed with "*Borat* is so gut-bustingly funny it should carry a health warning."[24] Britain's *Daily Telegraph* warned, "The only guarantee for anyone who sees *Borat* is that once you start laughing, it will be impossible to stop."[25] Colin Covert of *Knight Ridder* wrote "*Borat* is unquestionably, honestly, literally the funniest film I have ever seen."[26] The late film critic Joel Siegel of ABC agreed auspiciously noting, "[I]t's one of the funniest movies I have ever seen."[27] *USA Today* hailed it as a "shockingly hilarious satire that knows no bounds."[28] *The San Francisco Chronicle* affirmed, "The first thing that must be said about *Borat* is that it's screamingly, hysterically, laugh-through-the-next-joke, laugh-through-the-next-week funny."[29] Even those reviews which found the movie utterly tasteless admitted it was, at the very least, funny.

Going beyond a simple reading of whether or not *Borat* was funny, a holistic interpretation of the film's critical reception presents a mosaic of political orientation on American "wedge issues," i.e., those social concerns which divide liberals from conservatives, or in terms of the political geography of the United States, "Red States" from "Blue States." In recent years, the most divisive issues have been gay marriage, abortion, and prayer in schools. Gene Maeroff, senior fellow at the Hechinger Institute at Teachers College, Columbia University, argues that the root of the various wedge issues is the holy triumvirate of "patriotism, religion, and sexual mores."[30] *Borat* taps all three for humor. The political overtones of the film are so blatant that even the fluff rag *Entertainment Weekly* declared it a "psychopolitical *Jackass* . . . in which Borat, the old-world specimen of *masculis ignoramus* from an underdeveloped half-Muslim nation, stands in for a world we didn't have to think about much before 9/11, and the people Borat talks to become the symbolic heart of America—a place where intolerance is worn, increasingly, with pride." Given the film's ability to expose American xenophobia and prejudice, it should come as no surprise that reviews outside the US focused on the movie as a barometer of the current state of affairs within the world's only superpower. In the coming pages, I attempt to deconstruct the highly politicized, academically robust, and ideologically variegated critical receptions given a film which, had it premiered at another time, might have been completely ignored by pundits, politicos, and the public-at-large. I also offer some of my own analysis of the film's politics and why it was so resonant.

Perhaps the most paradoxical reception of *Borat*, given the fact that the film significantly increased News Corp's bottom line in 2007, came from *FOX News'* film critic, Mike Straka.[31] While admitting the film is funny, Straka lashes out at the Left, growling, "America haters will love how Cohen uses Michael Moore-type scenarios to get his point across."[32] Even the most cursory viewing of *FOX News* will provide the watcher with a clear understanding of documentarian Michael Moore's locus within the cable network's pantheon of villains: slightly less evil than Osama bin Laden but certainly more heinous than Benedict Arnold. Rupert Murdoch's other media properties were a bit kinder (or at least promotive of corporate synergy).

The *Sun* declared, "It's not only a masterpiece of character comedy but of comic timing" and Lou Lumenick of the *New York Post* hailed *Borat* as the "funniest film of the year."[33]

Just as the conservative Rupert Murdoch was of two minds on *Borat* (producing the film and using his media empire to market it on the one hand, while allowing his more conservative media properties to trash it publicly), the American right wing was ambivalent towards *Borat.* Most traditional conservatives categorically condemned the film, while neo-conservatives tended to side with the Left in regards to the merits of Baron Cohen's humor. Writing in the *American Conservative*, one of the few remaining bastions of paleo-conservatism, Steve Sailer took Baron Cohen to task for propagating "traditional Ashkenazi anti-gentilism" and its depiction of "Borat as the ultimate goyishe kop" ('fool,' *literally* 'Gentile head').[34] Sailer's argument is that *Borat* is nothing more than anti-American, cosmopolitanism with a strong dose of anti-Christian invective. He dismissed the notion that *Borat* was an "Important Message Movie" simply because it "portrays Kazakhs—and Red State Americans—as anti-Semites."[35]

The ultra-conservative weekly *Human Events* eviscerated the film in its review entitled "Gratuitous America-Bashing for Lining Pocket of Overrated Sacha Cohen." The journal's movie reviewer Ned Rice opined that *Borat* was not even the funniest movie of the week (its only competitor was the moribund *Santa Clause 3: The Escape Clause*), much less of all time, before going on to make apologies for the flagrant racism and homophobia that Baron Cohen's alter ego uncovers. He proudly declares—against strong evidence to the contrary—that the US is the country "where racial equality was, to a great extent, invented" before launching into a jingoist rant reminiscent of the shameful French-baiting which preceded the Iraq War.

> I don't think a Brit is any position to lecture me on race relations, thanks very much. Instead of making yet another movie about what a racist hellhole America is, my British friend, how about you stop bashing Pakis and go brush your teeth? If you've got a problem with that, slip into something red and we'll meet you back at Yorktown—we'll be the guys dressed in buckskin. If you've got a problem with that—and I can see how you might—go boil something, you smug limeys.[36]

The *American Spectator* also received the movie poorly with not one, but two negative reviews: one by James Bowman and the other by Greg Gutfeld. Bowman's critique focused on Baron Cohen's British anti-Americanism suggesting that the film artificially accentuates the level of "stupidity, credulity, and bloodthirstiness of the Bush-supporting American heartland" in order to "pander to the elite European opinion."[37] Strangely, Bowman's review also made a fumbled attempt to decipher traditional Kazakh culture. He accused Baron Cohen of making mistakes with regard to Borat's fantasies about "sex without consequence or responsibility," suggesting that a "traditional" Kazakh would instead want to kidnap Pamela Anderson so she might "bear him fine strong sons."[38] It is obvious that Bowman is out of his depth since he clearly failed to understand that *Borat*, at least on some level, is also a critique of the globalized mélange culture which MTV, YouTube, and satellite TV have transmitted to the developing world. Borat, like many overseas viewers of American media, has been de-

luded by the myth that America is a land of sex without consequences populated by bikini-clad beach bunnies.

Greg Gutfeld's treatment of the movie was no more kind, and just as
peculiar as his wooly critique wanders into a number of intellectual cul-de-
sacs. Gutfeld labels the film "a massive cop out" too fearful to make Borat
into one of the "Mad Mullahs" that populate contemporary Londonistan.[39]
"If Cohen had made Borat a radical Muslim, then it would have been funny,
scarily real, and actually quite dangerous. Here it's just funny. But in London, where few people speak about the real Borats around them, it seems
also kind of lame."[40] Such a curious treatment of the film shows the lengths
to which conservative political commentators went to find a place for *Borat*
in journals. While Baron Cohen might have been pleased by the level of
exposure he received, it begs the question: why does the right care so much
about this joker?

While traditional conservatives lambasted *Borat*, neo-conservative
commentators rallied in support of Borat's mission, though some of their
interpretations of the film were as equally muddled and/or far-reaching as
those of their traditional conservative counterparts. In order to understand
why neo-cons found common cause with a left-leaning British comedian, a
bit of background is in order. The history of the neo-conservative movement
can be told through the political progression of a few key American thinkers
including Irving Kristol, founder of the influential foreign policy magazine
National Interest, and Norman Podhoretz, editor-at-large of the journal
Commentary.[41] The platform of neo-conservatism is based on an activist
foreign policy which includes the use of military force to remove dictatorial
leaders and destroy totalitarian regimes.

After the fall of communism in Eastern Europe and the former Soviet
Union, the focus of the movement turned to the Middle East where corrupt
regimes were the norm. The one state in the region which was solidly democratic and capitalist was Israel. As a large percentage of neoconservatives
were Jewish and also supported avidly pro-Israel policies in the Middle
East, neo-cons soon came into conflict with the libertarian wing of the
American conservative movement. Until the rise of the neo-conservatives,
the Republican Party generally supported a comparatively isolationist policy, or at the most, a *realpolitik*-based approach of supporting key allies
such as the UK, Germany, and Japan. The so-called paleo-conservatives, led
by the previously-discussed commentarian Patrick Buchanan, have criticized the neo-cons for putting the interests of Israel above those of the US.[42]
Due to the strong dichotomy between the traditional conservatives and the
neo-conservatives, the Republican establishment has become fractured with
some supporting intervention abroad and others calling for a more Ameri-
can-centric approach to world affairs.

This intra-party division manifested itself in the reception of *Borat.*
While noted neo-conservative thinkers extolled the virtues of the film, their
traditionalist counterparts denounced it in the harshest terms. John Podhoretz, son of one of neo-conservatism's founding fathers, offered nothing
short of a paean to Sacha Baron Cohen. In his review "The 'Borat' Show" in
The Weekly Standard, the flagship publication of the neo-con movement,
Podhoretz proclaimed the work to be "one of the four or five funniest films
ever made."[43] He reveled in Baron Cohen's remarkable ability to simultaneously "savage" political correctness and the notion that "political correct-

ness is humorless twaddle."[44] On the various condemnations of the film, he argues, "Borat is a satire of anti-Semitism—a riposte and retort to it in every conceivable way." His article paints Baron Cohen as a later-day Jonathan Swift who similarly did not "explain that he was being facetious," thus causing the solons of then and now to "scream in horror."[45]

Podhoretz's father's magazine *Commentary* featured an in-depth piece on the Borat phenomenon by Joshua Muravchik. A scholar at the American Enterprise Institute and signatory to the "Project for the New American Century," Muravchik is arguably one the most renowned neoconservative thinkers operating today.[46] Muravchik begins his observations by recounting his own experiences with Sacha Baron Cohen in the guise of Ali G. Before the foreign policy expert could be bombarded with too many of Ali's fatuous queries, he headed for the door, missing his opportunity for global fame via *Da Ali G Show*. He then goes on to extol certain neo-conservative virtues via the ill-fitting medium of Borat. According to Muravchik, *Borat* satirizes the Third World and its failure to match up to the one which he and Baron Cohen inhabit. "As the movie makes wholly explicit, the differences between those two worlds are in fact all too real. They consist not only in disparities of wealth but also in something less readily mentioned: namely, the respective quality of social norms, especially as these are evidenced in the treatment of Borat's two favorite topics, women and minorities."[47] Muravchik then invokes the (rare) practice of bride kidnapping in "historically Muslim" Kazakhstan and "open hostility" towards Jews in Baron Cohen's native England to prove his point.[48]

As a journal founded by the American Jewish Committee in 1945, it is not surprising that the article provoked a wealth of responses, mostly condemnatory of both Muravchik and Baron Cohen. In the April issue of *Commentary*, one respondent to Muravchik's piece applied the eternal acid test "Is it good for the Jews?" to *Borat*. The answer was resoundingly negative, despite Muravchik and others' protestations to the contrary. In a well-written and insightful letter, Stephen Schwartz took Muravchik to task for impugning Kazakhstan's reputation as potentially hostile to Jews due to its Muslim connections and "absolving drunken Americans from bellowing a Jew-baiting song" by raising the canard of bride kidnapping.[49] According to one of Muravchik's critics, "The Borat travesty constitutes a gratuitous slur on a country prepared to make invaluable contributions to Jewish-Muslim reconciliation as well as to the war on terror."[50]

David Horowitz's pro-Israel, anti-leftist periodical *FrontPage Magazine* also defended Borat's antics as "the most effective satire of anti-Semitism since Archie Bunker."[51] In his review "Free Borat," Ben Johnson chided the Anti-Defamation League for its earlier criticisms that Baron Cohen's work may inadvertently promote anti-Semitism. He writes, "Their absurdity lies in holding a guiltless actor liable for the reaction of the audience. By this logic, Jodie Foster was guilty of shooting President Reagan."[52] He casts Baron Cohen in the mold of Jewish comedian and filmmaker Mel Brooks whose life-long affirmation has been to "make the world laugh at Hitler" as an inoculum against a breakout of future Hitlers.[53] While Podhoretz and Muravchik's analyses come across as measured and learned, Johnson's arrant sloppiness (he implies that Kazakhs are Arabs) and alarmist hyperbole (e.g., bemoaning "Europe's continual march to *dhimmitude*") weaken the thrust of his argument.[54]

The *National Review*, founded by William F. Buckley, Jr., also lauded the motion picture. Though not normally grouped together with unabashedly neo-conservative publications like *The Weekly Standard* and *Commentary*, the *National Review* has been roundly criticized by the libertarian wing of the Right for supporting planks of the neo-con platform including global free markets, a strong state, and "a neo-Jacobin ideology" of violent regime-change abroad. Certainly, Peter Suderman's review of *Borat*, "Learning from Culture," evoked comparisons with the neo-con view of Borat as campaigner against small-mindedness and for internationalism. "It's a shiv to the guts of appeasement, and it just might be the best—and certainly the funniest—deconstruction of American pretensions ever." Reflecting both neo-con and Ivy-league conservatism (in opposition to Patrick Buchanan's homespun, late-19th century *Weltanschauung*), Suderman chortles, "It's an all-American comedy of non-manners, with cultural conflicts, not-so-hidden biases, and the insular pompousness of various subgroups out for the world to see. The country's clashing sects each get tricked into shooting themselves in the foot simply by forcing them to explain themselves to a mystified outsider." In a final jibe, he notes: "The joke's not on us—it *is* us." Such comments evince the ideological orientations of the neo-cons towards the world beyond America's insulating borders. Unlike traditional conservatives, they hope to push the American polity towards a greater understanding of the global village, undoubtedly an insoluble ideological vestige of their Trotskyite heritage.

One of the few dissenters among the neo-con crowd was Charles Krauthammer. The Pulitzer Prize-winning columnist condemned Baron Cohen's humor as a reflection of the "unfortunate attitude of many liberal Jews toward working-class American Christians, especially evangelicals."[55] Echoing the sentiments of the traditional right-wing critics of *Borat*, Krauthammer, who is of Franco-Jewish descent, decried the notion that the American heartland is the global locus of anti-Semitism. He directed that blame instead at the regimes of Mahmoud Ahmadinejad and Hugo Chavez, even striking out at France and Norway.[56] Krauthammer stated, "America is the most welcoming, religiously tolerant, philo-Semitic country in the world. No nation since Cyrus the Great's Persia has done more for the Jews. And its reward is to be exposed as latently anti-Semitic by an itinerant Jew looking for laughs and, he solemnly assures us, for the path to the Holocaust?"[57] *New York Times* columnist David Brooks elaborated on this point shortly after the film's premiere, "We Jews know all about Borat's Jewish snobbery—based on the assumption that Middle America's acceptance of Jews must be a mirage, and that underneath every Rotarian there must be a Cossack about to unleash a continental pogrom."[58] Hyperbole aside, the film did function as an effective—albeit unorthodox—vehicle for introducing novel discourses of anti-Semitism in the American cultural sphere.

Every major conservative magazine in America found ample space to publish reviews, opinion pieces, and full-blown articles about *Borat*. The same cannot be said for their left-wing counterparts. In fact, the liberal *American Prospect*, the progressive *Mother Jones*, the pacifist *Progressive*, and the alt-culture *Utne Reader* all passed on the opportunity to review *Borat*. However, the bastion of modern liberalism *The New Republic* dedicated a page to Borat's defense prior to the release of the film by attacking the Anti-Defamation League for its "kvetching" on Borat. Curiously echoing

FrontPage Magazine's neo-con review of the film, TNR's editors declare: "The freedom to offend, of course, is an artistic freedom that can be abused. But it can also serve to clarify and reveal things about those it offends."[59] However, there was no follow-up review of the film when it premiered a month later. As such, we will never know how the editors felt about watching Sacha Baron Cohen inadvertently· perform anallingus on his 300-lb co-star.

Fortunately, the flagship of the left, *The Nation*, did have something to say about Borat's cross-country carnival of delights. Stuart Klawans anointed *Borat* the movie of year in his review "Coming to America!" As the self-declared "cinematic guinea pig of the American left," Klawans proclaimed, "Mere anarchy is loosed, and its name (bless him!) is Borat."[60] While much of the content of Klawans' essay echoed those of his neo-con rivals, there was a whiff of sneering cynicism which was totally absent in neo-conservative views of Borat's interactions with "normal" Americans. With a bit of *Schadenfreude*, he affirms that while Borat may brag about his country's (i.e., Kazakhstan's) "race hatred" and "religio-jingoism," the United States is, in fact, the "actual site of these grotesqueries."[61] Whereas Muravchik and Podhoretz pine for a more enlightened America post-Borat, Klawans gleefully basks in the celluloid glow of "punishment meted out (with breathtaking peremptoriness) for the crime of complacency about slavery."[62]

In his review for Lincoln Center's *Film Comment*, Nathan Lee joyously declared the aim of *Borat* was to "stick it" to Bush country. He writes of Borat/Baron Cohen, "The man with a plan [Borat] serves one with an agenda [Sacha Baron Cohen]."[63] According to Lee, "*Borat*'s giggling assault on the real world is closer to *Fahrenheit 9/11* than *Talladega Nights*. Ditto its politics."[64] To underscore his point, he quotes a bevy of gloomy statistics about perceptions of America abroad with descriptors like "vulgar," "uncultured," and "ignorant." In a half-hearted attempt to assure his audience that all is not lost, he states, "Happily, [*Borat*] arrives just in time for the conservative meltdown. The family-values set has not been pleased by the revelation that Republican Congressmen lust after teenage cock just like everyone else."[65]

Nancy Condee similarly invoked repressed right-wing homosexuality in her review of the film, "Borat's New Blackface."[66] However, the thrust of her argument lies in how the film is ultimately an exposition of America's multi-layered self-deception. Armed simply with a bad suit, a worse accent, and a bevy of medieval notions, Borat undermines the myths of Americanism, specifically the strength of its civil society, tolerance, and gender relations. She argues that while Borat cannot be redeemed, the film proves that America's own obsession with pseudo-redemption will allow its people to continue to assuage their own guilt over such travesties as Abu Ghraib, the legacy of slavery, etc. "Borat's marginalized land stands in for the marginalized things we prefer to disown: anti-Semitism, homophobia, racism, never mind rape, incest and non-stop (so to speak) toilet humor. Assigned to Borat, these practices are no longer really ours; they are his, although—with a nudge and a wink—the U.S. citizens of Borat's faux-documentary signal their private sympathy for 'Kazakh' prejudice of any stripe."[67]

The major left-of-center publications also chimed in with some equally far-reaching political navel-gazing. *The New Yorker*'s film critic Anthony

Lane reckons that Baron Cohen is "outraged by the business of our being human."[68] In his slaughter of sacred cows, Lane writes, "His task is not so much to insult his fellow Jews, or the African-American community, as to register amazement at a culture that turns race relations into an article of faith—that seems to believe, against the run of history, in legislating our lower, more brutish instincts out of existence. In the mind of Sacha Baron Cohen, they are here to stay."[69] The *New York Times* likened Borat to General William Tecumseh Sherman "laying waste to a sizable swath of the South" with his ribald satire and trade on "cultural and regional stereotypes."[70] In its discussion of the "bigots, creeps, and idiots" Borat encounters in his "Red State" peregrinations, *San Francisco Chronicle* critic Mick LaSalle noted that the "picture takes the country's temperature at a rather fraught period" and finds a "streak of poison in American life."[71] *NPR*'s Kenneth Turan notes that Baron Cohen's mean-spirited humor is "very much of and about our time." He states, "We deserve each other and we might as well laugh."[72]

My own anecdotal experiences with the film bear similar conclusions. I saw the film at a sold-out showing in central New Jersey on the evening of its American premiere. Exiting the theatre, I overheard a young male commenting to his companion, "Can you believe how backward those people are in the middle of the country?" Rather than making observations on "Kazakhs" or foreigners in general, the film had caused the viewer in question to engage in introspection which evoked shades of the "red/blue" divide in his own country. *New York* magazine described this phenomenon as such: "We laugh at [Borat's victims] for thinking that they are superior to him— for their noblesse oblige."[73] Prior to the premiere of the film, the Borat character had heaped derision on Kazakhstan; after November 2006, it was America in the crosshairs.

The British Take on Borat

Anti-Americanism is surging in Great Britain at a time when it is trending downward on the European continent.[74] This can partially be explained by the post-Blair hangover, which involved waking up to the realities of an unwinnable war in the Middle East. Unable to blame Blair any longer (current PM Gordon Brown condemned the war from the start), Britons have turned their ire at George W. Bush and the Americans who voted for him (twice!). Not surprisingly, the debased opinions Britons now have of their American cousins effervesced in most British reviews of *Borat*. Oxford chancellor (Newcastle University) and the last British governor of Hong Kong Chris Patten recently commented, "There is now stronger anti-Americanism in Britain than there has been in my lifetime."[75] According to John O'Sullivan, "Traditional anti-Americanism in Britain has been of two kinds: a left-wing political anti-Americanism rooted in anticapitalism, and a right-wing hostility based on the decline of British power and the resentment at being displaced by the U.S. Neither was politically important."[76] However, he concludes that since the Iraq War, a strong—almost religious—anti-Americanism has manifested in Britain's center-Left politics, which resonates among large swaths of the general populace.

The current tenor of European anti-Americanism, unlike that of the 1980s or 1990s, is not confined to criticism of the country's political elites. In other words, anti-American invective is not simply directed at Bush II and his cronies. Rather, such vituperation is increasingly being directed at those who voted for him, i.e., everyday Americans. This can be witnessed in a number of quarters. Angst over Washington's refusal to abide by the Kyoto Protocols on greenhouse gas reduction has spilled into vociferous criticism of the American lifestyle replete with McMansions, gas-guzzling Hummers, and irreverence for their over-sized "carbon footprints." The United States' pertinacious refusal to fully adhere to international conventions such as the International Criminal Court (ICC) and the Ottawa Treaty banning land mines is now seen as an elite complement to Americans' workaday "better than thou" esprit vis-à-vis the rest of the world. Horror at the White House's arrogance in its prosecution of the Iraq War has filtered down to a general disgust for "Dirty Harry-style" American chest-thumping in the fields of business, education, etc. Revulsion at Bush's Manichean, biblically-inflected righteousness (e.g., "you are either with us or against us") has translated into a pernicious mistrust of American religiosity in all its forms: Evangelical, Catholic, Jewish, etc.

With such a sea change in mind, it not surprising that the left-of-center *Independent* review "Hitting the Bigot Time" noted how well "Borat's absurdly offensive bigotry . . . conforms to a certain American mindset."[77] Humming the same tune, Britain's radical weekly magazine, *New Statesman*, expressed shock at the "tacit" reactions of Americans to Borat's "ghoulish requests."[78] Ryan Gilbey notes, "There's an ageing cowpoke who requires only the mildest of prompts to endorse the murder of gays and Muslims. Others indict themselves as much by what they don't say as what they do. . . . Trying to find the ideal car for mowing down gypsies, or seeking the best gun for killing Jews, he encounters only compliance among America's salespeople."[79] The images and exchanges have much greater resonance after six years of the Bush presidency than they might have had a decade earlier.

Borat provides a remarkably expressive canvas for painting a picture of America which evokes and then confirms European prejudices against the hoi polloi of "Red State" America. Borat exposes a snake pit of Bible-thumping, intolerant mouth-breathers everywhere he travels and many Europeans simply leaned back in their cineplex seats and chortled, "I knew it." While some may ponder how many hours of "useless" footage ended up on the cutting room floor, e.g., scenes of erudite Americans questioning Borat's Kazakhness, their refusals to suffer his nonsense, etc., it is an undeniable fact that many Europeans wallowed in the final pastiche because it confirmed their deepest prejudices. America did find one British/European defender in the form of the iconoclastic journalist Christopher Hitchens, who took the *New Statesman* to task for its jaundiced, anti-American review of *Borat*.[80] In his commentary on the film's reception, he suggested that the real message of the film was that "Americans are almost pedantic in their hospitality and politesse."[81]

There is an additional wrinkle as well. *Borat* appeared at a time when, according to *Daily Mail* columnist Melanie Phillips, "anti-Semitism is on the rise in Britain" and the "biggest single cause of British anti-Americanism . . . is Israel."[82] A film by an observant British Jew who is decidedly pro-Israel and uses his art to mock American anti-Semitism by engaging in it could hardly have come at a more complicated time. Writing in the left-wing *Guardian*, Peter Bradshaw framed the issue succinctly:

> Borat . . . is an anti-semite, and for cinemagoers who have become used to the unwritten convention that anti-semitism is not represented on screen other than in the period garb of Nazi Germany, it is almost a physical shock to feel the swipe of Borat's contemporary bigotry. The last time I experienced this was listening to Terry Jones's sentimental cleaning-lady in Monty Python's *The Meaning of Life* in 1983: "I feel that life's a game, you sometimes win or lose/And though I may be down right now, at least I don't work for Jews." But this really is something else.[83]

Bradshaw's comments suggest how deeply embedded political correctness has become in England, while at the same time surreptitiously expressing some level of approbation that a taboo has been broken. This is not to say that Bradshaw approves of anti-Semitism; most likely, he does not. Instead, he advocates a widening of the public sphere, especially at a time when it is so common to parody other groups, mentalities, and orientations.

Samizdat Success: How the Russian and Kazakhstani Bans Brought Borat to Eurasia

While the government of Kazakhstan modified its position on Baron Cohen's Boratistan parody in advance of the film's premiere, not all was forgiven. The organization which manages the majority of Kazakhstan's theatres made the decision not to buy or show the film in the country. Ruslan Sultan, distribution manager for the country's largest movie chain Otau Cinema, condemned the feature film as such: "We consider this movie offensive, a complete lie, and nonsense."[84] Speaking of the decision, Roman Vassilenko of Kazakhstan's Embassy to the US stated:

> I suspect they made this decision without seeing the film and based their decision on the current media outcry associated with the depiction of Kazakhstan. I doubt, however, that they would have changed their minds upon seeing the film. It offers nothing to a Kazakh audience. It would not be funny. It would be lost in translation—both literally and figuratively. Not only the issues associated with Sacha Baron Cohen's speech which uses Polish, Hebrew, and gibberish or [his co-star Ken Davitian's] use of Armenian. The jokes are based on a sophisticated understanding of the nuances of American culture. The movie offends particular layers and groups within the US population. It would not be appealing given the mentality of Kazakhs.

Recognizing the importance of local sensitivities, Twentieth Century Fox's regional distribution subsidiary, Gemini Films, agreed not to attempt to show the film in Kazakhstan.[85] The indirect ban did not, of course, prevent intrepid Kazakhstanis from viewing the longtime *bête noire* of their government. Pirated versions of the DVD were available for purchase in the markets soon after the film's premiere in Western theatres.[86] In addition to pirated copies, the *Borat* DVD made a killing in Kazakhstan once it entered into legal distribution. Online retailer Amazon's spokesperson Rakhi Parekh noted, "With the controversy the film caused around the world, it seems residents of Kazakhstan are now desperate to see what all the fuss is about—so much so that they are willing to pay the 505 Kazakhstani tenge ($4) charge to have the DVD delivered from the U.K."[87]

Kazakhstan gingerly sidestepped the harshest form of international opprobrium by thrusting the responsibility of "banning" the film onto a private agency, thus effectively making it a "market-based" issue rather than governmental censorship. Such an approach stands in stark contrast to the reception the film received in the Middle East. Every Arab country, with the sole exception of Lebanon, banned the film. In the United Arab Emirates, several censors even walked out of the screening in disgust.[88] However, President Nursultan Nazarbayev is keen on gaining the Organization for Security and Co-operation in Europe (OSCE) presidency for his country in the future and it would have been untoward for an organization charged with improving democratic practices and improved governance as having been responsible for banning such trivial fare as *Borat*. Kazakhstan's media regime is, in fact, one of its great weaknesses in the eyes of Western observers. Since independence, several media figures have died under suspicious circumstances or been the victims of unsolved murders. Until the premiere of *Borat*, the most famous motion picture associated with Kazakhstan was *Killer* (1998), which depicts the downward spiral of an unemployed chauffeur who is railroaded into killing an investigative journalist before meeting his own demise at the hands of the mafia.

While Astana took a tentative approach to *Borat*, their northern neighbor was less subtle. Russia's Federal Culture and Cinematography Agency declined to certify the film for public distribution in the country. Blaming a recent series of hate-crimes directed against Caucasians and Central Asians, the agency's spokesperson Yury V. Vasyuchov cited the possibility that the film might enflame "religious and ethnic feelings" and thus posed a danger to public safety.[89] It was the first time a non-pornographic film had been banned in the second Russian republic.[90] As such, the news that the film would not run in the 300 theatres which were planning on showing it was received as a political issue among Russia's population. Yerzhan Ashykbayev, the Kazakhstani official who famously threatened Baron Cohen with "legal action" back in 2005, quickly denied that his government had asked the Kremlin to take such actions.[91]

While Russian officials denied the decision constituted a ban, it was reported in the Russian media as such, including the influential English-language daily the *Moscow Times*. The movie, which would have likely fallen flat in Russia had it not been banned, was an instant hit. According to sociologist Peter Meylakhs of the Center for Independent Social Research in St. Petersburg, Russia, *Borat* DVDs were "literally flying off the shelves" due to the oversized caption which stated the film had been "banned in the Russian theatres."[92] Under the Soviet Union's totalitarian media regime, government-suppressed literature, music, and other works of art were often produced in self-published or *samizdat* form.[93] The allure of such forbidden fruit continues to this day in post-Soviet Russia, as the success of *Borat* proves. The question remains whether the ban on *Borat* was, as one analyst framed it, "a unique case,"[94] or an ominous harbinger of President Vladimir Putin's growing control over all aspects of Russian media.[95]

Borat Goes to Court

Arguably, *Borat: Cultural Learnings of America for Make Benefit Glorious Nation of Kazakhstan* has stimulated more lawsuits than any motion picture in recent memory. While films like *The Da Vinci Code* (2006) and *The Passion of the Christ* (2004) inflamed religious sensibilities and provoked protests, none have done so while simultaneously fueling a micro-industry of civil litigation like *Borat*. Even before *Borat*'s premiere, two of the three USC frat boys discussed earlier in this chapter filed for an injunction against the film. In their wake came a deluge of supporting "actors" seeking damages for the film's destructive impact on their lives, from an entire Romanian village to a Manhattan executive. While some of the lawsuits were simply frivolous attempts to profit off the film's unexpected financial success, other cases—such as those brought by a musician whose work was used without permission—represented genuine headaches for Sacha Baron Cohen, his team of lawyers, and Twentieth Century Fox.

The Romani villagers who appeared in the movie's opening scenes exemplify the problematic nature of Baron Cohen's global minstrelsy. Genetic and linguistic data suggest the ancestors of contemporary Roma and Sinti began migrating from the Punjab region of the Indian subcontinent around 1050 C.E.[96] Over the past millennium, the Romani people (often referred to as Gypsies) have generated a fantastic array of perceptions, images, and prejudices among Europeans.[97] While the Roma have been envied for their perceived freedom, vivre, and adherence to traditions, they have simultaneously been excoriated for their secretiveness, chicanery, poverty, and lack of hygiene. Everywhere Roma are viewed as a (usually undesirable) minority living on the fringes of society and modernity. In Europe, they were consigned to a subservient position within society, taking up professions such as horse-traders, coppersmiths, and entertainers.[98]

The 20th century proved traumatic to the Romani peoples. In the 1940s, the Nazis systematically murdered hundreds of thousands of Roma in what has come to be called the *Porrajmos*. Shortly thereafter, the newly-established Communist governments of Eastern Europe forcibly sedentarized the Roma, a process which destroyed key aspects of their traditional support networks but failed to fully integrate them into "socialist society." After the democratic revolutions of 1989, Gypsies emerged a scapegoat for many of the evils of post-totalitarian Europe. As a result, 21st century Roma suffer from economic marginalization, and are frequently the victims of institutionalized discrimination, as well as ethnic violence. Over time, negative stereotypes of the Roma became deeply ingrained in the European world view, something Baron Cohen subtly taps into with his own humor.

In Romania, as well as other Central European states, Roma tend to live together in low-income urban housing or, alternatively, in small "Gypsy towns." Glod, Romania—the site of the opening scenes of *Borat*—is one such village. Located in Dâmbovița County some 80 miles north of the capital Bucharest, the hamlet of approximately 1,500 is poor and unkempt. When scouting a location for the film, Kazakhstan was rumored to have been ruled out not only for political reasons, but also due to aesthetic concerns. Kazakhstani towns, villages, and the countryside in general tend to be better kept than those of Romania. Despite its European Union status, it is not uncommon to see litter-strewn riverbeds, horse-drawn carriages on main thoroughfares, and (speaking from personal experience) the odd granny defecating in public.

Glod's residents are clearly of European stock. However, they are noticeably swarthy, thus evoking the subtle Orientalist prejudices of the "Balkan other."[99] According to famed postcolonial theorist Edward Said:

> The development and maintenance of every culture require the existence of another, different and competing alter ego. The construction of identity . . . involves the construction of opposites and "others" whose actuality is always subject to the continuous interpretation and reinterpretation of their differences from "us."[100]

The Roma—perhaps more than any other entity, with the possible exception of the "Jew" and the "Turk"—represent that alter ego for modern Europeans. While the swarthy but undeniably European Roma struck just the right chord for the film, Asiatic Kazakhs would have certainly short-circuited the desired presentation of Sacha Baron Cohen's "Boratistan" by inevitably triggering the question "Are those people Chinese?" from uninitiated American viewers. Ethnographer Dickie Wallace describes the artificial landscape created by the use of a Romani village as an "orientalized palimpsest" that trots out all of Western Europe's prejudices towards the Balkans as an immediately recognizable site of barbarism, filth, overt sexuality, and hyper-masculinity.[101]

Having selected Glod as the site of the film, Baron Cohen and his production team went to work creating a sufficiently medieval backwater to explain Borat's origins. Glodeni, who were paid about six dollars apiece for their troubles, were outraged by the presentation of their town as a place where the school yard is littered with AK-47s, cows are kept inside the house, and the local abortion doctor's instrument of choice is an acetylene torch. Resentful at her neighbors being cast as stand-ins for the unfortunate nation of Boratistanis, Dana Luca lamented, "We thought they came here to help us—not mock us . . . we are a poor people, but we are still people."[102] Lawyers filed a $30 million lawsuit in a Manhattan court on behalf of Nicolae Todorache and Spiridom Ciorebea stating that the Glod residents had been misled by the film's producers, who claimed to be making a "documentary about extreme poverty in Romania that would fairly depict their lives, living conditions, occupations, community, heritage and beliefs."[103] Gregg Brilliant, a spokesman for Twentieth Century Fox, countered stating, "The movie was never presented to anyone in Romania as a documentary."[104] It has been argued that by filming in Romania prior to EU accession, the film's legal team was able to avoid a number of "good faith" practices required of filmmakers in other parts of Europe and the United States. Regardless, the case seems to stand on weak ground.

Ironically, the lawsuit has had the exact opposite of its stated intent. Ostensibly, the villagers were upset by the fact that they and their little town were portrayed in such a negative light. However, it was not until the case became public that the international press began to focus on Glod itself (until that point Kazakhstan was still the site of the mischief except for only the most careful readers of the film's credits). Soon journalists were streaming into the Carpathian town asking questions, taking pictures, and seeking interviews. Sadly, press coverage of the story tapped into well-established narratives in the West of Gypsies as perennial victims on one hand and prone to connivance in business dealings on the other. The unwanted attention eventually provoked hostility "with crowds of angry, shouting villagers repeatedly gathering around reporters."[105] According to *Independent* reporter Simon Calder, Glod's residents should stop trying to renegotiate the terms of their contract with Baron Cohen and threatening journalists, instead "they should celebrate the worldwide success of the movie, and the way their village has transcended other Glods in the Romanian pantheon" (there are four others).[106] In his essay "Why Romanians are Sitting on a Glod Mine," Calder playfully (and condescendingly) predicted a bright future for the locality with a Borat Bar and Grill, a Kazakh Hotel, and campy tours in horse-drawn carts.

Borat's explicit denigration of Gypsies also sparked controversy for the film outside of Romania. The European Center for Antiziganism Research, a not-for-profit organization dedicated to combating prejudice against Gypsies, filed a complaint against the film claiming it violated Germany's anti-discrimination laws. The non-governmental organization accused Baron Cohen of "defamation and inciting violence against Sinti and Roma."[107] Borat brands himself as a "former Gypsy catcher" and provocatively asks a used car salesman how fast he would need to drive a Hummer to ensure that he would kill any Gypsies he hit. Marko Knudsen, the group's leader, asked for an injunction to stop the film from being shown in Germany after failing to achieve action at the market level. "We called the distributors, but they laughed at us."[108] The state ultimately failed to intervene as well, though advertisements for the film stopped carrying clips from the above-referenced scene.

In an interview with the *Chronicle of Higher Education*, Ian F. Hancock, the leading American scholar on the Romani people, stated that he liked the film. However, the scholar was saddened to see how little criticism *Borat*'s antiziganism triggered, especially in relation to the condemnations of the film for its attacks on Jews, blacks, gays, and women. He claimed that in America being a Gypsy is seen in the same terms as being a hippie, you can start and stop.[109] Unfortunately, in the European context, this is far from the case as Gypsies are denied jobs and proper housing based on their ethnic background.

While his days as Ali G had certainly prepared him for the potential backlash of *Borat*, even the veteran comedic offender Baron Cohen must have been shocked by the sheer volume of complaints, controversies, and court cases his 2006 film generated. Reflecting on such contentiousness, Baron Cohen used his acceptance speech at the Golden Globes to wryly thank "every American who has not sued me so far." Even before its premiere, *Borat* had to face down two of its own stars in court. "John Doe One" and "John Doe Two" (i.e., two of three previously-mentioned USC frat boys) filed a case against the film in Los Angeles Superior Court West claiming fraud, rescission of contract, common law false light, statutory false light, appropriation of likeness, and negligent infliction of emotional distress. The complaint opens with the misspelled, but self-evident assertion: "Sasha Baron Cohen is a prankster."[110]

According to the plaintiffs, the production company interviewed a number of members of their fraternity before deciding on the outspoken troika that ultimately appeared in the film. They were promised that neither their names nor the fraternity's name would be mentioned and that the film would only be distributed in Europe. They further claimed to have been "loosened up" with alcohol prior to signing their consent forms, and that heavy drinking continued during filming. Based on their belief that the film would not be distributed in the US, the plaintiffs then participated in "behavior that they otherwise would not have engaged in." As such, the plaintiffs sought an injunction against the use of their likenesses and unspecified damages for the malicious infliction of "humiliation, mental anguish, and emotional and physical distress, loss of reputation, goodwill and standing in the community in which the PLAINTIFFS live, work and learn." The crux of their argument was that the film had falsely depicted them as being "insensitive to minorities." Evidently, the plaintiffs did not see a need to distance themselves from their throaty misogyny as no mention of their offensive comments about women is to be found in the claim. Despite the fact that the case was thrown out, the stage was set for a raft of additional lawsuits.[111]

Claiming that her "business is in ruins," etiquette coach Cindy Streit, who hosted the film's comedy-of-errors dinner party, sought relief under California's Unfair Trade Practices Act. In a press conference with her attorney, Streit announced, "I am mortified at forever being portrayed in an R-rated movie with the most horrifying, pornographic scene imaginable to me."[112] At the time of writing the owner of Etiquette Training Services in Birmingham, Alabama was still seeking "a disgorgement of the profits" of the film and was also considering a civil suit against Baron Cohen and the film's producers. Another etiquette coach, Kathie Martin, who prepped Borat for the dinner party similarly made public her intentions to sue in the wake of negative publicity generated by her appearance. Jeffrey Lemerond, a New York-based financial analyst, also filed a lawsuit stating he suffered "public ridicule, degradation, and humiliation" as a result of being filmed fleeing in apparent terror as Borat tries to kiss him on a Manhattan street. Lemerond's case may have some merit since he never signed a release form which might therefore violate New York State's privacy laws. Another suit was filed by a South Carolina man who was filmed in a restaurant bathroom where Borat posed as an attendant. Borat's prurient comments about the fellow's masculine endowments did not make it into the final cut but were posted on *YouTube*.

While Jeffrey Lemerond and the embarrassed South Carolinian may have some grounds for a lawsuit against Twentieth Century Fox, most entertainment lawyers have suggested that the producer's consent forms are airtight. One America Productions, Baron Cohen's longtime shill for his various projects, carefully protected the film against lawsuits arising from the participants' distaste over their portrayal. Under American law, the written content of a consent form always trumps any spoken agreement. While the producers somewhat unorthodox practice of denying the signatories a copy of the document and misrepresenting the scale and scope of the film's distribution have cast some doubt on the inviolability of the contract, thus far, the consent forms have held up. Timing of the signing was important and also explains why most participants failed to secure a copy of the agreement. According to *Newsweek*, "The producers usually pulled it out just before the cameras rolled, at a moment of maximum bustle. . . . Most of the folks contacted by *Newsweek* admit they barely read the release. Even if they did, they might not have grasped the legalese . . . which is a nifty way of getting people to agree that it's OK to defraud them."[113]

The text of the consent form refers to the project as a "documentary-style film" and not a documentary (as many aggrieved participants have suggested). And while the producers may have told Cindy Streit, the John Does, and others that the film would be confined to the Stalin-era cinemas of Belarus, they signed a contract which stipulated:

> The Participant agrees that any rights that the Participant may have in the Film or the Participant's contribution to the Film are hereby assigned to the Producer, and that the Producer shall be exclusively entitled to use, or to assign or license to others the right to use, the Film and any recorded material that includes the Participant without restriction in the media throughout the universe in perpetuity and without liability to the Participant, and the Participant hereby grants any consents required for those purposes.[114]

In other words, we can use your likeness wherever and whenever we want. Certainly recognizing that a bit of verbal prestidigitation would be necessary to prompt some of the "cast" to sign the documents, the following clause was also included in the release: "the Participant is not relying upon any promises or statements made by anyone about the nature of the Film or the identity of any other Participants or persons involved in the Film." According to a top entertainment lawyer speaking on the Borat controversy, the consent form is a contractual legal doctrine that supersedes any oral representation relayed.[115] Furthermore, the film's participants also signed away their rights to sue in order to gain their fifteen minutes of fame:

> The Participant specifically, but without limitation, waives, and agrees not to bring at any time in the future, any claims against the Producer, or against any of its assignees or licenses or anyone associated with the Film, that include assertions of (a) infringement of rights of publicity or misappropriation (such as any allegedly improper or unauthorized use of the Participant's name or likeness or image), (b) damages caused by "acts of God" (such as, but not limited to, injuries from natural disasters), (c) damages caused by acts of terrorism or war, (d) intrusion (such as any allegedly offensive behavior or questioning or any invasion of privacy), (e) false light (such as any allegedly false or misleading portrayal of the Participant), (f) infliction of emotional distress (whether allegedly intentional or negligent), (g) trespass (in property or person), (h) breach of any alleged contract (whether the alleged contract is verbal or in writing), (i) allegedly deceptive business or trades practices, (j) copyright or trademark infringement, (k) defamation (such as any allegedly false or misleading statements made on the Film), (l) violations of Section 43(a) of the Lanham Act (such as allegedly false or misleading statements or suggestions about the Participant in relation to the Film or the Film in relation to the Participant), (m) prima facie (such as alleged intentional harm to the Participant), (n) fraud (such as any alleged deception or surprise about the Film or the consent agreement), (o) breach of alleged moral rights, or (p) tortuous or wrongful interference with any contracts or business of the Participant.

The alphabetized clauses above read like a laundry list of the lawsuits and threats of legal action that dogged the movie; however, they also present a solid defense against such claims. Curiously, the form also requires that if any claim is brought, it must be filed in the State of New York. To date, the film's participants have received little legal traction against the well-prepared legal team which initially greenlighted the release of the film.

While ironclad consent forms may have protected Sacha Baron Cohen & Co. from legal claims emanating from embarrassed bit players, no such protections existed for the film's copyright infringements. *Borat*'s unexpected success at the box office and international resonance quickly stimulated new controversies. Mahir Çağrı best exemplifies this trend.

Çağrı has been labeled cyberspace's "first famous non-f......us person." The amateur Web developer and comedian achieved some measure of global fame in 1999 with his roughhewn Web site "I Kiss You."[116] Like the three-dimensional "Dancing Baby" and the "Hamster Dance," Çağrı's site emerged as one of the late 1990s' preeminent Internet memes, i.e., a unit of cultural information faddishly transmitted via email, blogs, social networking sites, or instant messaging. While today almost anyone can achieve overnight, albeit fleeting, fame via *YouTube*, such celebrities were comparatively rare a decade ago. Çağrı's site included him engaging in a game of ping pong, lounging in a speedo, and declaring "I like sex": all elements of the prologue to the *Borat* film. Furthermore, Borat bears a striking resemblance to Çağrı with his Semitic features, bad suit, love of travel, and prodigious height. According to the *Guardian*, "Both men struggle with the English language and are wildly enthusiastic about the prospect of meeting women and sexing them . . . the similarities are too strong to be coincidental."[117]

Despite the fact that Kristo (Borat's conceptual forebear) appeared on British television as earlier as 1997, Çağrı has consistently maintained that he was the inspiration for Borat. In the immediate wake of the film's global premiere, Çağrı traveled to London with the intent of obtaining a share of the film. Shortly before meeting with lawyers, he declared to the international press, "The world knows he is copying Mahir. . . . I am not saying this—the world is. I have received so many e-mails from people in the United States who tell me he is imitating me. The bombshell is going to fall. [Baron Cohen] is making money by using me."[118] In reality, the claims of a lawsuit were little more than a mass-mediated gimmick to revive Çağrı's moribund fame. The Turk deftly used the success of the Borat movie to leverage his longtime goals of making his own movie and publishing an autobiography.[119] The gamble paid off. After a week of Borat-bashing, he exclaimed, "I have five offers to make movie of myself from the States and UK came in last week. My life story as a book is ready, and now ready for producement (sic). It will show the real Mahir. When I do my movie people will see and see that it is not like Borat."[120]

Baron Cohen may face a stiffer legal battle with the Israeli comedian Dovale Glickman. Glickman is suing the Borat creator for allegedly stealing one of his catchphrases: "Wa Wa Wee Wa." Borat uses the phrase to suggest his amazement and/or admiration of certain key cultural findings he uncovers in his travels. However, Glickman coined the nonsensical interjection in 1991 while on the Israeli television program *Zehu Zeh* ('That's It'). He also used it in a series of television commercials for the Israeli equivalent of the yellow pages phone directory. According to a number of reports,

the phrase is still common today on the streets of Israel, which could ultimately hinder any efforts at litigation.

The film's most obvious infringement of intellectual property came
with its use of the song "Čaje Šukarije" by the Macedonian singer Esma
Redžepova. In late 2006, she told the Serbian daily newspaper *Politika* of
her intention to sue the comedian for 800,000 euros or more than one million dollars. The song, which has been re-recorded by other musicians, is
one of her best known. Redžepova is one of the most prominent Roma sing-
ers in the Balkans and was outraged by the song's usage without permission
stating, "I am fed up with the fact that everyone is using my song without
even informing me about it, not even mentioning that it is my song, the one
I once wrote and was the first to sing."[121] The emotionally-charged tune is
used as a leitmotiv for Borat's "Kazakhstan," played in the opening segment
and when the protagonist remembers his village at later points in the film.
According to *Agence France-Presse*, "A tune by another famous Balkan
musician, Goran Bregovic, can also be heard during the film, but reports say
his financial demands had been satisfied prior to the movie's distribution."[122]

While Redžepova will likely settle out of court and the two comedians
addressed above will find few courts willing to hear their cases, the collective existence of such controversies further underscores the global nature of
the Borat phenomenon. From Tel Aviv to Vladivostok and from Cairo to
Los Angeles, Borat has proved to be a cultural, political, and social lightning rod.

Notes

1. Due to its almost total reliance on unwitting participants rather than professional actors, many characterized the film as a documentary in the style of Michael
Moore's films *Bowling for Columbine* (2002) and *Fahrenheit 9/11* (2004). Others
have likened the film to mocking, faux documentaries like Christopher Guest's *Wait-
ing for Guffman* (1996) and *Best in Show* (2000). Neither the rubric of documentary
nor the mockumentary label perfectly fit *Borat* since Baron Cohen's methodology
involves a small core of actors whose job is to provoke "real people" into embarrassing themselves on camera.

2. There is some dispute over the actual name of the village. The producers of
Borat thanked the inhabitants of Moroieni in the credits and, according to the *Independent,* the town has changed its name to differentiate it from the other Romanian
villages named 'Glod;' see Simon Calder, "Why Romanians are Sitting on a Glod
Mine," *Independent,* 23 June 2007. According to the dictionary edited by the Romanian Academy, which is the body that decides what is what in the Romanian language, the correct meaning of the word is 'moist ground, road, soil, etc.' The etymology can be traced back to the Russian word "gluda." The author wishes to thank
Paul Chiş for this helpful translation.

3. The very notion of a Ministry of Information carries extensive Cold War baggage. It was through such government bureaus that Eastern European Communist
Parties monopolized power in the wake of World War II. In recent decades, many
countries in Europe and elsewhere abolished (or at least renamed) their Ministries of
Information to avoid the stigma of propaganda, thought control, and state censorship
of the press.

4. In the 1940s, the pair starred in four successful films of rollicking misadventures: *Road to Zanzibar* (1941), *Road to Morocco* (1942), *Road to Utopia* (1946), and *Road to Rio* (1947).

5. David Laderman, *Driving Visions: Exploring the Road Movie* (Austin: University of Texas Press, 2002), 1-2.

6. Nancy Condee, "Borat: Putting the Id Back in Identity Politics," *Slavic Review* 66, no. 1 (Spring 2008): 84-87.

7. Dharma Arthur, the producer of the Channel 16 WAPT's noon-time news show lost her job over the gaffe. Arthur later commented, "Because of him, my boss lost faith in my abilities and second-guessed everything I did thereafter. . . . I spiraled into depression, and before I could recover, I was released from my contract early. It took me three months to find another job, and now I'm thousands of dollars in debt and struggling to keep my house out of foreclosure;" Roger Friedman, "Dharma and . . . Borat? A 'Victim' Complains," *FOX News*, 2 November 2006, http://www.foxnews.com/story/0,2933,226960,00.html (7 August 2007).

8. Rowe later told *Salon.com*, "As long as [homosexuals] don't mess with me and get me involved, if that's their choice, just have at it. Just don't come in my household and try to demand, as they're doing now, all sorts of things. All this marriage and this mess. If you want to go live together, go live together, but don't drag everyone else into it. It's, like, before you could just pump your gas, but the thieves ruined it for everyone. Now everyone has to go pay for their gas first. Homosexuals, they want their rights for marriage and all this stuff, and they want respectability. If you want to live that life, live that life, but don't involve the whole rest of the country;" see David Marchese and Willa Paskin, "What's real in 'Borat'?" *Salon.com,* 10 November 2006, http://www.salon.com/ent/feature/2006/11/10/guide_to_borat/ (10 August 2007).

9. See Laurence Hammack, "Rodeo in Salem Gets Unexpected Song Rendition," *Roanoke Times*, 9 January 2005.

10. Anthony Lane, "In Your Face," *New Yorker* 82, no. 36 (6 November 2006): 106-109.

11. Steven S. Lee suggests this is an exceptionally effective scene for exposing Southern racism towards blacks since Luenell, as "a poor, black prostitute," is actually "more offensive than shit in a bag;" Lee, Steven S. "*Borat*, Multiculturalism, *Mnogonatsional'nost'*," *Slavic Review* 66, no. 1 (Spring 2008): 19-34.

12. Marchese and Paskin, "What's real in 'Borat'?"

13. Despite the appearance of sexual congress between the traveling partners, the scene is not coded as the realization of a simmering homosexual relationship, but instead functions as the ultimate affirmation of what Dickie Wallace describes as the "Balkan and east European crudeness and masculinity" that pervades the film; Dickie Wallace, "Hyperrealizing 'Borat' with the Map of the European 'Other,'" *Slavic Review* 66, no. 1 (Spring 2008): 35-49.

14. Interestingly, this now infamous scene pushed documentarian Michael Moore to go even further in his own incendiary filmmaking. After the Toronto Film Festival where Baron Cohen stated his admiration for Moore's own style of provocative filmmaking, Moore decided to revise portions of his most recent film *Sicko*. Moore told the *Associated Press*, "So after I saw 'Borat,' if he says I was an inspiration for those things, I now have to up the ante for him. So we sailed into the mined waters of Guantánamo Bay with sick 9/11 workers and a bullhorn." The stunt earned Moore industry kudos and an investigation from the US Department of the Treasury's Office of Foreign Assets Control for violations of the trade embargo against Cuba; see Reed Saxon, "Borat Emboldened Moore to Visit Guantanamo," *Associated Press,* 28 June 2007.

15. Upon learning about the nomination, Baron Cohen had notified the gala's organizers that Borat himself would be unable to attend, stating, "I have been trying to let Borat know this great news but for the last four hours both of Kazakhstan's

telephones have been engaged. Eventually, Premier Nazarbayev answered and said he would pass on the message as soon as Borat returned from Iran, where he is guest of honor at the Holocaust Denial Conference."

16. Campbell writes, "The hero, instead of conquering or conciliating the power of the threshold, is swallowed into the unknown and would appear to have died;" Joseph Campbell, *The Hero With a Thousand Faces* (Princeton: Princeton University Press, 1973), 90.

17. This branch of Christianity grew out of Methodism, but has a decidedly stronger emphasis on the personal relationship with God. This manifests most visibly in "speaking in tongues" and other forms of personal spontaneity during church services.

18. See "The UPCI and the Movie Borat," *Spiritual Abuse* web site, http://www.spiritualabuse.org/issues/borat.html (10 August 2007).

19. A staple of evangelical Christianity, "testimony" is a verbal profession of faith given in front of the congregation. It often involves a detailed description of one's abandonment of God or refusal to embrace His grace, and may even include titillating details of one's past indiscretions.

20. Curiously, Pamela Anderson filed for divorce from her husband, the musician Kid Rock, after he became enraged upon seeing the film.

21. Bride-kidnapping in Kazakhstan was once an endemic practice, due to the strict prohibitions against endogamy which made finding a suitable mate in the local community rather difficult. However, the Soviets effectively banned the practice in most of the country. Today, it continues almost exclusively through a consensual form of the practice—a highly ritualized form of elopement. Young Kazakh lovers have even been known to text one another in advance of the kidnapping to work out the details.

22. See Campbell, *The Hero With a Thousand Faces.*

23. According to a lawsuit filed on behalf of two of the film's "supporting cast," *Borat* was the only film to "gross over $26 million while playing at less than 1,000 locations:" see John Doe 1, an individual; John Doe 2, an individual v. One America Productions, Inc. *et al.* No. SC091723 (Cal. Sup. Ct., L.A. - West, Santa Monica, 2006).

24. Joe Morgenstern, "With Insults for All," *Wall Street Journal,* 3 November 2006, W1; Tom Charity, "Review: 'Borat' is Most Excellent Comedy," *CNN.com,* 2 November 2006, http://www.cnn.com/2006/SHOWBIZ/Movies/11/02/review.borat/index.html (15 August 2007).

25. Sukhdev Sandhu, "Review: Borat," *Daily Telegraph,* 27 October 2006, 26.

26. Colin Covert, "Movie Review: 'Borat' Just Might Be the Funniest Movie Ever," *Knight Ridder Tribune Business News,* 3 November 2006.

27. Joel Siegel, "Review: 'Borat'—Offensive, Juvenile, and Very, Very Funny," *ABC News,* 3 November 2006 at www.abcnews.go.com/Entertainment/JoelSiegel/story?id=2624468 (accessed 15 August 2007).

28. Claudia Puig, "It Bears Repeating: 'Borat' is Funny," *USA Today,* 3 November 2006, E7.

29. Mick LaSalle, "'Borat' Explores America, Finds a Very Funny Place," *San Francisco Chronicle,* 3 November 2006, E1.

30. See Gene I. Maeroff, "The 'Wedge Issues' of 2004," *Education Week* 23, no. 16 (7 January 2004): 60.

31. See Cecile Daurat, "'Borat' Leads Revenue Gains for News Corp." *International Herald Tribune,* 8 February 2007.

32. Mike Straka, "'Borat' Would Be Better on YouTube," *FOX New.com,* 3 November 2006, http://www.foxnews.com/story/0,2933,227136,00.html (4 November 2006).

33. Johnny Vaughan, "Eeeza Nizah," *Sun*, 3 November 2006, http://www.thesun.co.uk/article/0,,2003080003-2006510080,00.html (15 August 2007); Lou Lumenick, "Kazakh It To Me!," *New York Post*, 2 November 2006, 65.

34. Paleo-conservatives are distinguished from their neo-conservative counterparts by their contempt for free trade in global markets, strident anti-immigration positions, and a strong anti-interventionist orientation in foreign policy; Steve Sailer, "21st Century Polish Jokes," *American Conservative*, 4 December 2006, http://www.isteve.com/Film_Borat.htm (4 August 2007).

35. Sailer, "21st Century Polish Jokes."

36. Ned Rice, "Gratuitous America-Bashing for Lining Pocket of Overrated Sacha Cohen," *Human Events* 62, no. 40 (20 November 2006): 20.

37. James Bowman, "Conventional Cuts," *The American Spectator*, 39 no. 10 (December 2006/January 2007): 86-7.

38. Bowman, "Conventional Cuts," 87.

39. 'Londonistan' is a term often used by certain quarters of the security community to refer to Britain's hitherto lenient policies towards radical groups, especially Islamist organizations.

40. Greg Gutfeld, "Impostors," *The American Spectator* 39, no. 10 (December 2006/January 2007): 62-4.

41. Intellectually, neo-conservatism is rooted in the works of Leo Strauss, a political philosopher at the University of Chicago from 1949-69; however, the genesis of the movement lies in a small group of Jewish, Trotskyite intellectuals who, in the context of the Cold War, came to realize the futility of changing the world through a Marxist-Leninist internationalist revolution. Kristol famously noted that he was a "liberal mugged by reality." The movement's leaders eventually began publishing small circulation magazines and journals espousing their novel world view based on an activist foreign policy, lowered taxes, and a circumscribed view of the first amendment. During the 1970s, a few key thinkers began to embrace the foreign policy of Richard Nixon, including the Vietnam War and a hard line against the Soviet Union. As their ideology evolved, it became differentiated from other forms of international relations theories such as realism, idealism, and Marxism.

42. Historically, the Republican Party has supported a Washingtonian foreign policy. In his departing address, the first American president noted, "The great rule of conduct for us in regard to foreign nations is in extending our commercial relations, to have with them as little political connection as possible. So far as we have already formed engagements, let them be fulfilled with perfect good faith. Here let us stop."

43. Prior to the release of the film, *Weekly Standard* writer Philip Terzian also penned a piece ostensibly about Borat. In fact, the essay "Steppes in Time" was little more than a litany of complaints about the author's visits to Kazakhstan where he was inconvenienced by local hospitality and "bundles of straw" on board his Kazakh Air flight; see Philip Terzian, "Steppes in Time," *Weekly Standard* 12, no. 3 (2 October 2006): 4; John Podhoretz, "The 'Borat' Show," *Weekly Standard* 12, no. 7 (30 October 2006): 36.

44. Podhoretz, "The 'Borat' Show," 36.

45. Podhoretz, "The 'Borat' Show," 36.

46. While PNAC is now a non-profit think tank, it began as an open letter sent on 3 June 1997 condemning President Bill Clinton's "incoherent" foreign policy and "isolationism" in the ranks of the right-wing. The 25 signatories included future Bush advisors and appointees Dick Cheney, I. Lewis "Scooter" Libby, Zalmay Khalizad, Aaron Friedberg, Paul Wolfowitz, and Donald Rumsfled, as well as a short-list of the neo-con establishment including Norman Podhoretz, Francis Fukuyama, Midge Decter, Elliot Abrams, and Donald Kagan. See the New American Century website at http://www.newamericancentury.org/statementofprinciples.htm.

47. Joshua Muravchik, "Borat!" *Commentary* 123, no. 1 (January 2007): 44-47.

48. Muravchik, "Borat!" 46.

49. Stephen Schwartz et. al., "No Laughing Matter?" Commentary 123 no. 4 (April 2007): 16-20.

50. Schwartz et. al., "No Laughing Matter?" 17.

51. Ben Johnson, "Free Borat," FrontPage Magazine, 3 November 2006. Available online at http://frontpagemagazine.com (11 August 2007).

52. Johnson, "Free Borat"; Ronald Reagan's would-be assassin John Warnock Hinckley, Jr. wrote to the actress shortly before his attempt on the president's life stating, "The reason I'm going ahead with this attempt now is because I cannot wait any longer to impress you."

53. Maclean's, Canada's leading news magazine, drew a similar analogy in its review of the film, "Did Bunker Beget Borat?" recalling Brooks' Springtime for Hitler, as well as All in the Family's Archie Bunker and Eric Cartman of the Comedy Central series South Park; see Jaime J. Weinman, "Did Bunker Beget Borat?" Maclean's 119, no. 44 (6 November 2006): 62-64.

54. Dhimmitude is a neologism derived from 'servitude' (or 'attitude') and dhimmi (a non-Muslim minority living under Islamic rule). The concept carries a decidedly negative connotation as it is associated with an environment of fear, subservience, and persecution on the part of the non-Muslim people in question.

55. Charles Krauthammer, "Just an Anti-Semitic Laugh? Hardly," Washington Post, 24 November 2006, A41.

56. In a 2005 Christmas speech, Chavez stated that "a minority, the descendants of the same ones that crucified Christ . . . has taken possession of all the wealth of the world . . . ownership of all of the gold of the planet, of the silver, of the minerals, the waters, the good lands, oil, of the wealth, and have concentrated the wealth in a few hands."

57. Krauthammer, "Just an Anti-Semitic Laugh?"

58. David Brooks, "The Heyday of Snobbery," New York Times, 16 November 2006, 35.

59. "By the Horns," New Republic, 235, no. 16 (16 October 2006): 7.

60. Stuart Klawans, "Coming to America!" Nation 283, no. 19 (4 December 2006): 32-36.

61. Klawans, "Coming to America!"

62. Klawans, "Coming to America!" 33.

63. Lee, "Persona Non Grata," 22.

64. Lee, "Persona Non Grata," 24.

65. Lee, "Persona Non Grata," 24.

66. While Nathan Lee's essay simply alluded to disgraced former Congressman Mark Foley (R-FL), Condee's piece mentioned Pastor Ted Haggard by name. The latter stepped down as leader of the National Association of Evangelicals after allegations of homosexuality and drug use were made public by a male prostitute.

67. Nancy Condee, "Learnings of Borat for Make Benefit Cultural Studies," Pittsburgh Post-Gazette, 12 November 2006, H6.

68. Anthony Lane, "In Your Face," New Yorker 82, no. 36 (6 November 2006): 106-109.

69. Lane, "In Your Face," 107.

70. William Tecumseh Sherman served as a general in the Union Army during the American Civil War (1861–65). He is infamous in the American South for the harshness of the "scorched earth" policies and conducting total war against the Confederate States; Manohla Dargis, "Satire is Not Pretty," New York Times, 3 November 2006, W1.

71. Mick LaSalle, "'Borat' Explores America, Finds a Very Funny Place," San Francisco Chronicle, 3 November 2006, E1.

72. Kenneth Turan, "'Borat' Offends, Entertains While Mirroring Society," NPR Morning Edition, 3 November 2006.

73. David Edelstein, "So Funny It Hurts," *New York,* 6 November 2006, 91-92.

74. Philippe Roger, "Global Anti-Americanism and the Lessons of the 'French Exception,'" *Journal of American History* 93, no. 2 (September 2006): 448-451.

75. Chris Patten, "Epiphanies," *Foreign Policy* 161 (July/August 2007): 19.

76. John O'Sullivan, "State of the Cousins," *National Review* 57, no. 9 (23 May 2005): 22-24.

77. Anthony Quinn, "Hitting the Bigot Time," *Independent,* 3 November 2006, 6-7.

78. Ryan Gilbey, "Thongs of Freedom," *New Statesman* 135, no. 4817 (6 November 2006): 45.

79. Gilbey, "Thongs of Freedom," 45.

80. Hitchens, who eschews the oft-applied neoconservative label, is well known for his pro-American views in the realm of foreign policy, specifically support for the Iraq War, combating "Islamo-fascism," and remaking the Middle East.

81. Christopher Hitchens, "Kazakh Like Me," *Slate,* 13 November 2006, http://slate.com/id/2153578/ (14 November 2006).

82. Melanie Phillips, "Britain is Turning on the U.S.—at Its Own Peril," *USA Today,* 24 October 2006, 13.

83. Peter Bradshaw, "Bear-Baiting in Bushville," *Guardian,* 27 October 2006, 7.

84. Pallavi Gogoi, "Banning Borat," *Business Week Online,* 7 November 2006.

85. Steven Lee Myers, "'Borat' is Not Approved for Distribution in Russia," *New York Times,* 10 November 2006, 9.

86. In a nod to such practices, the (legal) DVD version released in regions 1 and 2 (North America and Western Europe/Middle East, respectively) mimics foreign bootlegs in outward appearance. The DVD menu facetiously warns viewers that "selling piratings of this moviedisc will result in punishment by crushing."

87. "'Borat' DVD selling nicely in Kazakhstan," *Reuters News,* 12 March 2007.

88. See Ali Jaafar, "'Borat' Gross-outs Fall Flat in Mideast," *Variety,* 30 November 2006.

89. Myers, "'Borat' is Not Approved," 9.

90. "'Offensive' Borat Movie Banned," *St. Petersburg Times,* 10 November 2006.

91. "Borat Banned From Russian Movie Theaters," *Moscow Times,* 9 November 2006.

92. Peter Meylakhs, personal correspondence, 2 January 2007.

93. An interesting example of such samizdat was the phenomena of "ribs" or "bones," i.e., homemade recordings of forbidden Western music on X-ray sheets pilfered from hospitals. When he performed in Red Square in 2003, singer Paul McCartney was presented with a "ribs" recording of an early Beatles album by a fan who had horded the contraband for decades.

94. Myers, "'Borat' is Not Approved," 9.

95. See, for instance, Masha Lipman, "Constrained or Irrelevant: The Media in Putin's Russia," *Current History* 104, no. 684 (October 2005): 319-24.

96. See Radu P. Ioviță, and Theodore G. Schurr. "Reconstructing the Origins and Migrations of Diasporic Populations: The Case of the European Gypsies," *American Anthropologist* 106, no. 2 (June 2004): 267-281.

97. The etymology of 'Gypsy,' increasingly seen as a pejorative descriptor though still embraced by many Roma, stems from the mistaken assumption that the Roma were of Egyptian origin; see David Mayall, *Gypsy Identities 1500-2000: From Egipcyans and Moon-men to the Ethnic Romany* (London and New York: Routledge, 2004).

98. In Wallachia and Moldavia, the core states of modern-day Romania, they were enslaved from the 1300s until the mid-19th century.

99. See Maria Todorova, *Imagining the Balkans* (Oxford: Oxford University Press, 1997) for more on Western European obsessions with "Balkanism."

100. Edward Said, *Orientalism* (New York: Vintage Books, 1979), 331-2.

101. See Wallace, "Hyperrealizing 'Borat' with the Map of the European 'Other.'"

102. "Romanians Say 'Borat' Misled Them," *Associated Press*, 14 November 2006.

103. One of the litigants, Todorache, is an amputee; he appears in the film with a rubber sex toy attached to his stump. The other, Ciorebea, was portrayed as the town's "mechanic and abortionist;" see "New York Judge Questions Viability of Villagers' 'Borat' Lawsuit," *Associated Press*, 4 December 2006.

104. Thomas Zambito, "Gypsies Sue 'Borat' for $30m for Making Them Look Like Glods," *New York Daily News*, 21 November 2006, 2.

105. "Romanians Say," *Associated Press*.

106. Calder, "Why Romanians are Sitting on a Glod Mine."

107. "German Gypsies in Legal Bid against Borat Creator," *Reuters News*, 17 October 2006.

108. "German Gypsies," *Reuters*.

109. See Peter Monaghan, "Verbatim," *Chronicle of Higher Education* 53, no. 15 (1 December 2006): A13.

110. See *John Doe 1, an individual; John Doe 2, an individual v. One America Productions, Inc.* et al. No. SC091723 (Cal. Sup. Ct., L.A. - West, Santa Monica, 2006).

111. Earlier in the year, Baron Cohen had to deal with a harbinger of the lawsuits to come. Heddi Cundle, who made the acquaintance of the comedian when they visited Israel as teenagers, sued *Da Ali G Show* for Ali G's use of her name. The character called her a "minger" and a "bitch" and claimed to have impregnated her in a conversation with Gore Vidal. The complaint stipulated that the show had caused her "loss of reputation, stress, worry, physical pain, humiliation, shame, mortification, and hurt feelings." Subsequent releases of the *Da Ali G Show* bleeped out her name; see James Tapper, "Why is You Calling Me a Minger, Ali," *Mail on Sunday*, 4 March 2007, 47.

112. Lisa Sweetingham, "Etiquette Expert is Latest to Lash Out at 'Borat' Creator, Claiming Humiliation," *Court TV* web site, 17 November 2006, http://www.courttv.com/people/2006/1116/borat_ctv.html (accessed 25 August 2007).

113. Devin Gordon, "Behind the Schemes," *Newsweek* 148 no. 16 (16 October 2006): 74-75.

114. See TMZ Staff, "Borat's Release—Anything But Sexy Time," *TMZ.com*, 14 November 2006.

115. Solvej Schou, "With Flap over 'Borat' Methods, Experts Weigh in on Consent Forms," *Associated Press*, 17 November 2006.

116. See http://www.ikissyou.org/.

117. "The Real Borat," *Guardian*, 28 October 2006.

118. Suzan Fraser, "Turkish Man Says He's the Real Borat," *Associated Press*, 7 November 2006.

119. See Michele Norris, "Is the Real Borat Being Shut Out of the Limelight?" *NPR: All Things Considered*, 19 December 2006.

120. Jane Clinton, ". . . And Upset the 'Real Borat' in the Process," *Express on Sunday*, 12 November 2006, 10.

121. "Macedonian Songstress to Sue 'Borat' Filmmakers," *Agence France-Presse*, 15 December 2006.

122. "Macedonian Songstress," *AGP*.

Afterword
The Global Minstrel Show

Sacha Baron Cohen owes his career to two things: an uncanny talent for crafting and maintaining outrageous characters, and his ability to parlay controversy into professional success. Regarding the latter, he has been serendipitously aided by major structural changes in international politics, global communications, and the infrastructure of mass media. In an interconnected world where cultural disorientation is the norm not the exception, Ali G, Bruno, and Borat unexpectedly emerged as mirrors of the age. While Baron Cohen may have initially performed simply for his countrymen, his pantomime ultimately reached across the world with massive ramifications. Whether it was intentional or not, Baron Cohen has created a new form of comedy: global minstrelsy.

In recent years, satellite television, the Internet, the proliferation of mobile phones, and manifold applications which connect all three have revolutionized the consumption of entertainment, news, and information. Predictably, there has been a concurrent broadening of the geographic scope of Western media products far beyond what has traditionally been labeled "the West." Corporate consolidation of media companies has reduced the global diversity of all media. Consequently, more people in more places have access to the same media sources, and thus concern themselves with the same issues. Political changes since 1989 have also contributed to this new milieu, creating an environment more open to the global spread of a creolized cultural mélange.[1] The dismantling of the so-called Iron Curtain that divided Soviet-dominated Eastern Europe from its Western, American-influenced counterpart is the most obvious manifestation of this new world order. However, the past several decades have also seen the marketization of the People's Republic of China, the democratization of most of Latin America, and the spread of neo-liberalism across generous swaths of the developing world. Taken collectively, these phenomena have gone a long way in realizing the "global village" Marshall McLuhan predicted in the 1960s.[2] In his seminal text *The Gutenberg Galaxy*, McLuhan observed that electronic mass media were collapsing space and time barriers in human communication, thus enabling people to communicate on a global scale.

Whether one laments or celebrates this turn of events, it is undeniable that certain cultural norms have now become global. Today, this phenomenon is disproportionately manifested among the world's youth, many of whom are now versed in key elements of the same popular culture. From Parisian *banlieue* to Istanbul's *gecekondus* to the *favelas* of Rio de Janeiro, earnest expropriations of American rap culture have been integrated into local identity just as references to MTV, Britney Spears, and *The Sopranos* pepper the discourse of urban elites from Bangalore to Moscow to Mexico City.[3] Consequently, the influence of Sacha Baron Cohen's avatars—Ali G, Bruno, and Borat—have greater reach and influence today than they could have possibly attained at any time in the past. In today's world of deterritorialized, decentralized, and denationalized media products, cultural lodestones like Ali G are created and disseminated at a mind-boggling rate, regardless of their merit. More importantly, each new global meme is more easily distributed than the last, allowing (though not guaranteeing) penetration far beyond its country of origin into nearly every corner of the global marketplace.

I do not suggest that such flows go unquestioned or uncontested. In his seminal essay "Jihad and McWorld," political scientist Benjamin Barber identified two powerful forces that are tearing at the fabric of contemporary, nationally-oriented societies: globalism and tribalism.[4] On the one hand, formerly national polities are today being knitted together by global markets, products, threats, and media. This results in a decidedly global outlook among certain segments of the population, especially upwardly-mobile, urban elites. Simultaneously, certain elements of globalization are being challenged by champions of parochialism, who mobilize along local, social, regional, and religious lines. Consequently, there has been a transnational embrace of Baron Cohen's humor among certain groups, while others have voiced sharp criticisms of the comedian. In the latter camp, we find such varied players as media regulators, adoptive parents, Pentecostals, anti-discrimination activists, and partisan political pundits. In each case, the virulent reaction to Baron Cohen's humor stemmed from a desire to protect a particular image (personal, occupational, local, religious, national, etc.) in the global marketplace of ideas. Undoubtedly, this attention to reputation was most keenly felt in Kazakhstan's response to the Boratistan farce, which evinced the new consciousness towards brand that currently pervades postmodern diplomacy. Kazakhstan, however, is not alone in defending its country image against globally-disseminated threats to the nation.

Ali G once stated, "International relations is not just about having a Bangladeshi cousin." His fatuous reflection underscores the complex nature of foreign policy and diplomacy that, in the current era of globalization, involves a complex web of state and non-state actors. International relations are now, by definition, both public and private. Consequently, the importance placed on brand management of country image has become something of a fetish for certain governments as Kazakhstan's response to Baron Cohen's pantomime has proven. In a case which somewhat parallels that of the battle over Borat, the American director Eli Roth incurred the wrath of the Slovakian state for his portrayal of the country in his 2005 horror film *Hostel*. In Roth's own words, the film depicts Slovaks as "a bunch of insane, chainsaw-wielding maniacs who torture people."[5] Bratislava's Ambassador to the US, Ratislav Káčer, described the characterization as "unfair" and an insult "touching the pride of the nation."[6] Slovakian MP Tomáš Galbavý stated, "I am offended by this film. I think that all Slovaks should feel offended."[7] Clearly trying to protect his state's brand, he went on to describe the film as a "monstrosity that does not at all reflect reality [and does] damage the good reputation of Slovakia."[8] In response, Roth was unapologetic in his choice of the central European republic as the backdrop for his grue-some film; "I set it in Slovakia especially because Americans don't know anything about that country. . . . But you know what, at least Americans know the country now. That's a start."[9] While Roth did not require reaction from Bratislava for *Hostel* to succeed, Baron Cohen's provocations of As-tana seemed to be an integral part of his artistic project. The fact that Ka-zakhstan took the bait sets a dangerous precedent. By participating in a global dialogue about Kazakhstan and its national image, the country granted Baron Cohen publicity he could never have attained otherwise. Ul-timately, both parties benefited from the fray. I predict that such a symbiotic outcome of this global minstrel show will be rare in the future.

Importantly, Roth's "Slovakia" and Baron Cohen's "Kazakhstan" re-flect the ability of entertainers, comedians, and filmmakers to create spuri-ous national stereotypes out of whole cloth—creations which ultimately serve their art but impugn the images of the countries involved. In today's world of over-stimulated, under-educated, culturally-confused youth, a country's image seems to be only as good as its last reference in popular culture. Given such unhappy realities, a nation's image-makers would be unwise to ignore Baron Cohen, Roth, or any other interlopers into their spa-tial and conceptual territory. Assisted by global flows of information and entertainment, non-state actors can influence millions (if not billions) with their "art." Employing a real country in one's artistic project has serious ramifications, as the two nations mentioned above have learned in recent years. Prior to the advent of the purported global village, a country's image was determined by factors that were predominately under the control of its national elites. This is less true today than at any time in the past. Conse-quently, national pantomime is no laughing matter—a maxim which may soon become painfully obvious to Austrians if the Bruno movie is even half as successful as *Borat: Cultural Learnings of America for Make Benefit Glorious Nation of Kazakhstan.*

Sacha Baron Cohen is a new type of comedian practicing an old form of comedy: satire. He lampoons, he ridicules, and he mocks; however, this is not just for laughs. Baron Cohen has an agenda, and Ali G, Bruno, and Bo-rat all tell us something about the life and times of the global village in which we live. Often, we do not like what we hear and see, but that is how Baron Cohen prefers it. He has been called a squirmist because he makes us uncomfortable. Our distress stems from the political questions he raises, rather than his humor as such. In the 21st century, the important questions of identity, morality, and authority have all been transformed by multicultural-ism, postmodern politics, and cultural change. While Baron Cohen does not provide any definitive answers, he certainly has found a way to make us sit up and take notice.

Notes

1. Jan Nederveen Pieterse, *Globalization & Culture: A Global Mélange* (Lan-ham, MD: Rowman & Littlefield, 2003).

2. See Marshall McLuhan, *The Gutenberg Galaxy: The Making of Typographic Man* (Toronto: University of Toronto Press, 1962).

3. According to Jeff Chang, "Hip-hop is a lingua franca that binds young people all around the world, all while giving them a chance to alter it within their own national flavor." Jeff Chang, "It's a Hip-Hop World," *Foreign Policy* 163 (Nov-Dec 2007): 58-65.

4. See Benjamin R. Barber, "Jihad vs. McWorld," *Atlantic Monthly* 269, no. 3 (March 1992): 53-65.

5. The subject of the film is a hostel whose guests become fodder for a pay-to-play torture chamber. The themes which gird the narrative are European anti-Americanism and American fears of the unknown and primitive "East" (though the principal villain is, in fact, an accomplished, globetrotting Dutch businessman). It may be of some interest to the reader to learn that in the "Featurettes" portion of the *Hostel* DVD, there is a scene in which director Eli Roth teaches a young Czech extra Ali G's standard catch-phrases such as "Boyakasha" and "respek," as well as a tutorial on how to talk like Borat.

6. "Slovakian Reaction to the Film 'Hostel,'" *The World*, Public Radio International, 25 January 2006.

7. "Slovakia Angered by Horror Film," *BBC News* web site, 27 February 2006.

8. *BBC News,* "Slovakia Angered."

9. "Slovakian Reaction," *The World.*

Bibliography

Abdygaliyeva, Gauhar. "My 'Glorious Nation of Kazakhstan,'" *Washington Post,* 7 November 2006.

Ahmad, Ali Nobil. "Ali G—Just Who Do *We* Think He Is? A Response to Rachel Garfield," *Third Text* 56 (Autumn 2001): 79-81.

Aitmatov, Chingiz. *The Day Last More than a Hundred Years.* Translated by John French. Bloomington: Indiana University Press, 1988.

Allan, Vicky. "Ali G Indahouse: Wigger Happy TV," *Scotland on Sunday,* 17 March 2002, 7.

Allen, Robert Clyde. *Horrible Prettiness: Burlesque and American Culture.* Chapel Hill: University of North Carolina Press, 1991.

Alleva, Richard. "British Invasion," *Commonweal* 133, no. 22 (15 December 2006): 15-16.

Alonso, Alex A. "Tricked into Silly Interview with Wanna Be Gangster Ali G of Britain," *Streetgangs.com Magazine,* 12 March 2002, http://www.streetgangs.com/topics/2002/031202aligshow.html.

Alpion, Gëzim "Images of Albania and Albanians in English Literature from Edith Durham's *High Albania* to J. K. Rowling's *Harry Potter,*" *BESA Journal* 6, no. 2 (Spring 2002): 30-34.

Andersen, Michael. "TV Comedian's Satire Falls Flat in Almaty," *Index on Censorship,* 1 December 2005.

Anderson, Benedict. *Imagined Communities: Reflections on the Origin and Spread of Nationalism.* London: Verso, 1991.

Andrews, Nigel. "Rude, Appalling, Irresistible," *Financial Times,* 2 November 2006, 13

Anholt, Simon. "Forward," *Brand Management* 9, nos. 4-5 (April 2002): 229-239.

———. "Nation Branding: A Continuing Theme," *Brand Management* 10, no. 1 (September 2002): 59-60.

———. "Anholt-GMI Nation Brands Index: Second Quarter, 2005." PDF available at http://www.gmi-mr.com/gmipoll/docs/NBI_Q2_2005.pdf (last accessed 25 August 2005).

———. *Competitive Identity: The New Brand Management for Nations, Cities and Regions.* New York: Palgrave Macmillan, 2007.

Bakhtin, Mikhail. *Rabelais and His World,* translated by Helene Iswolsky. Cambridge, MA: The MIT Press, 1968.

Barber, Benjamin R. "Jihad vs. McWorld," *Atlantic Monthly* 269, no. 3 (March 1992): 53-65.

Barfield, Ana. "Sculpting The Nation: A Comparative Look at the Impact of Past Legacies on the Emerging National Identities in Central Asia," B.A. Thesis, Department of Sociology, Princeton University (April 2004).

Barney, Katharine. No title. *Evening Standard,* 2 December 2005, 3.

Baron Cohen, Sacha. *The Black-Jewish Alliance—A Case of Mistaking Identities: The Involvement of Jewish Organizations and Jewish Students in the Black Civil Rights Movement 1960-1967.* Cambridge: Christ's College, 1993.

———. "Two Cents," *Broadcasting & Cable,* 134, no. 29 (19 July 2004): 40.

Baum, Matthew A. "Sex, Lies, and War: How Soft News Brings Foreign Policy to the Inattentive Public," *The American Political Science Review* 96, no. 1. (March 2002): 91-109.

Bauman, Zygmunt. *Postmodern Ethics*, Oxford: Blackwell, 1993.

Baxter, Sarah. "We Are Not Liking This Ali G Joke, Says Kazakhstan," *Sunday Times*, 19 September 2004.

Baym, Geoffrey. "*The Daily Show*: Discursive Integration and the Reinvention of Political Journalism," *Political Communication* 22, no. 3 (July 2005): 259–276.

Becker, Jonathan. "Lessons from Russia: A Neo-Authoritarian Media System," *European Journal of Communication* 19, no. 2 (June 2004): 139-163.

Benn, Tony. "How I Tamed Ali G," *Guardian*, 30 March 2000, 17.

Bennett, Lance. *News: The Politics of Illusion*, Seventh ed. New York: Longman, 2007.

Berger, Peter L. *Redeeming Laughter: The Comic Dimension of Human Experience*. New York and Berlin: Walther De Gruyter, 1997.

Berkowitz, Lana. "Cover Story: Borat," *Houston Chronicle*, 5 November 2006.

Best, Steven and Douglas Kellner. "Dawns, Twilights, and Transitions: Postmodern Theories, Politics, and Challenges," *Democracy & Nature: The International Journal of Inclusive Democracy* 7, no. 1 (March 2001): 101-117.

Bhabha, Homi K. *The Location of Culture*. London: Routledge,1994.

Bilgrami, Akeel. "Notes toward the Definition of 'Identity,'" *Daedalus* 135, no. 4 (Fall 2006): 5-16.

Binelli, Mark. "Idiot Power," *Rolling Stone* 918 (20 March 2003): 34-35.

Bly, Laura. "Finding the Real Kazakhstan," *USA Today*, 16 November 2006.

Borenstein, Eliot. "Our Borats, Our Selves: Yokels and Cosmopolitans on the Global Stage," *Slavic Review* 66, no. 1 (Spring 2008): 1-7.

Boulding, Kenneth E. "National Images and International Systems," *Journal of Conflict Resolution* 3, no. 2 (June 1959): 120-131.

Bourdieu, Pierre. "La sociologie de la culture populaire," in *Le Handicap socioculturel en question*. Paris: ESF, 1978.

Bowman, James. "Conventional Cuts," *American Spectator* 39 no. 10 (December 2006/January 2007): 86-7.

Bradley, John R. "Outrageous Comic Has Last Laugh," *Straits Times*, 16 January 2006.

Bradshaw, Peter. "Bear-Baiting in Bushville," *Guardian*, 27 October 2006, 7.

Brand, Madeleine. "Kazakhstan Not Laughing at TV's 'Ali G,'" *NPR*'s Day to Day, 17 November 2005.

Brandle, Lars. "New Ingredients Spice Up MTV Europe Show," *Billboard*, 19 November 2005.

Brandon-Bravo, Joel. "Israel, My Pride and My Shame," *Sunday Times*, 21 April 2002.

Braun, Aurel. "All Quiet on the Russian Front?" in *The New European Diasporas: National Minorities and Conflict in Eastern Europe*, edited by Michael Mandelbaum. New York: Council on Foreign Relations Press, 2000.

Brayton, Sean. "MTV's Jackass: Transgression, Abjection and the Economy of White Masculinity," *Journal of Gender Studies* 16, no. 1 (March 2007): 57-72.

Brookhiser, Richard. "Jokers Wild and Mild," *National Review* 55, no. 2 (10 February 2003): 52.

Brooks, David "The Heyday of Snobbery," *New York Times*, 16 November 2006, 35.

Brubaker, Rogers. *Nationalism Reframed: Nationhood and the National Question in the New Europe*. Cambridge: Cambridge University Press, 1996.

Burkeman, Oliver. "Problem with Your Country's Image?" *Guardian*, 11 November 2006.

Byers, David. "Sacha Baron Cohen among 20 most powerful men in UK," *European Jewish Press*, 4 February 2007.

Calder, Simon. "Why Romanians are Sitting on a Glod Mine," *Independent*, 23 June 2007.

Callan, Jessica and Eva Simpson. "3am—Reigns Massive," *Mirror*, 21 March 2002, 12

Campbell, Joseph. *The Hero With a Thousand Faces*. Princeton: Princeton University Press, 1973.

Carvajal, Doreen. "Kazakh Officials Don't See Spoof's Humor," *International Herald Tribune*, 15 December 2005.

Chang, Jeff. "It's a Hip-Hop World," *Foreign Policy* 163 (Nov-Dec 2007): 58-65.

Charity, Tom. "Review: 'Borat' is Most Excellent Comedy," *CNN*, 6 November 2006.

Clifford, Michael. "The Great Pretender . . . Innit?" *Sunday Tribune*, 24 March 2002, 15.

Clinton, Jane. ". . . And Upset the 'Real Borat' in the Process," *Express on Sunday*, 12 November 2006, 10.

Clough, Ralph N. *Reaching across the Taiwan Straight: People-to-People Diplomacy.* Boulder, CO: Westview Press, 1993.

Cohen, Rich. "Hello! It's Sexy Time!" *Vanity Fair* 556 (December 2006): 262-270.

Colapinto, John. "Mad Dog," *Rolling Stone* 956 (2 September 2004): 104-111.

Collins, Kathleen. *Clan Politics and Regime Transition in Central Asia.* Cambridge: Cambridge University Press, 2006.

Collins, Michael. "Hold on to Your Hats," *Guardian*, 27 March 2000, 2.

Condee, Nancy. "Learnings of Borat for Make Benefit Cultural Studies," *Pittsburgh Post-Gazette*, 12 November 2006, H6.

——— . "Borat: Putting the Id Back in Identity Politics," *Slavic Review* 66, no. 1 (Spring 2008): 84-87.

Conquest, Robert. *The Nation Killers: The Soviet Deportation of Nationalities.* London: Macmillan, 1970.

Cook, Richard. "The White DJ in Black Culture," *New Statesman* 128, no. 4447 (2 August 1999): 18-19.

Cook, Robin. "Robin Cook's Chicken Tikka Masala Speech: Extracts from a Speech by the Foreign Secretary to the Social Market Foundation in London," *Guardian Unlimited*, 19 April 2001.

Cook, William. "After Ali: The IOS Profile: Sacha Baron Cohen," *Independent on Sunday*, 22 August 2004, 19.

Cooper, Glenda. "Secret world of Sacha B," *Daily Mail*, 19 March 2002.

Cornwell, Tim. "Wish You Were Here, Mr Borat," *Scotsman*, 20 October 2006.

Covert, Colin. "Movie Review: 'Borat' Just Might Be the Funniest Movie Ever," *Knight Ridder Tribune Business News*, 3 November 2006, 1.

Crews, Robert D. *For Prophet and Tsar: Islam and Empire in Russia and Central Asia.* Cambridge, MA: Harvard University Press, 2006.

Cummings, Sally N. *Kazakhstan: Power and the Elite.* New York: I.B. Tauris, 2005.

Dargis, Manohla. "Satire is Not Pretty," *New York Times*, 3 November 2006, D1.

Daurat, Cecile. "'Borat' Leads Revenue Gains for News Corp." *International Herald Tribune*, 8 February 2007.

Dave, Bhavna. "National Revival in Kazakhstan: Language Shift and Identity Change," *Post-Soviet Affairs* 12, no. 1 (1996): 51–72.

David, Miriam E. "Sue Lees: An Appreciation," *Gender and Education* 15, no. 1 (March 2003): 3-4.

Davies, Christie. *The Mirth of Nations.* New Brunswick, NJ: Transaction Publishers, 2002.

Davis, Michael. *The Poetry of Philosophy.* South Bend, IN: St Augustine's Press, 1999.

Davis, Natalie Zemon. *Society and Culture in Early Modern France.* Stanford: Stanford University Press, 1975.

Deutsch, Karl. *Nationalism and Social Communication: An Inquiry into the Foundations of Nationality.* Cambridge: The Technology Press of the Massachusetts Institute of Technology, 1953.

de Vicente, Jorge. *State Branding in the 21st Century,* Master of Arts in Law and Diplomacy Thesis, The Fletcher School of Diplomacy at Tufts University, May 2004.

Diener, Alexander C. "Kazakhstan's Kin State Diaspora: Settlement Planning and the Oralman Dilemma," *Europe-Asia Studies* 57, no. 2 (March 2005): 327-348.

Djumaev, Aleksandr ."Nation-Building, Culture, and Problems of Ethnocultural Identity in Central Asia: The Case of Uzbekistan," in *Can Liberal Pluralism be Exported?: Western Political Theory and Ethnic Relations in Eastern Europe,* edited by Will Kymlicka and Magda Opalski. Oxford, Oxford University Press, 2001.

Dowd, Maureen. "America's Anchors," *Rolling Stone* 1013 (16 November 2006): 52-139.

Dyke, Peter. "Da Real Ali G's a Shy Geezer Innit," *Daily Star*, 20 March 2002, 19.

Dzenovska, Dace. "Remaking the Nation of Latvia: Anthropological Perspectives on Nation Branding," *Place Branding* 1, no. 2 (March 2005): 173–186.

Eboda, Michael. "We Can Take Ali G's Humor in Our Stride," *Independent*, 12 January 2000, 4

Eckardt, A. Roy. "The Heirs of Itzhak," *Society* 24, no. 4 (May/June 1992): 34-42.

Edelstein, David. "So Funny It Hurts," *New York* (6 November 2006): 91-92.

Elber, Lynn. "British Comic Lowers the Satire Bar in HBO's 'Da Ali G Show,'" *Associated Press*, 19 February 2003.

Ellis, Frank. "Political Correctness in Britain: A Blueprint for Decline," *Academic Questions* 7, no. 5 (Fall 1994): 77-101.

Evans, Richard. "Is It 'Cos We is Welsh?" *Western Mail*, 22 March 2002, 11.

Farley, Christopher John and Simon Robinson, "Dave Speaks," *Time* 165, no. 21 (23 May 2005): 68-73.

Freebury, Jane. "Ali G Ready to Save the World," *Canberra Times* (20 July 2002), 13.

Friedman, Dan. "Genuine Authentic Gangsta Flava," *Zeek: A Jewish Journal of Thought and Culture* (April 2003): 1-4, http://www.zeek.net/.

Friedman, Roger. "Dharma and . . . Borat? A 'Victim' Complains," *FOX News*, 2 November 2006.

Fraser, Suzan. "Turkish Man Says He's the Real Borat," *Associated Press*, 7 November 2006.

Gamson, Joshua. *Freaks Talk Back: Tabloid Talk Shows and Sexual Nonconformity*. Chicago: University of Chicago Press, 1998.

Garfield, Rachel. "Ali G: Just Who Does He Think He Is?" *Third Text* 54 (Spring 2001): 63-70.

Gasperetti, David. "The Carnivalesque Spirit of the Eighteenth-Century Russian Novel," *Russian Review* 52, no. 2 (April 1993): 166-183.

Gellner, Ernst. *Nations and Nationalism*. Ithaca: Cornell University Press, 1983.

George, Alexandra. *Journey into Kazakhstan: The True Face of the Nazarbayev Regime*. Lanham, MD: University Press of America, 2001.

Gilbey, Ryan. "Thongs of Freedom," *New Statesman* 135, no. 4817 (6 November 2006): 45.

Gilmore, Fiona. "Spain—A Success Story of Country Branding," *Brand Management* 9, nos. 4-5 (April 2002): 281-293.

Gilroy, Paul. "Ali G and the Oscars," *Open Democracy* Web site, 4 April 2002.

————. *After Empire: Melancholia or Convivial Culture*. Oxford: Routledge, 2004.

Gogoi, Pallavi. "Banning Borat," *Business Week Online*, 7 November 2006.

Goldstein, Patrick. "Out of Character," *Los Angeles Times*, 9 January 2007.

Goldstein, Richard. "The Tao of Borat," *Nation* 283, no.17 (20 November 2006): 8.

Goodman, Clive. "Mummy's Little Boyakasha," *News of the World*, 24 March 2002, 14.

Gordon, Devin. "Behind the Schemes," *Newsweek* 148 no. 16 (16 October 2006): 74-75.

Gordon, Devin and Ginanne Brownell. "The Brain Behind Borat," *Newsweek* 148, no. 20 (13 November 2006): 69.

Graff, Vincent. "It's a Free Country, But This Ali G Guy Has Got It All Wrong," *Evening Standard*, 3 April 2000, 36.

Gray, Geoffrey. "Kazakh Elites Divided over Borat," *New York Magazine*, 28 August 2006.

Grimes, William. "Japan as the 'Indispensable Nation' in Asia: A Financial Brand for the 21st Century," *Asia-Pacific Review* 12, no. 1 (May 2005): 40-54.

Gross, Terry. "Interview: Jody Rosen," Fresh Air from WHYY on *NPR*, 2 January 2007.

————. "Meet the Real Sacha Baron Cohen," Fresh Air from WHYY on *NPR*, 4 January 2007.

Gudjonsson, Hlynur. "Nation Branding," *Place Branding* 1, no. 3 (July 2005): 283–298.

Gudkov, Lev. *Negativnaya Identichnost*. Moscow: Novoe Literaturnoe Obozrenie, 2004.

Gutfeld, Greg. "Impostors," *American Spectator* 39, no. 10 (December 2006/January 2007): 62-64.

Halkin, Hillel. "Why Jews Laugh at Themselves," *Commentary* 121, no. 4 (April 2006): 47-54.

Hall, Sarah. "Kazakhstan Strips Borat of Site," *Yahoo! News*, 13 December 2005.

Hammack, Laurence. "Rodeo in Salem Gets Unexpected Song Rendition," *Roanoke Times*, 9 January 2005.

Harris, John. "When Ali G Went to Kazakhstan (Or How a Cult Comedian Fell Out with an Entire Country," *Independent*, 26 April 2000, F1.

Hayes, Dominic. "Why We Is All Now Talkin' Like Ali G," *Evening Standard*, 10 April 2006, 3.

Heffernan, Virginia. "The Cheerful Confessions of Ali G, Borat and Bruno," *New York Times*, 15 July 2004, A/C1.

Hernandez, Tyler. "It's Nice! Very Nice!" *Tulane Hullabaloo*, 10 November 2006.

Hess, Mickey. "Metal Faces, Rap Masks: Identity and Resistance in Hip Hop's Persona Artist," *Popular Music and Society* 28, no. 3 (July 2005): 297–311.

Hickson, Jill E. "Using Law to Create National Identity: The Course to Democracy in Tajikistan," *Texas International Law Journal* 38, no. 2 (Spring 2003): 346-379.

Himes, Stephen. "Review of Talladega Nights," *Flak Magazine*, 18 August 2006, http://www.flakmag.com/film/talladega.html.

Hirano, Tetsuyuki. "Design and Culture: Developing a Nation's Brand with Design Management," *Design Management Review* 17, no. 1 (Winter 2006): 15-20.

Hirsch, Francine. *Empire of Nations: Ethnographic Knowledge and the Making of the Soviet Union.* Ithaca and London: Cornell University Press, 2005.

Hitchens, Christopher. "Kazakh Like Me," *Slate*, 13 November 2006.

Holsti, Ole R. "The Belief System and National images: A Case Study," *Journal of Conflict Resolution* 5, no. 3 (September 1962): 244-252.

Holton, Gerald. "Einstein and the Cultural Roots of Modern Science," *Daedalus* 127, no. 1 (Winter 1998): 1-44.

Horovitz, David. 'In My Country There Is Problem—With Borat," *Jerusalem Post*, 1 December 2006, 24.

Howe, Darcus. "Ali G is a Great Act," *New Statesman* 129, no. 4469 (17 January 2000): 12.

Howells, Richard. "'Is It Because I Is Black?': Race, Humor and the Polysemiology of Ali G," *Historical Journal of Film, Radio and Television* 26, no. 2 (June 2006): 155–177.

Hroch, Miroslav. *Social Preconditions of National Revival in Europe: A Comparative Analysis of the Social Composition of Patriotic Groups among the Smaller European Nations.* Cambridge: Cambridge University Press, 1985.

Huhn, Tom. "Heidegger, Adorno, and Mimesis," *Dialogue and Universalism* 11-12 (November-December 2003): 43-52.

Huizinga, Johan. *Homo Ludens: A Study of the Play-Element in Culture.* Boston: The Beacon Press, 1950.

Hunt, Tristram. "Why Britain is Great," *New Statesman* 134, no. 4751 (1 August 2005): 12-14.

Hutchison, Robin. "Ali G Pulling 'Em In Staines Massive," *Daily Star*, 1 April 2002, 25.

Idrissov, Erlan. "Sacha Baron Cohen Exploits the West's Ignorance of Kazakhstan," *Guardian*, 4 October 2006.

———. "We Survived Stalin and We Can Certainly Overcome Borat's Slurs," *Times*, 4 November 2006.

Ioviţă, Radu P. and Theodore G. Schurr. "Reconstructing the Origins and Migrations of Diasporic Populations: The Case of the European Gypsies," *American Anthropologist* 106, no. 2 (June 2004): 267-281.

Jaafar, Ali. "'Borat' Gross-outs Fall Flat in Mideast," *Variety*, 30 November 2006.

Jaworski, Stefan Paul and Don Fosher, "National Brand Identity & Its Effect on Corporate Brands: The Nation Brand Effect," *Multinational Business Review* 11, no. 2 (Fall 2003): 99-113.

Johnson, Ben. "Free Borat," *FrontPage Magazine,* 3 November 2006.

Juni, Samuel and Bernard Katz, "Self-Effacing Wit as a Response to Aggression: Dynamics in Ethnic Humor," *Journal of General Psychology* 128, no. 2 (April 2001): 119-142.

Kahn, Jeremy. "A Brand-New Approach," *Foreign Policy* 157 (November-December 2006): 90-92.

Kamp, Marianne. "Women, Marriage, and the Nation-State: The Rise of Nonconsensual Bride Kidnapping in Post-Soviet Kazakhstan," in *The Transformation of Central Asia: States and Societies from Soviet Rule to Independence*, edited by Pauline Jones Luong. Ithaca: Cornell University Press, 2004.

Karin, Erlan and Andrei Chebotarev, "The Policy of Kazakhization in State and Government Institutions in Kazakhstan," M.E.S. Series No. 51: *The Nationalities Question in Post-Soviet Kazakhstan, Institute of Developing Economies*. Chiba: IDE-Jetro, 2002.

Kelaart, Lucy. "Inside Story: 'Is It Cos I Is Kazakh?'" *Guardian*, 11 April 2003, 7.

Kelso, Paul. "Race Protest at Ali G's Film Premiere," *Guardian*, 21 March 2002, 7.

Kennedy, Lisa. "Masochism's Light Side," *Denver Post*, 26 December 2006, F1.

Keohane, Robert. *After Hegemony: Cooperation and Discord in the World Political Economy*. Princeton: Princeton University Press, 1984.

Kimberlee, Richard H. "Why Don't British Young People Vote at General Elections?" *Journal of Youth Studies* 5, no. 1 (March 2002): 85-98.

Kitwana, Bakari. *Why White Kids Love Hip-Hop: Wankstas, Wiggers, Wannabes, and the New Reality of Race in America*. New York: Basic Civitas Books, 2005.

Klawans, Stuart. "Coming to America!" *Nation* 283, no. 19 (4 December 2006): 32-36.

Kleppe, Ingeborg Astrid. "Country Images in Marketing Strategies: Conceptual Issues and an Empirical Asian Illustration," *Brand Management* 10, no. 1 (September 2002): 61-74.

Kohn, Hans. *The Idea of Nationalism: A Study in its Origins and Background*. New York: Macmillan, 1944.

Kolstø, Pål. "Anticipating Demographic Superiority: Kazakh Thinking on Integration and Nation Building," *Europe-Asia Studies* 50, no. 1 (January 1998): 51-70.

Kononenko, Natalie and Svitlana Kukharenko. "Borat the Trickster: Folklore and the Media, Folklore in the Media," *Slavic Review* 66, no. 1 (Spring 2008): 8-18.

Kotkin, Stephen. "Trashcanistan," *New Republic* 226, no. 14 (15 April 2002): 26-38.

Kotler, Philip and David Gertner, "Country as Brand, Product, and Beyond: A Place Marketing and Brand Management Perspective," *Brand Management* 9, nos. 4-5 (April 2002): 249-261.

Kotwal, Kaizaad. "Booyakasha!" *Gay People's Chronicle*, 16 March 2007.

Krauthammer, Charles. "Just an Anti-Semitic Laugh? Hardly," *Washington Post*, 24 November 2006, A41.

Kravitz, Derek. "Cockney Accent Being Swept Aside in London by New Hip-Hop Inspired Dialect," *Associated Press Newswires*, 13 April 2006.

Laderman, David. *Driving Visions: Exploring the Road Movie*. Austin: University of Texas Press, 2002.

Laitin, David. *Identity in Formation: Russian-Speaking Populations in the Near Abroad*. Ithaca: Cornell University Press, 1998.

Lampert, Nicole. "Ali G Star's 'Anti-Semitic' Song Starts a TV Storm," *Daily Mail*, 20 August 2004, 36.

Lane, Anthony "In Your Face," *New Yorker* 82, no. 36 (6 November 2006): 106-109.

Larmer, Brook. "The Center of the World," *Foreign Policy* 50 (September-October 2005): 66-74.

LaSalle, Mick. "'Borat' Explores America, Finds a Very Funny Place," *San Francisco Chronicle*, 3 November 2006, E1.

Lea, Andy. "Come Home Borat, All Is Forgiven," *Daily Star*, 20 November 2005.

Lebedenko, Vladimir. "Russia's National Identity and Image-Building," *International Affairs: A Russian Journal of World Politics, Diplomacy & International Relations* 50, no. 4 (September-October 2004): 71-77.

Lee, Nathan. "Persona Non Grata," *Film Comment* 42, no. 6 (November/December 2006): 22-24.

Lee, Steven S. "*Borat*, Multiculturalism, *Mnogonatsional'nost'*," *Slavic Review* 66, no. 1 (Spring 2008): 19-34.

Leibovitz, Liel. "Did Ali G Go Too Far?" *Jewish Week*, 13 August 2004.

Leiby, Richard. "The Reliable Source," *Washington Post*, 16 January 2005, D03

Lemann, Nicholas. "Fear Factor," *New Yorker* 82, no. 6 (27 March 2006): 32-37.

Lenart, Silvo and Harry R. Targ, "Framing the Enemy," *Peace & Change* 17, no. 3 (July 1992): 341-362.

Leslie, Esther. "Modernism and Cultural Studies: Address to Modernist Studies Association," Birmingham, 26 September 2003.

Lewis, Philip. "Between Lord Ahmed and Ali G: Which Future for British Muslims," in Wasif A. R. Shahid and P. Sjoerd van Koningsveld, eds., *Religious Freedom and the Neutrality of the State: The Position of Islam in the European Union*. Leuven: Peeters, 2002.

Lewis-Smith, Victor. "A Kazakhstanding Ovation," *Mirror*, 29 April 2000, 6.

Lipman, Masha. "Constrained or Irrelevant: The Media in Putin's Russia," *Current History* 104, no. 684 (October 2005): 319-324.

Lipovetsky, Mark and Daniil Leiderman, "Angel, Avenger, or Trickster?: The 'Second-World Man' as the Other and the Self," in Stephen Hutchings (ed), *Screening Intercultural Dialogue: Russia and its Other(s) on Film*. London: Palgrave, forthcoming.

Lloyd, John. "Cool Britannia Warms Up," *New Statesman* 127, no. 4376 (12 March 1998): 10-11.

Lumenick, Lou. "Kazakh It To Me!," *New York Post*, 2 November 2006, 65.

MacNeille, Suzanne. "Oh, The Places You'll Go!" *New York Times*, 18 September 2006, F1.

Maeroff Gene I., "The 'Wedge Issues' of 2004," *Education Week* 23, no. 16 (7 January 2004): 60.

Marchese, David and Willa Paskin. "What's Real in 'Borat'?" *Salon.com*, 10 November 2006.

Marre, Oliver. "Sacha Baron Cohen: Our Man from Kazakhstan," *Observer*, 10 September 2006.

Martel, Ned. "Booyakasha! Is You Ready for Ali G?" *Financial Times*, 4 April 2003.

Martin, Terry. *The Affirmative Action Empire: Nations and Nationalism in the Soviet Union, 1923-1939*. Ithaca and London: Cornell University Press, 2001.

Martinović, Stjepo. "Branding Hrvatska—A Mixed Blessing that Might Work," *Brand Management* 9, nos. 4-5 (April 2002): 315-322.

Masanov, Nurbulat "Perceptions of Ethnic and All-National Identity in Kazakhstan," M.E.S. Series No. 51: *The Nationalities Question in Post-Soviet Kazakhstan, Institute of Developing Economies*. Chiba: IDE-Jetro, 2002.

Maxwell, Bill. "Look at Borat, Then Look at Yourself," *St. Petersburg Times*, 26 November 2006, 3.

Mayall, David. *Gypsy Identities 1500-2000: From Egipcyans and Moon-men to the Ethnic Romany*. London and New York: Routledge, 2004.

McLuhan, Marshall. *The Gutenberg Galaxy: The Making of Typographic Man*. Toronto: University of Toronto Press, 1962.

Michaels, Paula A. "If the Subaltern Speaks in the Woods and Nobody's Listening, Does He Make a Sound?" *Slavic Review* 66, no. 1 (Spring 2008): 81-83.

Millar, John. "Mail Movies: Ali G Has Wild Time in Jungle Romp," *Sunday Mail*, 10 July 2005, 31.

Mohan, Dominic. "Madonna Called But I Thought It Was A Joke," *Sun*, 10 June 2000, 25.

Monaghan, Peter. "Verbatim," *Chronicle of Higher Education* 53, no. 15 (1 December 2006): A13.

Monetti, Sandro. "Why British Stars are Laughing All the Way to America," *Express on Sunday*, 11 March 2007, 49-51.

Moore, Robert E. "From Genericide to Viral Marketing: On 'Brand,'" *Language and Communication* 23, nos. 3-4 (July-October 2003): 331-357.

Morgan, Nigel, Annette Pritchard, and Rachel Piggott, "New Zealand, 100% Pure. The Creation of Power Niche Destination Brand," *Brand Management* 9, nos. 4-5 (April 2002): 335-354.

Morgenstern, Joe. "With Insults for All," *Wall Street Journal*, 3 November 2006, W 1.

Morrissey, Brian "MySpace Rolls Out 'Black Carpet' for Movies, *AdWeek*, 15 September 2006.

Mühleisen, Susanne, "What Makes an Accent Funny, and Why? Black British Englishes and Humor Televised" in Reichl, Susanne and Mark Stein, *Cheeky Fictions: Laughter and the Postcolonial*. Amsterdam: Rodopi, 2005.

Mullan, John. "Lost Voices," *Guardian*, 18 June 1999.

Muravchik, Joshua. "Borat!" *Commentary* 123, no. 1 (January 2007): 44-47.

Musto, Michael. "Sarah Silverman Is My Kind of Cunt," *Village Voice*, 23 January 2007.

Myers, Steven Lee. "'Borat' is Not Approved for Distribution in Russia," *New York Times*, 10 November 2006, 9.

Nayak, Anoop. "After Race: Ethnography, Race and Post-Race Theory," *Ethnic and Racial Studies* 29, no. 3 (May 2006): 411-430.

Nazarbayev, Nursultan. *V potoke istorii*. Almaty: Atamura, 1999.

———. "Who Needs Borat?" *Spectator*, 25 November 2006.

Nekrich, Alexander M. *The Punished People: The Deportation and Fate of Soviet Minorities at the End of the Second World War*. New York: W.W. Norton, 1978.

Nilsen, Alleen Pace and Don L. F. Nilsen. "Just How Ethnic is Ethnic Humor?" *Canadian Ethnic Studies* 38, no. 1 (2006): 131-139.

Norris, Michele. "Is the Real Borat Being Shut Out of the Limelight?" *NPR: All Things Considered*, 19 December 2006.

Nye, Jr., Joseph S. *Soft Power: The Means to Success in World Politics*. New York: Public Affairs, 2004.

O'Callaghan, Luke. "War of Words: Language Policy in Post Independence Kazakhstan," *Nebula* 1, no. 3 (December 2004 – January 2005): 197-216.

Olcott, Martha Brill. "The Emergence of National Identity in Kazakhstan," *Canadian Review of Studies in Nationalism* 8 (Fall 1981): 285-300.

———. *The Kazakhs*. Stanford: Hoover Institution Press, 1987.

———. *Kazakhstan: Unfulfilled Promise*. Washington, DC: Carnegie Endowment for International Peace, 2002.

Olins, Wally. "Branding the Nation—The Historical Context," *Brand Management* 9, nos. 4-5 (April 2002): 241-248.

O'Neill, Brendan. "Backstory: Borat Write Thesis," *Christian Science Monitor* 98, no. 250 (21 November 2006): 20.

O'Reilly, Sally. "Dead Funny," *Art Monthly* 302 (December 2006-January 2007): 7-9.

O'Sullivan, John. "The Real British Disease," *New Criterion* 24, no. 1, (September 2005): 16-23.

———. "State of the Cousins," *National Review* 57, no. 9 (23 May 2005): 22-24.

Papadopoulos, Nicolas and Louise Heslop, "Country Equity and Country Branding: Problems and Prospects," *Brand Management* 9, nos. 4-5 (April 2002): 294-314.

Patten, Chris. "Epiphanies," *Foreign Policy* 161 (July/August 2007): 19.

Payne, Matt. "The Forge of the Kazakh Proletariat?: The Turksib, Nativization, and Industrialization during Stalin's First Five-Year Plan," in Suny, Ronald G. and Terry Martin, *A State of Nations: Empire and Nation-Making in the Age of Lenin and Stalin*. Oxford: Oxford University Press, 2001.

Pearson, Allison. "Da Importance of Not Being Earnest," *Evening Standard*, 29 March 2000, 15.

Penketh, Anne. "After Nazarbayev: The Dictator, His Daughter, and a Dynasty at War," *Independent*, 30 May 2007.

Peterson, J. E. "Qatar and the World: Branding for a Micro-State," *Middle East Journal* 60, no. 4 (Autumn 2006): 732-748.

Phillips, Melanie. "Britain is Turning on the U.S.—at Its Own Peril," *USA Today*, 24 October 2006, 13a.

Pieterse, Jan Nederveen. *Globalization & Culture: A Global Mélange*. Lanham, MD: Rowman & Littlefield, 2003.

Pink, Daniel H. "The Brand Called UK," *Fast Company* 22 (January 1999): 172-172.

Podhoretz, John. "The 'Borat' Show," *Weekly Standard* 12, no. 7 (30 October 2006): 46-47.

Poole, Oliver. "Ban Borat, Say Offended Kazakhs," *Telegraph,* 23 April 2000.
Powell, Lawrence Alfred and Lloyd Waller. "Politics as Unusual," *Communication World* 24, no. 2 (March/April 2007): 20-23.
Preston, Peter. "Freedom from 'Britain': A Comment on Recent Elite-Sponsored Political Cultural Identities," *British Journal of Politics and International Relations* 9, no. 1 (February 2007): 158–164.
Puig, Claudia. "It Bears Repeating: 'Borat' is Funny," *USA Today,* 3 November 2006, E7.
Purdy, Jane-Ann. "Spoof or Dare," *Scotsman,* 15 May 1999, 6.
Quinn, Anthony. "Hitting the Bigot Time," *Independent,* 3 November 2006, 6-7.
Rayner, Jay. "The Observer Profile: Sacha Baron Cohen: Mutha of Invention," *Observer,* 24 February 2002, 27.
Rice, Ned. "Gratuitous America-Bashing for Lining Pocket of Overrated Sacha Cohen," *Human Events* 62, no. 40 (20 November 2006): 20.
Risen, Clay. "Branding Nations," *New York Times Magazine* 155, no. 53425 (11 December 2005): 61.
Rivers, William P. "Attitudes towards Incipient Mankurtism among Kazakhstani College Students," *Language Policy* 1, no. 2 (May 2002): 159–174.
Robbins, Christopher. *In Search of Kazakhstan: The Land that Disappeared,* London: Profile Books, 2007.
Roger, Philippe. "Global Anti-Americanism and the Lessons of the 'French Exception,'" *Journal of American History* 93, no. 2 (September 2006): 448-451.
Ro'i, Yaacov. "Introduction," in Y. Ro'i, ed., *Democracy and Pluralism in Muslim Eurasia.* London: Frank Cass, 2004.
Rojek, Chris. *Celebrity.* London: Reaktion Books, 2001.
Roseanne. "The TIME 100: Sacha Baron Cohen," *Time* 169, 20 (14 May 2007): 143.
Rosen, Jody. "Borat Owes Me 97 Dollars," *Slate,* 3 November 2006.
Rosen, Steven. "Will Offensive Volley Miss Its Mark?" *Denver Post,* 3 November 2006, F3.
Roy, Olivier. *The New Central Asia: The Creation of Nations.* New York: New York University Press, 2000.
Rusciano, Frank Louis. "The Construction of National Identity—A 23-Nation Study," *Political Research Quarterly* 56, no. 3 (September 2003): 361-366.
Sabol, Steven. "The Creation of Soviet Central Asia: The 1924 National Delimitation," *Central Asian Survey* 14, no. 2 (June 1995): 225-241.
Said, Edward. *Orientalism.* New York: Vintage Books, 1979.
Sailer, Steve. "21st Century Polish Jokes," *American Conservative,* 4 December 2006.
Sandhu, Sukhdev. "Review: Borat," *Daily Telegraph,* 27 October 2006, 26.
Sardar, Ziauddin and Barin Van Loon. *Introducing Cultural Studies.* Cambridge, Icon Books Ltd., 1999.
Saunders, Robert A. "Denationalized Digerati in the Virtual Near Abroad: The Internet's Paradoxical Impact on National Identity among Minority Russians," *Global Media and Communication* 2, no. 1 (Spring 2005): 43–69.
———. "Unweaving the Web of Identity," PhD dissertation, Rutgers, The State University of New Jersey, May 2005.
———. "Happy Slapping: Transatlantic Contagion or Home-grown, Mass-mediated Nihilism?" *Static* 1, no. 1 (October 2005): 1-11.
———. "In Defence of *Kazakshilik*: Kazakhstan's War on Sacha Baron Cohen," *Identities: Global Studies in Culture and Power* 14, no. 2 (May 2007): 225-255.
Saxon, Reed. "Borat Emboldened Moore to Visit Guantanamo," *Associated Press,* 28 June 2007.
Sayid, Ruki. "It's Ali in De Mirror . . . Ali in De Mirror," *Mirror,* 12 January 2000.
Schatz, Edward. "The Politics of Multiple Identities: Lineage and Ethnicity in Kazakhstan," *Europe-Asia Studies* 52, no. 3 (May 2000): 489-506.
———. "Transnational Image Making and Soft Authoritarian Kazakhstan," *Slavic Review* 66, no. 1 (Spring 2008): 50-62.
Schechner, Sam. "Respek! How Does Ali G Keep Conning Famous Guests?" *Slate,* 20 September 2004, http://www.slate.com.

Schou, Solvej. "With Flap over 'Borat' Methods, Experts Weigh in on Consent Forms," *Associated Press*, 17 November 2006.

Schutz, Charles. "The Sociability of Ethnic Jokes," *Humor* 2, no. 2 (April 1989): 165–177.

Schwartz, Stephen *et. al.* "No Laughing Matter?" *Commentary* 123 no. 4 (April 2007): 16-20.

Siegel, Joel. "Review: 'Borat'—Offensive, Juvenile, and Very, Very Funny," *ABC News*, 3 November 2006.

Siegel, Robert. "Ali G: Fooling Serious Interviewees, All for a Laugh," All Things Considered, *NPR*, 23 July 2004.

Sinha Roy, Ishita. *"Worlds Apart*: Nation-branding on the National Geographic Channel," *Media, Culture & Society* 29, no. 4 (July 2007): 569-592.

Smith, Anthony. *National Identity*. Reno: University of Nevada Press, 1991.

Smith, Emily. "Borat Spanked by Angry Yank," *Sun*, 13 November 2006.

Socor, Vladimir. "A Model for Central Asia," *Wall Street Journal*, 2-4 December 2005, 13.

Sollors, Werner. *Beyond Ethnicity: Consent and Descent in American Culture*. New York: Oxford University Press, 1986.

Soucek, Svat. *The History of Inner Asia*. Cambridge: Cambridge University Press, 2000.

Stratton, Jon. *Coming Out Jewish: Constructing Ambivalent Identities*. London and New York: Routledge, 2000.

Strauss, Neil. "The Man Behind the Moustache," *Rolling Stone* 1014 (11 November 2006): 58-70.

Suny, Ronald. "Making Minorities: The Politics of National Boundaries in the Soviet Experience," in *The Construction of Minorities: Cases for Comparison across Time and around the World*, edited by André Burguière and Raymond Grew. Ann Arbor: University of Michigan Press, 2001.

Surucu, Cengiz. "Modernity, Nationalism, Resistance: Identity Politics in Post-Soviet Kazakhstan," *Central Asian Survey* 21, no. 4 (December 2002): 385-402.

Sutherland, Claire. "Voice Squad," *Herald-Sun*, 15 September 2005, I5.

Sweetingham, Lisa. "Etiquette Expert is Latest to Lash Out at 'Borat' Creator, Claiming Humiliation," *Court TV*, 17 November 2006.

Tapper, James. "Why is You Calling Me a Minger, Ali," *Mail on Sunday*, 4 March 2007, 47.

Taylor, Teddy. "Wicked! The Day Ali G Made Me Look a Clown," *Mail on Sunday*, 16 January 2000, 55.

Terzian, Philip. "Steppes in Time," *Weekly Standard* 12, no. 3 (2 October 2006): 4.

Thompson, Harry. "G Force," *Guardian*, 27 April 27 1999, 19.

Todorova, Maria. *Imagining the Balkans*. Oxford: Oxford University Press, 1997.

Topcik, Joel. "For Ali G, More Fame and Fewer Dupes," *New York Times*, 23 July 2005, 7.

Travers, Peter. "Comedy of the Year," *Rolling Stone* 1013 (16 November 2006): 134.

Turan, Kenneth. "'Borat' Offends, Entertains While Mirroring Society," *NPR* Morning Edition, 3 November 2006.

Tweedie, Neil and Thomas Harding, "The Polite Little Swot Who Grew into Ali G," *Telegraph*, 8 March 2002.

Uberoi, Varun. "Social Unity in Britain," *Journal of Ethnic and Migration Studies* 33, no. 1 (January 2007): 141-157.

van Ham, Peter. "The Rise of the Brand State: The Postmodern Politics of Image and Reputation," *Foreign Affairs* 80, no. 5 (September-October 2001): 2-7.

———. "Branding European Power," *Place Branding* 1, no. 2 (March 2005): 122-126.

Vaughan, Johnny. "Eeeza Nizah," *Sun*, 3 November 2006.

Wallace, Bruce. "Cool Britannia," *Maclean's* 110, no. 17 (28 April 1997): 38-41.

Wallace, Dickie. "Hyperrealizing 'Borat' with the Map of the European 'Other,'" *Slavic Review* 66, no. 1 (Spring 2008): 35-49.

Wang, Jian. "Localising Public Diplomacy: The Role of Sub-national Actors in Nation Branding," *Place Branding* 2, no. 1 (January 2006): 32–42.

Warner, Jamie. "Political Culture Jamming: The Dissident Humor of 'The Daily Show With Jon Stewart,'" *Popular Communication* 5, no. 1 (2007): 17-36.

Waxman, Sharon. "Equal-Opportunity Offender Plays Anti-Semitism for Laughs," *New York Times*, 7 September 2006, E1.

Weaver, Hilary N. "Indigenous Identity," *American Indian Quarterly* 25, no. 2 (Spring 2001): 240-255.

Weaver, Simon. "Comprehending Ambivalence: Ali G and Conceptualisations of the 'Other.'" Paper presented at Connections Conference, University of Bristol, 2005.

Weinman, Jaime J. "Did Bunker Beget Borat?" *Maclean's* 119, no. 44 (6 November 2006): 62-64.

Westwood, Sallie. "Re-Branding Britain: Sociology, Futures and Futurology," *Sociology* 34, no. 1 (February 2000): 185-202.

White, Roland. "Borat's Easy . . . Being Me is Odd," *Sunday Times*, 21 January 2007.

Whitfield, Stephen J. "Towards an Appreciation of American Jewish Humor," *Journal of Modern Jewish Studies* 4, no. 1 (March 2005): 33–48.

Wills, Sara and Kate Darian-Smith. "Beefeaters, Bobbies, and a New Varangian Guard? Negotiating Forms of 'Britishness' in Suburban Australia," *History of Intellectual Culture* 4, no. 1 (2004): 1-18.

Wiltenburg, Mary. "Backstory: The Most Unwanted Man in Kazakhstan," *Christian Science Monitor*, 30 November 2005, 20.

Windolf, Jim. "Ali G for Real," *Vanity Fair* 528 (August 2004): 178-192.

Winner, David. "Minimum Respect," *Jerusalem Report* 11, no. 8 (14 August 2000): 42.

Worthington, TJ. "Review: Ali G Before He Was Massiv," *Off The Telly*, 27 March 2002.

Yessenova, Saulesh. "'Knowing the Road That Leads You Home:' Family, Genealogy, and Migration in Post-Socialist Kazakhstan," *Silk Road Newsletter* 1, no. 2 (December 2003).

———. "'Routes and Roots' of Kazakh Identity: Urban Migration in Postsocialist Kazakhstan," *Russian Review* 64 (October 2005): 661–679.

Zambito, Thomas. "Gypsies Sue 'Borat' for $30m for Making Them Look Like Glods," *New York Daily News*, 21 November 2006, 2.

Index

About the Author

Robert A. Saunders is an Assistant Professor in the Department of History, Economics & Politics at the Farmingdale State College, a campus of the State University of New York. He received his Ph.D. from the Division of Global Affairs at Rutgers University in 2005. He is a regular contributor to *Transitions Online* and his articles have appeared in the *Nations and Nationalism, Identities: Global Studies in Power and Culture, Nationalism & Ethnic Politics, Russia in Global Affairs, Journal of Global Change and Governance, East Asia: An International Quarterly, Global Media and Communication*, and *Slavic Review*.

He has contributed chapters to the following edited volumes: *Playing Politics with Terrorism: A User's Guide* (2007); *International Migration and the Globalization of Domestic Politics* (2005); and *Cul'tura "Post": At the Crossroads of Cultures and Civilizations* (2004). He is currently completing work on his manuscript *The Web of Identity: Minority Nationalism and Ethnopolitics in Cyberspace*, which is to be published in 2009. His next book project is a *Historical Dictionary of Contemporary Russia*, co-authored with Vlad Strukov.

Prior to completing his doctorate, he held the position of Director at The Eastern Management Group, an international consultancy specializing in information and communications technology. While at TEMG, he was a frequent guest on National Public Radio and his articles, editorials, and analysis appeared in *BusinessWeek, Washington Post, Forbes*, and other publications. Dr. Saunders holds an M.A. in Russian History from the State University of New York at Stony Brook and a B.A. in History from the University of Florida.